# ZACHARY TAYLOR
*Soldier of the Republic*

### In Full Dress Uniform

This oil painting of Zachary Taylor, by an unknown artist, hangs in the Pentagon, Washington. Reproduced by permission of the United States Army Signal Corps.

# ZACHARY TAYLOR

## SOLDIER OF THE REPUBLIC

### by Holman Hamilton

Zachary Taylor was a brave old feller,
  Brigadier-general, A. No. 1.
He fought twenty thousand Mexicanos;
  Four thousand he killed, the rest they "cut and run."

In the thickest of the fight old Zachary appear-ed,
  The shot flew about him as thick as any hail,
And the only injury he there receiv-ed
  Was a compound fracture of his brown coat tail.

—CONTEMPORARY DOGGEREL

### ILLUSTRATED

## THE BOBBS-MERRILL COMPANY

*Publishers*

INDIANAPOLIS                    NEW YORK

To
ALLEN HAMILTON
*and*
HELEN KNIGHT HAMILTON

# CONTENTS

# ILLUSTRATIONS

# LIST OF MAPS

# INTRODUCTION

When Holman Hamilton, fresh from Williams College and succeeding me as the Editorial Writer of the Fort Wayne *Journal-Gazette,* confided to me his ambition to write a definitive biography of Zachary Taylor I was curious to know why he had selected the homespun soldier as his subject. When he replied that no serious biography had yet been written about a man who rendered yeoman service to the white man's civilization in the redemption of Indiana and neighboring states, and he wished to fill a gap in the biographical literature of the country, it seemed to me that he was inspired by the best possible motive in a biographer or historian.

And now he has conscientiously and exhaustively filled that important gap in the biographical history of the United States. Aside from the cheap campaign biographies published in the presidential campaign of 1848, and one or two superficial works, Taylor has been strangely ignored by the writers. In his generation and long afterward American history was largely the product of New England where there was not only little interest in the redemption of the western wilderness infested by the red men, but actual hostility as well. Even Taylor's colorful and dramatic military career in Mexico did not appeal, since the battles of Palo Alto and Monterey were long associated in the New England mind with the extension of the slave territory.

It is proper that the biographer of Taylor should come from one of the great and prosperous commonwealths that gratefully acknowledge their debt to this valiant master in Indian warfare, and especially from Indiana, so intimately associated with his work at Fort Harrison and Vincennes.

In these days when totalitarian madness is forcing us more and more to lean upon our Army, it is instructive to follow the trail of an officer of the Army of the United States, who, from patriotic motives, abandoned his supreme ambition—to live the quiet life of the planter—in order to serve his country. The biographer takes us from his earliest service in Indian warfare on the fringe of the frontier—when he distinguished himself by his valor and decision at Fort Harrison—to the completion of his great and stirring triumphs on the bloodstained fields of Mexico.

He has not permitted his admiration for this stout-hearted, self-sacrificing officer to lead him into an extravagant estimate of his military ability. Taylor was not a genius in tactics, as was Lee. He lacked the dashing qualities of Stonewall Jackson. He was deficient in the flare for dramatic leadership which was Andrew Jackson's gift. There was nothing debonair about him. He was not flashy on parade. He had no meteoric rise to fame and appreciation, for his was a slow, hard progress, far removed in the wilderness from the publicity on which others who achieved less have profited in history. Between his brilliant defense of Fort Harrison, which made Indiana safe for settlers, and the far-seeing and effective work he did in Florida stretch long years spent in the building of defenses, in the drilling of raw soldiers, in the negotiating and fighting with savages, in the loneliness of long separations from kith and kin, and in the torture of slow fever from the swamps.

And yet no single servant of the Republic did more, or as much, in negotiations or in battle to open the settlement of the white man of the rich commonwealths of Indiana, Illinois, Missouri, Wisconsin and Michigan.

The British romanticize the work of their soldiers on the out-skirts of their far-flung empire; we have no such intelligent appreciation of the soldiers of the Republic in the redemption of the West.

Pioneering is romantic only in perspective; the drama is the slow process toward the redemption of waste places, but the day by day routine of the pioneers was prosy and laborious. Its greatness is in the result to be seen long afterward.

"Old Rough and Ready," as Taylor affectionately was called by his men, was a professional soldier in the service of the nation. He could not pick and choose his arena of activity. He went where he was sent. He did as he was told. He pulled no wires in politics for the promotions that came too tardily on that account. But in this he was typical of the best type of the professional soldier—loyal, brave, resourceful, conscientious, able, dependable, and as unpretentious and simple in his tastes as Grant or Lincoln, both of whom, with Lee and Davis, were once under his command.

The author reveals that he was not a political soldier. No senator carried his knapsack. Through many years, stationed as he was on the edge of the wilderness at the farthest outposts and remote from home, he did not even vote. And but for the purely political conspiracy to rob him of the laurels so richly won in Mexico, politics would scarcely have touched his life. A Whig in politics, he yet conceived it the duty of the soldier to serve the Government in power regardless of its political complexion or policies. To him the constituted authority was the authentic voice of the nation. The voice of the nation was his master's voice. It was not until his really spectacular achievements at Palo Alto and Resaca de la Palma and on the bloody slopes of Monterey that he stirred the imagination of the masses and was swept into the presidency on a wave of popular acclaim.

Mr. Hamilton has painted a most appealing portrait of this staunch American. A disciplinarian but not a martinet, jealous of the rights of his men, and thoughtful of their comfort, deliberate of movement and of speech, careless in dress, unpretentious in manner as a simple planter for whom he often was taken by strangers—his homespun character stands out vividly. The years of his preparation for the great climax which the battlefields of Mexico gave to his military career, attain, in this biographer's handling, their full place of human interest and of national significance.

In the preparation of this work, Mr. Hamilton has explored every avenue for information about Taylor and his times, and has painted for the reader a clear panoramic picture of the then western frontier. His sources are in unpublished manuscripts, in rare long-forgotten volumes of western travel, in such newspapers of the period as have been preserved. Happily he cites his sources and thus places the stamp of authenticity on his narrative. And he tells the story with the straightforward simplicity of his subject.

The narrative ends with the close of the Mexican War just when Taylor began to figure in the calculations of the politicians. The story of his presidential nomination, favored by Lincoln, and the record of his presidency will follow in a second volume, and it is more than probable that the two volumes will become the definitive biography of the twelfth President of the United States.

Santiago, Chile.

# CHRONOLOGY

1744   Birth of Zachary Taylor's father, Richard Taylor.

1760   Birth of Zachary Taylor's mother, Sarah Dabney Strother.

1779   Marriage of Richard Taylor and Sarah Dabney Strother.

1784   Birth of Zachary Taylor in Orange County, Virginia, on November 24.

1785   Zachary Taylor is taken to Jefferson County, Virginia (Kentucky).

1808   Zachary Taylor is commissioned first lieutenant, United States Army.

1810   Marriage of Zachary Taylor and Margaret Mackall Smith, on June 21.
       Lieutenant Taylor is promoted to rank of captain.

1811   Birth of Ann Mackall Taylor.

1812   Captain Taylor successfully defends Fort Harrison, Indiana Territory.
       Captain Taylor is promoted to rank of brevet major.

1814   Birth of Sarah Knox Taylor.
       Brevet Major Taylor leads American troops in the battle of Credit Island, Illinois Territory.

1815   Brevet Major Taylor wins tardy promotion to lineal rank of major.
       Major Taylor is reduced to rank of brevet major and resigns from the United States Army.

1816   Zachary Taylor is restored to lineal rank of major, and is stationed at Fort Howard, Michigan Territory (Wisconsin).
       Birth of Octavia Pannill Taylor.

1818   Major Taylor relinquishes command of Fort Howard.

1819   Major Taylor is promoted to rank of lieutenant colonel.
       Birth of Margaret Smith Taylor, fourth daughter of Zachary Taylor.

1820    Lieutenant Colonel Taylor completes construction of Jackson Military Road, Mississippi.

Death of Octavia Pannill Taylor and Margaret Smith Taylor, third and fourth daughters of Zachary Taylor.

1821    Lieutenant Colonel Taylor is stationed at Cantonment Bay Saint Louis, Mississippi.

1822    Lieutenant Colonel Taylor establishes Fort Jesup, Louisiana.

Death of Mrs. Sarah Dabney Strother Taylor, mother of Zachary Taylor.

1823    Lieutenant Colonel Taylor is commandant at Baton Rouge, Louisiana.

Zachary Taylor purchases a cotton plantation in Feliciana (West Feliciana) Parish, Louisiana.

1824    Birth of Mary Elizabeth Taylor.

Lieutenant Colonel Taylor is superintendent general of the recruiting service, Western Department.

1826    Birth of Richard Taylor, only son of Zachary Taylor.

Lieutenant Colonel Taylor serves on the Militia Board in Washington.

1827    Lieutenant Colonel Taylor is stationed at Baton Rouge and New Orleans.

1828    Lieutenant Colonel Taylor is commandant at Fort Snelling, unorganized territory (Minnesota).

1829    Death of Richard Taylor, father of Zachary Taylor.

Lieutenant Colonel Taylor is commandant at Fort Crawford, Michigan Territory (Wisconsin).

Marriage of Ann Mackall Taylor and Dr. Robert Crooke Wood.

1830    Birth of John Taylor Wood, eldest grandson of Zachary Taylor.

1831    Zachary Taylor buys land in Wilkinson County, Mississippi, adjoining his plantation in West Feliciana Parish, Louisiana.

1832    Lieutenant Colonel Taylor is promoted to rank of colonel.

Birth of Robert Crooke Wood, junior, second grandson of Zachary Taylor.

Colonel Taylor participates in the Black Hawk War.

Colonel Taylor returns to Fort Crawford, where he remains almost continuously until 1836.

1834 Birth of Blandina Dudley Wood, eldest granddaughter of Zachary Taylor.

1835 Marriage of Sarah Knox Taylor and Jefferson Davis.
Death of Mrs. Sarah Knox Taylor Davis.

1836 Colonel Taylor assumes command of Jefferson Barracks, Missouri, and the right wing of the Western Department.

1837 Colonel Taylor reaches Tampa Bay, Florida Territory, to participate in the Second Seminole War.
Colonel Taylor routs Seminole and Mikasuki Indians in the battle of Okeechobee.

1838 Colonel Taylor is promoted to rank of brevet brigadier general.
Birth of Sarah Knox Wood, second granddaughter of Zachary Taylor.
General Taylor assumes command of all the troops in Florida Territory.
Zachary Taylor purchases additional land in West Feliciana Parish, Louisiana.

1840 General Taylor leaves Florida Territory, visits Pennsylvania and New York, and assumes command at Baton Rouge, Louisiana.

1841 General Taylor assumes command of the Second Department, Western Division, with headquarters at Fort Smith, Arkansas.
Zachary Taylor disposes of his property in West Feliciana Parish, Louisiana, and Wilkinson County, Mississippi.

1842 Zachary Taylor pays $95,000 for Cypress Grove Plantation, Jefferson County, Mississippi, and its eighty-one slaves.

1844 General Taylor is placed in command of the First Department with headquarters at Fort Jesup, Louisiana.

1845 General Taylor establishes the "Army of Occupation" at Corpus Christi, Texas.

1846 General Taylor leads the United States Army from Corpus Christi to the Rio Grande.
General Taylor defeats Mexican troops under General Ma-

riano Arista in the battles of Palo Alto and Resaca de la Palma.

General Taylor is promoted to lineal rank of major general, and for the first time is mentioned as a potential presidential candidate.

General Taylor defeats the Mexican force of General Pedro de Ampudia in the battle of Monterey, Mexico, and subsequently occupies Monterey.

1847 General Taylor turns back the legions of General Antonio López de Santa Anna in the battle of Buena Vista, near Saltillo, Mexico.

General Taylor returns to the United States, and is given a hero's welcome by the people of New Orleans.

# ZACHARY TAYLOR
*Soldier of the Republic*

# CHAPTER I

## Virginia Birth; Kentucky Growth

### 1

ZACHARY TAYLOR entered the White House at a moment when the sanctity of the Constitution and the inviolability of the Federal Union were being questioned. He was born before the Constitution was written, in an era when some of the leaders of thirteen semi-independent states voiced contempt for the general government. The United States of America was only eight years old. Three short years had elapsed since the surrender of Cornwallis at historic Yorktown. And the new nation was struggling along—with cards stacked against survival—under the vulnerable aegis of the Articles of Confederation. At such a time, on November 24, 1784, in Orange County, Virginia, a president was born.[1]

The log cabin tradition of Zachary's birth paints a perverted picture of his parents' financial and social status, for his birthright was the manor house and not the low log hut. Lieutenant Colonel Richard Taylor, late of the Continental Army, belonged to one of the first families of Virginia—a family high on the colonial social scale since the days of James Taylor, his immigrant great-grandfather.[2]

Although the Lieutenant Colonel counted among his forebears Elder William Brewster of *Mayflower* renown, the majority of his progenitors had little in common with the pundit of the Pilgrims.[3] Sternness with them was not a virtue, nor was sobriety the quintessence of the well-lived life; yet their business and agricultural achievements, coupled with civic and military leadership, testify to moderation as well as to ability and energy. Contrary to popular opinion, the Taylors, the Barbours, the Pendletons and the Lees did not spend all their time at the chase and in the banquet hall; nor

21

did Governor Alexander Spotswood invite ne'er-do-wells to participate in his exploring expedition into the Shenandoah Valley. James Taylor's son James was one of Spotswood's Knights of the Golden Horseshoe, and soon after his initial view of western Virginia he moved from the banks of the Mattaponi in fashionable Tidewater to the rich, red soil that borders on the Rapidan. There in 1722 he built Bloomsbury, the first frame house in rolling Orange County, and there he acquired many thousands of acres of heavily timbered virgin forest.

James Taylor, the second, was a useful subject of the crown. He was a prominent surveyor-planter, a soldier and a gentleman who served his king and served his church and was universally respected.[4] But when his daughter Frances married Ambrose Madison, and his son Zachary married Elizabeth Lee, no frontier prophet was on hand to tell this founder of a dynasty that two of his great-grandsons were destined to become presidents of the yet unborn United States.[5]

2

When James Taylor, the second, was gathered to his fathers, he was one of the wealthiest members of the landed gentry of Virginia. Wealth was land, and he had made the most of his opportunities. Hence there was no reason for his son, Zachary Taylor, the first, to plunge farther into the back country, since the improvement of his share of the estate was the business of a lifetime.

Zachary's vocation was to supervise the clearing of his forests and the planting of his fields with tobacco and corn. But this provincial aristocrat occupied a position in which he could also devote himself to the pleasures and privileges due a man of his station. Like many another leader he was Virginia's surveyor general. Like his father and grandfather, he was a member of the Church of England, serving as a vestryman and driving in on Sundays to Saint Thomas' near Orange Courthouse from his mansion, Meadow Farm, four miles away. A highly respectable member of a family noted for its respectability, the first Zachary Taylor was the only known Taylor ancestor of the President who was neither a soldier nor a pioneer.[6]

When the sons of Zachary Taylor, the first, reached manhood, the temptations of a life of ease could not keep them in Virginia. The lure of the frontier led them onward. The pioneering spirit of their grandfather and great-grandfather was part and parcel of their heritage. As early as 1769, Richard Taylor and his older brother Hancock ventured into the wilderness of the West on the first recorded trading voyage from Pittsburgh to New Orleans. At Pittsburgh, then an outpost of civilization, they procured a small boat. Accompanied by Abraham Haptonstall, a master woodsman, trapper and hunter, they set out on the dangerous journey down the Ohio and Mississippi Rivers.

Time was scarcely at a premium on this expedition, and the three young men did not hesitate to explore the Dark and Bloody Ground near the margin of the Ohio. On reaching the junction of the two rivers, they ascended the Mississippi to Fort Chartres, a handsome stone structure then occupied by British troops. After remaining a few days as guests of the regulars, the Virginians descended the Father of Waters to the mouth of the Arkansas, and pushed up this stream more than a hundred miles to a small French settlement near which they camped and hunted. With the coming of spring the trio separated, Hancock Taylor and Haptonstall dropping down the Mississippi to Natchez and New Orleans, while the youthful Richard—accompanied only by an Indian trader— traveled through the Chickasaw, Choctaw and Creek nations to Georgia for the purpose of examining a tract of land recently procured by that colony from the Creeks. Thence he worked his way overland through South and North Carolina, back to his Orange County home from which he had been absent more than a year.[7]

That it was Richard Taylor's intention to settle in the western country cannot be questioned, but another year elapsed before his brother returned from the South to compare notes on potential purchases. A second reason for postponement of the westward trek held even greater significance. Not only in Virginia, but elsewhere in the colonies, Americans were smarting under the iron heel of England. And Richard was not the sort of man to evade participation in the impending conflict. At the outbreak of the Revolution, he enlisted as a lieutenant in the First Virginia Regiment, serving with distinction from beginning to end of the nation's most momentous struggle and rapidly rising to the rank of major. White Plains, Brandywine, and Monmouth found him battling against the British. And his work against the Indians northwest of the Ohio was scarcely less important from the standpoint of the straggling settlements of Pennsylvania.[8]

### 3

With four years of stiff fighting to his credit and a lieutenant colonelcy due in December, Major Taylor took time out from the Revolution on August 20, 1779, to marry a young girl half his age. The bride was eighteen, the bridegroom thirty-five.[9]

To the typical Taylor background of war and pioneering, Sarah Dabney Strother introduced the subtle strain of a culture unusual for those times. Her brother was a poet, and Sally herself was the product of an education supervised by tutors imported from Europe. Left motherless in childhood, she had gone to Culpeper County, Virginia, to be reared with her cousins under the watchful eye of a paternal uncle who had climaxed a colorful public career by signing the first protest against the Stamp Act.[10] Though the lengthening vista of the years has dimmed her portrait, it is clear that Sally Strother's heredity, environment, and personal worth equipped her to meet the standards of the stalwart soldier whose six feet two inches of height, clear complexion, blue eyes, and strong features must have made him an attractive suitor.[11]

### 4

Hare Forest, within a mile of the roaring Rapidan, was the Orange County home of the Richard Taylors—their house standing on high ground in a small clearing, surrounded by stately cedars with chestnuts on the hill.

The summer of 1784 found two boy babies in the Taylor family.

Hancock, born in 1781, was named for his surveyor uncle, who had been killed by Indians in the West. William Dabney Strother Taylor, a year younger, bore the name of his mother's brother slain in the Battle of Guilford Courthouse. Sally was expecting a third child, too, but her husband's anxiety to claim his new lands in Kentucky before the coming winter prevented the youngster from being born at Hare Forest.

On an unrecorded day in the early autumn, the father, mother, and two small sons set out from their Virginia home accompanied by their slaves and probably by other whites. Montebello, the country place of a kinsman, was the destination of the first day's twelve-mile journey. There, according to tradition, an unnamed member of the party was taken ill, and during the ensuing delay Mrs. Taylor was confined. Since the dwelling was not pretentious, it is said that guests slept in outlying log cabins, in one of which twenty-three-year-old Sally gave birth to a third son. The infant was called Zachary in honor of his deceased grandfather, and the first seven months of his life were spent in his native Orange County.[12]

## 5

Meanwhile Richard Taylor had gone out to Kentucky to make his uncleared holdings habitable, returning eastward in the spring of 1785 to bring his wife and children to the Dark and Bloody Ground. Courageously the pioneers toiled overland to Redstone and then floated down the Monongahela and Ohio Rivers to reach the Falls of the Ohio before the second day of August. Their log house was situated on Beargrass Creek, five miles east of the swampy village of Louisville, on a four-hundred-acre place called Springfield which then amounted to little more than wilderness. Zachary was eight months old when he, his brothers, and his parents arrived at the new Kentucky home.[13]

Although nominally a part of the Commonwealth of Virginia, this frontier community had little in common with the seven hills of Richmond or the mansions on the James. The Kentucky of the

1780s was every bit as wild and woolly and heroically western as
the California of the Forty-niners. In the vicinity of Louisville,
these were the times that tried men's souls. The village proper and
its immediate environs could boast of only "one hundred inhabitants who had cleared and cultivated garden-spots around their
humble cabins. . . . All else was the primeval forest, with panthers
and bears and wolves and wildcats. The familiar song of the
Falls was sometimes disturbed by the yell of the savage, but all
else bore the solemn silence of the deep, dark woods around."[14]
If Richard Taylor and his neighbors fought few pitched battles
with the Indians, they were prepared for detached squads of irate
redskins who strove to perpetrate by stealth and cunning atrocities
comparable to those achieved in open conflict by their banded
brothers at Boonesborough and Harrodsburg.

At times, the settlers' struggles with the savages were calculated
to excite more merriment than woe. There was, for example, the
Battle of the Pumpkins in which Adam and Jacob Wickersham
made the most of frontier ingenuity to withstand two hostile
Indians who attempted to capture them. Working in their garden when the enemy approached, Jacob felled one aboriginal
with his bag of pumpkins, while Adam and his adversary raced
along in parallel formation on opposite sides of the fence surrounding the pumpkin patch. Reaching a deep ditch, Adam cleared it
with a bound, and the less agile Indian hurled his tomahawk at the
fleeing figure only to strike him with the handle instead of with
the blade. Both brothers reached the fort unharmed but not without a scare.[15] On another occasion, a Kentuckian named Squires
ventured out beyond the safety zone to the mouth of Beargrass
Creek, near the Taylor dwelling, where he treed a raccoon in the
branches of a sycamore. An Indian appeared, and a treadmill chase
began around the tree—the Indian after Squires and Squires after
the Indian. Eventually the same idea suddenly occurred to each,
and the red man and the white shot off in opposite directions.
Neither pursued the other; no one was hurt, and the raccoon went
scot-free.[16]

A land where grown men were forced to run for their lives was not exactly a protected playground for their sons and daughters. Although tradition has it that a party of children, of whom Zachary Taylor was one, was attacked by savages, the first reliable description of the lad depicts him as a happy normal youngster and not as the object of an Indian attack. When Zachary was five years old, Abraham Cleland arrived at Goose Creek, a branch of the Beargrass. "We were compelled, for want of better accommodation, to remain in our boat two weeks," his son, Thomas Cleland, wrote years later. "Afterward a small cabin, about twelve feet square, was obtained, a few miles out from the river, belonging to Colonel Richard Taylor. . . . This residence was on the edge of a dense cane-brake. Here we were saluted every night with the howling of wolves. In the meantime father had gone to look for his land. . . . He was absent more than six weeks without our knowing the cause. The family were in painful suspense. The Taylor family, old and young, were very hospitable and kind to us. William, Hancock, and 'Little Zack,' as General Taylor was then called, were my playmates. Mrs. Taylor conceived a great fondness for my mother, and treated her as a sister."[17]

## 6

Zachary had other playmates. His father's friend, Colonel Richard Clough Anderson, was rearing a large family of children at Soldier's Retreat, his stone fortress-home three miles east of Springfield. With the Andersons lived the irrepressible Mrs. Chenoweth, who often startled and amused her youthful audience by displaying her bald head, "peeled like an onion by the Indians' bluntest scalping knife" and "shorn of her beautiful hair."[18]

While not everyone in the Beargrass region could boast of surviving bloody massacres, few boys had a prouder tradition than the Andersons' cousin, young George Croghan, who was seven years Zachary's junior but became his close friend as the years rolled on. Croghan lived at Locust Grove, the estate adjoining Springfield on the Louisville side and the home of Croghan's uncle, General George Rogers Clark, whose epochal exploits against

British soldiers had won him the title of the "Hannibal of the West." Tempting it is, to picture the two chums, George and Zachary, comparing and discussing their seniors' daring deeds— little dreaming that one was to become the gallant defender of Fort Stephenson and the other the victor of Buena Vista.[19]

Both Croghan and Taylor learned their lessons under the watchful eyes of Kean O'Hara. But before this celebrated Irish pedagogue came to Kentucky, Zachary already had studied his three R's with Elisha Ayer, an itinerant Connecticut schoolmaster whose specialty—if such it could be called—was arithmetic. Inoculated with the wanderlust, this shiftless, uncouth excuse for an educator vagabonded back and forth from New England to the Southwest on a mule—his long legs scraping the ground—and set up a school wherever he happened to be.[20] Ayer has left a graphic picture of the life near Louisville. "The Kentuckians were then a warlike and chivalrous people," he wrote, "and they were often engaged in offensive or defensive skirmishes with the Indians. A number [of Indians] were known to be in the woods not far distant from the school-house, and, on one occasion, one of them was shot, wearing a British uniform. In their hostility to the Americans, they were [believed to be] encouraged and sustained by the British authorities on the Northern frontier. There was a Mr. Whetsel, in the neighborhood of the school, who, having been once chased by three or four Indians, loaded his rifle while running, and successively shot them all. This exploit made Whetsel famous, and he became the instructor of the young men and boys in his mode of maintaining a running fire. Among his pupils, it is believed, was young Zachary."[21]

Although little is known of the youth's training in studies more academic than the firing of a muzzle-loader, Ayer testified many years afterward that his famous pupil was "quick in learning, and still patient in study,"[22] and the briefest association with such a teacher as O'Hara was enough to leave a lasting mark on any boy. An Irish Catholic gentleman and scholar, Kean O'Hara forsook his native land at the outbreak of the Revolution of 1798, taking charge of the academy at Danville, Kentucky, on the invitation of

Governor Isaac Shelby. He later moved to the vicinity of Louisville, where Taylor was among his pupils. O'Hara's fame as a classical scholar grew in later years when O'Hara's Institute at Frankfort became one of the fashionable centers of culture in the West. Transylvania University made him a Master of Arts, and he passed his genius on to a brilliant poet son, Theodore O'Hara, author of "The Bivouac of the Dead."[23]

Since a formal academic education was scarcely the be-all and end-all of frontier training, the probabilities are that Zachary did not have an opportunity to spend many years in such schools as the frontier offered. His earliest known letter, written at the age of twenty-three, discloses straggly, wavy writing and a decided inability to spell.[24] His correspondence of later life, however, bears eloquent evidence that the instruction of Ayer and O'Hara did not fall on barren soil. The hand is bold and firm, the mode of expression clear and forceful, if lacking in grace. Like many men whose own cultural experience has been curtailed, the proper training of his children became one of the ruling passions of Zachary Taylor's life. He sent his son to Edinburgh, to Paris, to an exclusive Massachusetts preparatory school, and to Yale College—a line of action followed by few Westerners in the 1840s.

7

When Zachary attained his twentieth year, his father's family included eight children. Hancock Taylor, aged twenty-three, led the list. The other brothers and sisters were William Dabney Strother Taylor, twenty-two; George, fourteen; Elizabeth Lee, twelve; Joseph Pannill, eight; Sarah Bailey, five; and Emily Richard Taylor, three.[25]

There were also innumerable boy and girl cousins, uncles and aunts, and distant kinsfolk who visited and were visited by the Taylors of Springfield. Across the river from Cincinnati lived Colonel James Taylor, the fourth, in the town of Newport which he had founded and of which he was the leading citizen.[26] Nearer to Springfield was Spring Hill in Shelby County where Major

William Berry Taylor, known as "Big Foot Billy," was developing a fine country place.[27] Commodore Richard Taylor of Revolutionary naval fame resided within five miles of the home of Zachary's father.[28] Over in Woodford County lived Zachary's uncle, Captain Zachary Taylor, junior, who had served with George Washington at Braddock's Defeat and who liked nothing better than to relate that he and Washington were the only members of the rangers who, standing at the bottom of the Natural Bridge in Virginia, could cast a stone to the very top.[29] Woodford County was also the home of Mrs. Taylor's aged father, William Strother, so that her children had abundant reason for visiting the beautiful bluegrass country near Lexington.[30]

Only one anecdote approaching reliability has come down to us concerning this frontier wife and mother, who bore nine children and was referred to with the deepest affection in later years by her soldier son. One day her niece, Sarah Taylor Woolfolk, was "assisting Aunt Dabney in molding bullets. In a ladle made of hard wood a coal of fire was placed, a piece of tallow was put on the coal and the lead put on to melt. Suddenly the cry 'Indians! Indians!' was heard. In the excitement Aunt Dabney turned the melted lead over [Sarah's hand]. . . . To her dying day her fingers were stiffened and crooked from the effect of the burn."[31]

But the horror of Indian raids gradually vanished, and Richard Taylor was reaping heavy harvests from farms carved out of forests. An indefatigable walker, he liked to stroll out over his fields of rich Silurian soil, invariably using a great pawpaw cane that reached to his shoulder. Tradition says that he always wore knee breeches and long stockings in preference to the rougher garb of his neighbors, but the queue and silver buckles were conspicuously absent.[32]

According to the standards of his day, Richard Taylor was well-to-do. At the turn of the century his property included ten thousand acres of improved and unimproved land in seven of Kentucky's counties, in addition to valuable lots in Louisville and the home plantation of seven hundred acres on Beargrass Creek. He had acquired twenty-six Negro slaves, and his spacious stables sheltered sixteen horses.[33] The log house with glassless holes for light had been replaced by a substantial brick dwelling, with high ceilings and thick walls and a garden out toward the muddy Ohio.[34]

Not only had the veteran of Brandywine prospered in the western country. He had also been honored time and again by state and nation. Justice of the Peace, Jefferson County Magistrate, delegate to the conventions of 1785 and 1788, he had taken part in framing the first and second constitutions of Kentucky and had represented his county at the initial session of the Kentucky legis-lature. From President Washington, he accepted appointment as Collector of the Port of Louisville, an important post in an era when Saint Louis and New Orleans were in the possession of Spain. Nor were Richard Taylor's activities limited to private business and civil service, for in November, 1792, he was wounded in the Battle of Greenville where the Indians of Little Turtle bested a body of Kentucky troops commanded by General John Adair.[35]

8

The village near which Lieutenant Colonel Richard Taylor lived, aged and prospered, contained seven hundred residents in 1804 and was fast developing into one of the important cities of the Union. Although Lexington was larger, Louisville had already achieved the distinction due the biggest and busiest Ohio River town west of Cincinnati.

From earliest times, its location at the Falls made it a natural tarrying place for travelers no matter where their eventual destination chanced to be. Ponds and marshes in the village proper, and on its outskirts, "gave the landscape the appearance of an archipelago." Cabins, "built of logs laid one above the other, with a space between filled with clay, and the roof of boards held in place by poles across them," were beginning to disappear, for Zachary Taylor's father was one of many settlers following the example of Frederick A. Kaye, who erected the first brick house in 1789. There were physicians in Louisville, and competent lawyers at the bar, but there was no church edifice until 1803 when Williams Kavanaugh conducted the Episcopal service in a small house on Second Street. The first newspaper had been printed. The first ship had arrived from the Monongahela with a cargo of peltry, meat and flour for New Orleans. The first dry goods store was there before the Taylors' arrival, and the years which followed witnessed a steady growth in the number of shops as well as improvement in the quality of articles on sale, ranging from calico dresses and straw bonnets for the belles, to the silverware and china then supplanting the wooden spoons and forks and noggins.[36]

When the first glass appeared in the windows of a Louisville residence, the townspeople were so unaccustomed to the sight that one small boy, running home to his mother, exclaimed, "O ma! There is a house down here with specs on!"[37] Other features of a developing civilization were inaugurated in those forgotten times: A pilot was officially appointed to conduct boats over the rapids; tobacco warehouses had begun to be examined by inspectors appointed by law; and "an act was obtained for the establishing of fire companies." Still neither free schools nor policemen had come into existence, and streets remained unpaved. Utopia was not an actuality at the Falls of the Ohio.[38]

Such was the stamping ground of Zachary Taylor in the days of his youth. He literally grew up with the town, participating in the free and easy pleasures of the place, yet fully familiar with frontier dangers. It was a period of feasting and whisky-drinking and dances after the feasts. And midnight found the transplanted Virginians cutting pigeonwings and trotting jigs. Zachary liked society; one of his earliest letters expresses keen regret at absence from Louisville festivities. But jigs and pigeonwings did not constitute the *summum bonum*. A man must attend to more serious business, especially when he cherished an ambition to enter the Regular Army.[39]

# CHAPTER II

## Baptism of Fire

### 1

HEREDITY and environment pointed twenty-three-year-old Zachary Taylor to a military career, and the times were auspicious. Although his elder brother William had served as a second lieutenant of Artillery for more than a year without promotion, higher rank awaited younger men who joined the Army in 1808.

It was an opportune hour. War with Spain was a possibility regarded by President Thomas Jefferson as scarcely remote; war with Great Britain even more immediate. Congress had provided for the establishment of a new regiment, the Seventh Infantry, and Kentucky's senators and representatives recommended "Zachariah Taylor" for a first lieutenancy in a joint petition to the Secretary of War.[1] On May 3, Zachary was officially commissioned.[2] A month wheeled by before the news reached Louisville, where a letter of acceptance was penned by a youth eager for action. It is his earliest communication known to be extant:

"LOUISVILLE KENTUCKY June the 6th 1808
"SIR
"I received your letter of the 4th of May in which you informed me that I was appointed a firs Lieutenant in the seventh regiment of Infantry in the service of the United States which appointment I doo accept.
"I am Sir with great respect
"your Obt. Servt.
"ZACHARY TAYLOR[3]
"*The Honrl. H. Dearborn S. at War.*"

His letter posted, Zachary waited five full months for instruc-

33

40353

tions. Plans of the War Department were none too clear, and mails to Washington City neither fast nor frequent. His acceptance left Louisville on June 26 but did not arrive at the capital until July 14. Autumn followed on the heels of summer before the subaltern was ordered by Colonel William Russell to assist with the recruiting service in Mason County, in the northeastern section of the state.[4] Reaching Washington, Kentucky, in mid-November, Lieutenant Taylor "found Capt. Hord . . . with a drum and a fife but no recruits." "He is in a very bad state of health and has given up the recruiting business entirely to me," Zachary wrote his father from Maysville, whither he had taken the drum and the fife, "as it is the place of most business."[5] On the same day—the twenty-fourth anniversary of his birth—Taylor informed the War Department that Hord "has not been furnished with Generall Orders no a form of weekyly return[.] I wish both of those to be forward to me at this plaice as soon as practicable[,] for untill I get them it is out of my power to comply with my instructions."[6]

Zachary's decision to make Maysville the recruiting rendezvous, his initial decision in the Army, may at first seem strange. Washington had the distinction accruing to county seats, was older, better established, and housed eight hundred souls—more than twice the population of its neighbor. A Philadelphia merchant, who visited the place three years before, described it as a thriving town of one hundred and fifty dwellings of which a dozen were brick or stone. As early as 1797 there were seventeen stores in Washington. And many families of future prominence resided there. Evidence of Washington's importance was found in its superior schools, including the West's outstanding female seminary conducted by the cultured wife of a distant relative of John Keats.[7]

But neither simpering schoolgirls nor deaf kinsmen of British poets interested Taylor as much as well-built men, five feet six or taller, who might make stout soldiers in the event of war. Washington was inland. Maysville's location on the Ohio River led pioneers to tarry there on their way west, and embryonic settlers were often embryonic fighters—adapted by temperament and by physique to the rigors of military service. Thus the demands of duty led the Lieutenant to Maysville, where he did not enjoy himself. "I am rather badly off here on the score of society," he admitted privately, "but a soldier ought not to repine at that circumstance for when he enters the army he ought to give up society entirely."[8]

## 2

Devoting his first winter in the Army to the dreary routine of recruiting, Lieutenant Taylor—whose pay at this time was thirty dollars per month, plus a twelve-dollar subsistence allowance— at length was ordered with his regiment to the South. In March or early April, 1809, his boat breezed down the Ohio from Newport, Kentucky, and into the Mississippi.[9] May found him in temporary command of Fort Pickering on the Chickasaw Bluffs at the site of the modern city of Memphis. History does not record with what mixed emotions Zachary Taylor climbed the steep log stairway leading up from the Mississippi River to the fort where his brother, William Dabney Strother Taylor, had been killed by Indians one year before.[10]

Shortly after Zachary's arrival, an English traveler, Fortescue Cuming, ascended the same stair to find "a trace of fresh blood the whole way up." "Arriving at the top," he recorded, "we saw . . . about fifty Chickasaw warriors, drest each according to his notions of finery, and most of them painted in a grotesque but not terrifick manner. . . . An idea started in my imagination that they had massacred the garrison; but on advancing a little farther I was agreeably undeceived by seeing a good looking young white sentinel in the American uniform, with his musket and fixed bayonet, parading before the gate of the fort. . . . We were ushered by a soldier to the officers' quarters where we were received by Lieut. Taylor the Commandant, with civility not unmixed with a small degree of the pompous stiffness of office. He however answered politely enough a few interrogatories we made respecting the Indians. He said they were friendly and made frequent visits to the garrison, but, except a few of the chiefs on business, none of them were ever admitted within the staccado, and that this was a jubilee or gala day on account of their having just received presents from the United States government. They have a large settlement about five miles directly inland from the river, but the most populous part of the Chickasaw nation is one hundred miles distant to the southeastward."[11]

Superseded by Captain William Swann, Zachary Taylor left Fort Pickering in June to rejoin his regiment. It was the hottest summer in twenty years, and disease stalked the unacclimated soldiers of General James Wilkinson on the narrow sidewalks of New Orleans. In search of health, Wilkinson mistakenly chose to canton officers and men in the swamps of Terre Aux Boeufs, thirteen miles south of the Crescent City. Here the General stood by helpless as his troops suffered, sickened, and died. The Kentuckians, who composed the Seventh Infantry and who had undergone the coldest winter within memory, succumbed even faster than their comrades. Conditions at camp beggared description. More men were sick than well, and it was impossible to care for all their needs. Sanitation did not exist. Spoiled food, supplied by seedy and frequently corrupt contractors, revolted those who were supposed to eat it. Attempts at burial were pitiful. Interred higgledy-piggledy in shallow graves, the protruding arms and legs of the deceased took the place of missing markers in reminding the living of the fate that might be theirs.[12]

Taylor sickened with the rest, discovering early in military life that diarrhea and dysentery could be quite as unpleasant as a body riddled by enemy bullets.[13] The end of his illness found him, however, not three feet under Louisiana soil, but homeward bound to regain his strength—more fortunate than his colonel, who informed the War Department that his right eye had become infected and "I have almost lost the sight of it."[14] Later, recuperating sufficiently to apply for active service, Zachary headed south once more—this time to Washington Village, near Natchez, in Mississippi Territory.[15] Meanwhile depleted ranks had been closed. New companies had been formed from the remnants of the old. And Taylor was shunted back to await further orders in Louisville.[16] Not all bugles and drums—this business of war! But the

Lieutenant returned to Springfield to use his leisure to good advantage.

## 3

Nothing could have fitted in more perfectly with Zachary's plans than a sojourn in and near Louisville. The preceding autumn, he had made the acquaintance of Miss Margaret Mackall Smith, who was visiting her sister, Mrs. Samuel Chew, in Jefferson County.

A member of a prominent Maryland family, whose home in Calvert County dated back to the days of her great-great-grandfather, the province's attorney-general under Oliver Cromwell, Peggy Smith was the daughter of Major Walter Smith, deceased, who had seen service in the War of the Revolution.

A slender young lady of twenty-one, she had been introduced to the broad-shouldered, stocky First Lieutenant by Dr. Alexander Duke. And the evidence is that she found his attentions to her liking. On June 18, 1810, Zachary Taylor secured their marriage license at the office of the Jefferson County clerk. Three days thereafter, on June 21, the wedding took place in a double log house two miles from Harrods Creek Station on the Wolf Pen Road.[17]

Information is lacking as to where they spent their honeymoon, or how long Zachary remained in the company of his bride before returning to the pursuit of his profession. But it is definitely known that their baby was born near Louisville on April 9, 1811, and that she was named Ann Mackall Taylor in honor of Peggy's mother.[18] Three hundred and twenty-four acres at the mouth of Beargrass Creek constituted Richard Taylor's wedding present to his son.[19] And in the November preceding Ann's birth, her soldier-father was promoted to the rank of captain in the Seventh Infantry.[20]

## 4

On the first day of July, 1811, Major George Rogers Clark Floyd instructed Captain Taylor to take charge of Fort Knox at Vincennes in Indiana Territory, to bring order out of chaos. Floyd's order was theoretically unorthodox, since the Captain was not under his immediate command. But the critical situation of the Fort Knox garrison cried out for a strong hand at the helm.

Captain Thornton Posey, the recent commandant, had consummated a long-standing personal feud with Lieutenant Jesse Jennings by shooting and killing Jennings, who had menaced him. Major Floyd apparently did not consider the sole remaining officers, Lieutenants Albright and Whitlock, competent enough to restore order among the privates. Accordingly, Taylor was sent for.

Captain Taylor reached Fort Knox on July 9, and assumed command on the following day. On the sixteenth he promptly called the attention of the Secretary of War to the "defenceless state of the Garrison and the alarm of the inhabitance of this Teritory from the appearance of hostilities from the Indians. . . . The men here are extreamly in want of Clothing[,] so much so that if they were ordered to march to any place at this time they must do so nearly naked unless they could be furnished befor they moved."[21]

Taylor immediately set about drilling his soldiers and strengthening his post, performing this duty so efficiently that three weeks of hard work brought that prized compliment of military men—the unstinted praise of an able superior. No sooner did Governor William Henry Harrison return to Vincennes than he dispatched a glowing report to the War Department: "Captain Z. Taylor has been placed in command of the Garrison near this. To all the qualities which are esteemed for an amiable man he appears to unite those which form a good officer. In the short time he has been a commander he has rendered the Garrison defensible—before his arrival it resembled anything but a place of defence."[22] Although Harrison recommended that "Capt. Taylor may be continued"[23] at Fort Knox, Washington authorities ordered otherwise. Harrison had "made the arrangement for me to take the command of about eighty light troops which would have been all the light troops belonging to the regular," the Captain later wrote.[24] Meanwhile, however, the War Department instructed him to appear as a defense witness at the trial of General Wilkin-

Louisville Kentucky June the 6th 1808

Sir I received your letter of the 4th of May in which you informed me that I was appointed a firs Lieutenant in the seventh regiment in infantry in the service of the United States which appointment I doo accept.

I am Sir with great respect your obt Servt

Zachary Taylor

The Honrl. H. Dearborn S. at War.

**FIRST LIEUTENANT, UNITED STATES ARMY**
Zachary Taylor's earliest known letter.

son.[25] Governor Harrison was mobilizing his forces for the historic march to Tippecanoe when Zachary departed for Frederick Town, Maryland, having lost his initial opportunity to fight the Indians in open battle.[26]

Although the principal charges preferred against Wilkinson concerned his alleged role in the Burr conspiracy, the prosecution also questioned the General's judgment in moving his fever-stricken troops from New Orleans to Terre Aux Boeufs during the epidemic of 1809. Taylor's testimony was probably confined to the Terre Aux Boeufs episode, with which he was familiar and in which Wilkinson had no ulterior motive despite the disastrous aftermath. On Christmas, 1811, the accused was acquitted on all counts. More than a month before, as soon as his presence was no longer required, Captain Taylor had left Frederick Town for the West. After having devoted December, January, February, and March to recruiting duty at Louisville,[27] he received an order in April, 1812, to take a broken company of the Seventh Infantry to Fort Harrison on the Wabash, and to assume command of that isolated post.[28] After scrambling through the uncleared wilderness of Indiana Territory, he reached the fort on or before May 3.[29] There he was the following month, when the United States declared war on powerful Great Britain.

5

America was unprepared for war. Right was on her side, but might was missing. If the Navy was notoriously feeble, the Army constituted a national joke. Old men and young boys served in the ranks, shoulder to shoulder with calloused criminals. Stealing and desertion prevailed. Pay was pitifully small, equipment poor, morale non-existent all along the line. Feuds and petty jealousies, gambling, duels, and whisky-drinking surfeited the service at the head of which stood Wilkinson, whom few liked and fewer trusted. President James Madison hoped to avenge: (1) The impressment of American seamen into His Majesty's Fleet; (2) Britain's sowing of sedition seeds in every corner of New England;

(3) Encouragement given the Indians to terrorize the pioneers.

The struggle started inauspiciously, especially in the West. July 17—Mackinac fell. August 15—Fort Dearborn was burned, its garrison massacred. August 16—Brigadier General William Hull, in charge of the northwestern army, surrendered at Detroit.[30] These events flung gates ajar for the onrush of redskin hordes, whom Tecumseh had taught to stand together, and the English had armed.

With only Fort Madison on the Mississippi, Fort Wayne on the Maumee, and Fort Harrison on the Wabash protecting American settlers from the exterminating tribes, the Indians planned to attack the three weak posts at once. Taking cognizance of rumors, Captain Taylor had dispatched a detailed message to General Harrison in May and another one in June;[31] and early in August he warned the Governor that Tecumseh was "preparing considerable force to strike an important blow somewhere against the white people. . . ."[32] "The full of the moon," Taylor wrote, "was the time fixed for . . . commencing hostilities."[33]

Fort Harrison lacked adequate defenses for hostilities of any kind. Situated in the heart of the Indian country, three miles above the site of Terre Haute, it was formed on three sides by single rows of pickets, and on the fourth by a range of log barracks flanked at each corner by a primitive blockhouse.[34] This rude fortress, hastily built the preceding October,[35] was pitifully undermanned, a dozen male civilians and Taylor's broken company of inexperienced soldiers comprising the potential fighting force. To make matters worse, many of the troops now suffered from fever so that the twenty-seven-year-old Captain, sick himself, could neither improve the stockade nor "mount a guard of more than six privates and two non-commissioned officers. . . . I had not conceived my force adequate . . . to the defence of this post should it be vigorously attack[ed], for some time past."[36]

6

Informed by friendly Indians that the followers of Tecumseh

and the one-eyed Prophet had taken the warpath, Zachary Taylor was anticipating the full fury of a wilderness attack when four shots punctured the evening stillness of September 3. Although he feared for the safety of two young frontiersmen who were making hay a quarter of a mile from Fort Harrison, the commandant did not "think it prudent to send out at that late hour . . . to see what had become of them." The danger was too great. Without a single commissioned officer to whom he might delegate authority, with nine women and children on his hands and a maximum of fifteen men capable of bearing arms, Taylor could ill afford the exposure of his garrison to butchery in the night. Instead, he waited watchfully till morning when the bodies of the haymakers were found, "each shot with two balls, scalped, and cut in the most shocking manner."

Twenty-four hours after the death of these unfortunates, a party of the Prophet's braves emerged from the forest and, waving a white flag, approached within hearing distance of Fort Harrison. Purposes of peace motivated them, they said, promising that one of their number would return for an interview on the morrow. Taylor agreed to talk to the emissary if and when he came, but privately he suspected treachery. Examining the soldiers' arms, he found them in good order and completed their cartridges to sixteen rounds per man. After drum and fife had sounded tattoo, the Captain cautioned the "guard to be vigilant, and ordered one of the non-commissioned officers . . . to walk round the inside . . . to prevent the Indians [from] taking any advantage of us. . . ." "As I had just recovered from a very severe attack of the fever," he wrote, "I was not able to be up much through the night."

Silence reigned until eleven o'clock, when the report of a sentinel's musket roused the commandant from his bed. Running out into the blackness he found the savages had set fire to the southwest blockhouse which contained provisions and other supplies. It was a time for quick, decisive action. Guns on both sides stormed away. Taylor told several of his men to bring water from the well to quench the fire, but the soldiers were discouragingly slow. In the hour of confusion, one of the women, Julia

Lambert, was equal to the emergency. She lowered herself to the bottom of the well and hoisted brimming buckets to the top. Already the blockhouse door was broken. Tongues of flame played havoc with the whisky. The blazing sheet sped upward to the roof, withstanding every effort of the fire fighters. "What from the raging of the fire, the yelling and howling of several hundred Indians, the cries of nine women and children . . . and the desponding of so many of the men . . . , I can assure you that my feelings were very unpleasant." Then, to cap the climax of misfortune, "two of the stoutest men in the fort . . . jumped the picket and left us."

Tomahawks and scalping knives at the stockade's threshold neither shook the Captain's confidence nor dimmed his hope. "My presence of mind did not for a moment forsake me." With the southwest blockhouse doomed, the single chance of white salvation lay in checking the fire before it reached the barracks. Detailing Surgeon William Clark to supervise civilians and convalescent privates as they ripped off sections of the barrack roof and waterlogged the rest, Taylor directed the able-bodied soldiers who shot steadily and well from the unharmed blockhouse and two bastions. These measures took effect both within the post and without. Inspired by their commandant's example, "never did men act with more firmness and desperation."

Redskins raged around the fort for seven solid hours, whooping bloody murder, charging and retreating, but never dashing far enough to dance their way inside. Private William Cowan bragged, "I killed an Indian!" He did not duck down fast enough, and an Indian killed him. A lone white man in Clark's command fell dead; two others were injured, brought down like sparrows as they strove to drench the roof. But casualties paid premiums; the barracks were out of danger. One of the deserters returned to beg admittance. Failing to recognize his voice, Taylor told "the men in the bastion, where I happened to be, to shoot him let him be who he would." The wretch escaped to another side of the fort where he hid behind a barrel, and later crawled within the picket line to display an arm crushed in the most shocking manner and to

Defence of Fort Harrison,
*Sept. 4th, 1812.*

THE DEFENSE OF FORT HARRISON
A wood engraving by Felter.

tell how his companion had been knifed to death while fleeing. Meanwhile tireless troops raised a sturdy breastwork where the blockhouse once had stood, and at six o'clock in the morning the Indians ceased fire. The fort was saved.[37]

## 7

The fort was saved. Forever or a day? A hundred miles from Vincennes, unfamiliar with the forests, aware that red sentinels would watch both road and river, Taylor subsisted his garrison on unnourishing green corn and delayed dispatching messengers for aid.

So pressing was the need of food, however, that on September 10 two soldiers paddled a short distance down the Wabash, to return almost immediately with the report that "the Indians had built a fire on the bank of the river . . . , which gave them an opportunity of seeing any craft that might attempt to pass, and were waiting with a canoe ready to intercept it."[38]

A second effort to communicate met with success. Leaving Fort Harrison under cover of darkness shortly after midnight of September 12, Taylor's orderly sergeant and a single companion plunged overland through the woods toward Vincennes, and handed their Captain's report of the attack to Acting Governor John Gibson three afternoons later.[39]

As events turned out, the orderly sergeant might as well never have stirred out of the fort, for already Colonel William Russell was heading northward by forced marches at the head of twelve hundred men.[40] And almost before the sergeant reached the territorial capital, Fort Harrison was being relieved and reprovisioned. Taylor's immediate duty was done when the Indians disappeared into their forest fastnesses. And Colonel Russell was the first to proffer congratulations.

William Russell did not stand alone in heaping laurels on Zachary Taylor's head. *The War,* a newspaper published in New York City, carried glowing accounts of the "gallant defence."[41] In Washington, the *National Intelligencer* devoted a full page to the official report of the attack.[42] Acting Governor Gibson of Indiana Territory declared that "the brave defense made by Captain Taylor . . . is one bright ray amid the gloom of incompetency which has been shown in so many places."[43] General Samuel Hopkins of the state of Kentucky grew even more eloquent. "The firm and almost unparalleled defence of Fort Harrison, by Capt. Z. Taylor," he wrote to Governor Shelby, "has raised for him a fabric of character not to be effaced by my eulogy. . . ."[44] Most important of all, precedents were shattered when the *Intelligencer* of October 31 announced that "the President has been pleased to confer the brevet rank of major on Captain Z. Taylor"—the first brevet of any kind ever awarded by the government of the United States.[45]

# CHAPTER III

## REDSKIN AND REDCOAT

### 1

SIGNIFICANTLY or not, Zachary Taylor's defense of Fort Harrison marked the turning point of the western campaign. Later events, bright with glory and wrought on a wider canvas, would be sure to outshine it in the perspective of history. Yet it is equally true that the young Kentuckian's determined stand on the east bank of the Wabash signalized the first American military victory in the War of 1812. And, in contrast to Mackinac, Fort Dearborn and Detroit, it served notice on the English and their Indian allies that not all Americans were incompetent or cowardly.

After this spectacular start, Taylor did not rest on his laurels. In mid-October he left Fort Harrison as aide-de-camp to General Hopkins on an expedition into what was destined to become the state of Illinois.[1] Although Hopkins lacked the leavening influence of United States Regulars, he hoped to attack and destroy the Kickapoo town on the Illinois River with the two thousand green mounted riflemen under his command. He ought to have known better. The best of his troops had been trained only in the militia mode, and they did not know the meaning of obedience.

Reaching the edge of the great prairie, the procession halted. The grass, Taylor wrote to his cousin, was "so entirely gone that our horses could not possibly subsist, and numbers of them began to fail. . . . Our provisions beginning to run short and our guides being at a loss for the precise course of the Town made the men very desirous to return."[2] In spite of the desire of Hopkins and Taylor to continue westward while the weather remained favorable, enthusiasm among the rank and file ebbed so low that when

45

the General called for a mere five hundred to volunteer for the forward march not a soldier spoke.[3]

## 2

Obliged to lead the unruly rabble back to Vincennes, Samuel Hopkins organized a more tractable force of twelve hundred infantrymen and headed them in the direction of the Tippecanoe battleground by way of Fort Harrison.[4]  At the latter post, Taylor found time on November 9 to write to General James Taylor: "We are now ready to start for tippecanoe and several small towns nearby. . . . I am fearful from the lateness of the season and the badness of the weather . . . we shall not be able to affect anything of importance. But rest assured that every thing that men can perform under similar circumstances will be performed."[5]

Although water now covered the entire countryside, Hopkins and Taylor set out from Fort Harrison on November 11, retraced the route taken by General Harrison, and arrived eight days later at Prophetstown near the mouth of the Tippecanoe. Here they destroyed three Indian villages together with a quantity of foodstuffs, but the troops did not meet a single aboriginal until November 21 when in a sharp encounter an American soldier lost his life. On November 22, lurking in ambush, the Indians slew eighteen members of Hopkins' army. Still they did not linger, but vanished into the north country. And Zachary Taylor's hope of fighting a pitched battle vanished with them.[6]

"After reconnoitring sufficiently, we returned to camp," General Hopkins informed Governor Shelby, "and found the ice so accumulated as to alarm us for the return of the [supply] boats. I had fully intended to have spent one more week in endeavoring to find the Indian camps; but the shoeless, shirtless state of the troops, now clad in the remnants of their summer dress; a river full of ice; the hills covered with snow; a rigid climate, and no operations . . . , orders were given and measures pursued for our return on the twenty-fifth. We are now progressing to Fort Harrison through ice and snow where we expect to arrive on the last day of this month. . . ."[7]

3

Throughout the winter of 1812-1813, except for a sick leave spent in Louisville, Brevet Major Taylor superintended the recruiting service in the territories of Indiana and Illinois—mustering and inspecting troops in preparation for the summer campaign.[8] With the advent of warm weather, he joined other officers in perfecting plans for a series of fast forced marches, designed to eliminate the savage menace at a single stroke. The army was to be smaller, more compact, capable of superior speed, less likely to desert on the first provocation. So the officers wisely planned.

Taylor did not participate in the first expedition, which Colonel Joseph Bartholomew led into the Illinois wilderness on June 11, 1813.[9] On July 1, however, he joined Colonel Russell at the head of five hundred and seventy-three sons of Indiana and Kentucky and with them he was disappointed in finding no Indians either at the Delaware towns or on the Mississinewa. After burning the encampments of the redskins, Russell and Taylor circled up and around the Eel River village, Winamac, Prophetstown, and the Winnebago settlement on Wildcat Creek, and thence dropped down to Fort Harrison.

Nowhere did the Brevet Major sight one Indian. Small parties of Americans trekked cross country in a southeasterly direction as far as the Ohio River. Still no Indians.[10] Now Taylor could not escape the conviction that the defense of Fort Harrison, together with subsequent campaigns, had proved effective. Following Tecumseh's example, the braves had all fled northward—many seeking succor from British agents at Malden. For the first time in United States history, the Indian stranglehold on Indiana Territory was broken.

4

Zachary Taylor saw no fighting of any kind in 1813. He chafed in the chains of inaction while luckier men courted immortality in more propitious quarters. Along the New York border, where senile generals competed for the mantle of disgrace, disaster followed on the heels of disaster. Farther to the east, on the New England coast, secession sentiment was rife. On the high seas, however, America had her heroes. In February James Lawrence joined his fellow captains, Isaac Hull and Stephen Decatur, in the naval hall of fame by sinking the British ship *Peacock* in South American waters, and in June he engaged the *Shannon* in a bitter battle. Here, however, fortune turned against him. His *Chesapeake* was captured. Captain Lawrence himself was mortally wounded. "Don't give up the ship!" the dying Lawrence cried. And the Navy had a slogan.

On inland waters, there was new encouragement. "We have met the enemy and they are ours: Two Ships, two Brigs[,] one Schooner & one Sloop," was Oliver Hazard Perry's terse report of the Battle of Lake Erie.[11] In May, a future president, William Henry Harrison, carried the defense of Fort Meigs to a successful termination. In November, another future president, fiery Andrew Jackson, won the battle of Talladega in what some day would be the state of Alabama. Most glamorous of all was the defense of Fort Stephenson, in Ohio Territory, by Taylor's boyhood friend George Croghan—the single colorful event in a career twisted by intemperance, and one entitling Croghan, in General Jackson's opinion, "to be drunk for the rest of his life."[12]

Taylor took no conspicuous role in this portion of the war. During the greater part of the time he commanded at Fort Knox, which he considered secure enough to have his wife join him, bringing their two-year-old daughter Ann. "Peggy . . . says she is very lonesome," the young soldier wrote his brother Hancock, "and is in hopes that you will be as good as your word in paying us the visit you promised. . . . If you come over[,] Peggy says you must bring her some cotton for nitting which [she] wants mother to have spun for her. . . ."[13] No threat of an Indian attack broke the monotony of life at old Vincennes. A garrison of forty-six officers and men[14] stolidly waited for something to happen. And Brevet Major and Mrs. Taylor had no alternative but to wait with them.

Action came at last. In the spring of 1814, an order led Taylor westward to Saint Louis to assume command of all the troops in Missouri Territory. This assignment was a temporary one, but the Kentuckian was retained at Saint Louis after being superseded by Brigadier General Benjamin Howard, who went out from head-quarters to strengthen American posts that dotted the frontier.[15] Both Howard and Taylor were apprehensive lest the English should sweep down toward Saint Louis in overwhelming numbers. And the threat of redskins, massing in large numbers at Credit Island, spread terror over the western countryside. Two catastrophes, each occurring on July 19, 1814, piled fuel on American fears: Several hours after the defeat of one United States lieutenant, John Campbell, by Indians on the Mississippi near its junction with Rock River, another lieutenant, Joseph Perkins, surrendered Fort Shelby at Prairie du Chien to the British. Of Campbell's com-mand, sixteen men died, more than twenty were wounded, and only the happiest coincidence saved the survivors from tomahawk and scalping knife.[16]

Now it was clear to Benjamin Howard that the most effective defense against the enemy lay in a militant American offense. Despite the paucity of seasoned troops, Howard planned accord-ingly. But in the hour of crisis the General fell victim to fever. Straightway the drastic duty of taking action devolved on Zachary Taylor.

## 5

Howard's orders were nothing if not explicit. "Major Taylor," he commanded, "will ascend the Mississippi as high as the Indian Vilages at the mouth of Rock River . . . [and] destroy the Vilages. . . . He will[,] after effecting or failing to effect the object at that place[,] drop down to the Demoine and erect . . . [a fort which] must be maintained untill further orders can be sent. . . ."[17] Thus the campaign had a twofold purpose: (1) Destroy the Indian property if possible; (2) Construct a new post. The first of these objectives was conditional, the second imperative. And Zachary Taylor left Saint Louis.

Gathering his forces at Fort Independence—eight miles above the mouth of the Cuivre—the Brevet Major embarked from that rendezvous at high noon on Monday, August 22,[18] with his little army of four hundred and thirty militiamen and rangers.[19] Advancing up the winding highway of the Mississippi in eight fortified keelboats, the frontier helmsmen followed the course charted by Taylor himself who reconnoitered in the foremost vessel. "We set out with hearts elated and sails filled untill Near sunset and encamped on the west side," Captain James Callaway jotted in his diary. At times the soldiers were forced to wade and pull the boats, heavy with supplies, over the shallow waters of the narrows. Often, too, when the wind died down, Taylor gave orders to ply the oars until "a Number of the men were readdy to feint with fateuge."[20] As if these hardships were not enough, measles began making inroads; by the end of August, dozens of officers and privates had fallen ill, and one of the latter was dead.

Sunday morning, September 4, found the expedition at the mouth of Rock River, where "the Indians began to make their appearance in considerable numbers; running up the Mississippi to the upper village and crossing the river below us." To date hostilities had not commenced. Taylor kept a white flag at his masthead in the hope of pacifying hostile Indians around a council fire. But no emissaries came. Indeed, conciliation seemed out of the question when the Americans saw "a considerable number of horses" on Credit Island and the western shore—placed there as decoys in a naïve attempt to lure frontier detachments within range of enemy guns.

Zachary Taylor ignored this invitation to certain casualty, concentrating his attention on the blistering wind which began to shift early in the afternoon and by four o'clock was blowing "a perfect hurricane." Aware of the weakness of his anchors, and fearing treacherous sandbars half-hidden by water, the young commander headed his fleet toward a small willow-covered island sixty yards above the upper end of Credit Island and near the middle of the Mississippi. To the accompaniment of wind and rain, thunder and lightning, Taylor and his men negotiated a landing, ate their hasty suppers, and prepared to spend a stormy night.[21]

6

Before daybreak on September 5,[22] Indians opened fire on the boats in which the men were sleeping on their arms, mortally wounding a sentinel of Captain Samuel Whiteside's company.[23] The die was cast. Americans returned the fire. But Taylor wisely waited till his troops could see their human targets before retaliating with a counter-offensive. No sooner was the wan light of dawning transmuted into day than the Brevet Major formed his command for action, pushing through the willows to the small island's southernmost tip in pursuit of the savages.

As the aborigines fled downstream to Credit Island, Whiteside raked them with a stiff barrage before they faded in between the trees. Simultaneously, Taylor instructed Captain Nelson Rector to drop down the river, ground his boat on Credit Island's western shore, pour broadside after broadside from his swivel guns, and fire on all canoes within his range. So successful was Rector in carrying out Taylor's order that not a single red man dared to show his face. Descending the Mississippi still farther, the Captain had just completed the destruction of several empty canoes when the Americans encountered trouble from an unexpected source.[24]

Ever since the outset of the expedition, Taylor had anticipated a massing of the Sauk and Fox warriors in the neighborhood of Rock River. For them he was prepared. From the British redcoats, on the other hand, neither he nor General Howard counted on opposition nearer Saint Louis than Prairie du Chien.[25] Although both the British and the Indians had obtained full information on their opponents' movements from the day of the departure from Fort Independence, the American commander was ignorant of the fact that Lieutenant Duncan Graham of the English Indian Department had brought thirty white soldiers, one brass three-pound gun and two swivels from Fort Shelby and had stationed them on Rock Island with a view to stopping Taylor, in case the latter should attempt to ascend the Mississippi all the way to Prairie du Chien. During the night which Taylor had been forced to spend on the willow-covered island, Graham—unbeknown to the American—had transplanted his battery to the western shore directly opposite the keelboats, and assigned a veteran sergeant, James Keating of the Royal Artillery Regiment, to man the three-pounder.[26]

Just as Rector's rangers were boarding their grounded vessel after destroying the canoes, Keating opened fire on the main body of Americans, the first ball pounding through the bow of Taylor's boat. Simultaneously, Graham's swivels blazed away, and a thousand-odd Indians suddenly appeared from nowhere, howling and shrieking and firing hit or miss.[27] From the very first, the gun served by Sergeant Keating produced a telling effect, bull's-eye accuracy adding to the unexpected nature of the attack. And the Americans' confidence was shaken.

Taylor's anchors were weak. The wind consistently blew up a dirty gale about him. Rangers and volunteers returned the fire none the less steadfastly. And Whiteside, under Taylor's order, dropped down to rescue Rector, who had driven back a large detachment of Indians after a well-contested quarter-hour action, but whose boat was drifting helplessly. At this critical juncture, Paul Harpole, one of Captain Rector's men, performed a feat long remembered in the annals of western warfare, leaping waist-deep into the boiling waters to throw a cable to Whiteside's craft near by. Having achieved his objective, Harpole cast caution to the winds. Instead of seeking shelter, he lingered in the stream where, exposed to enemy bullets, he shot off fourteen guns which his companions handed to him before "he himself was shot in the forehead, and tumbled forward into the river, when his body was obtained by the Indians, and cut up into a hundred pieces."[28]

# 7

With artillery odds against him, outnumbered three to one, and with the primary purpose of his expedition yet to be attained,

Brevet Major Taylor now gave the command to retreat for the first and only time in his career. In making this decision, he was motivated by the instructions which Benjamin Howard had issued prior to the expedition's departure from Fort Independence. Any attempt to destroy Indian property must depend entirely on conditions of time and place, the General had urged, whereas the erection of a new post in a strategic situation was imperative to the defense of the West. So it was that the frontier flotilla retreated down the river, facing and returning a murderous fire two miles of the way, and sailing on an additional mile "before a proper place presented itself for landing, as but few of the boats had anchors sufficient to stop them. . . ." American casualties were slight. Only one soldier, the intrepid Harpole, had been killed. Only ten were injured. While the wounded men received medical treatment, the damaged boats were mended. And the pursuing Indians, seeing Taylor's force drawn up for further action, fled "in as great a hurry as they [had] followed us."

Before arriving at a final decision between obedience to Howard on the one hand and recourse to reckless valor on the other, the American commander drew his fellow officers into consultation. Are three hundred and thirty-four troops, he asked them, able to fight the enemy with any prospect of effect, "which is to destroy their villages and corn"? The officers were of the opinion, Taylor wrote, that it was not practicable to attempt either object. "I then determined to drop down the river to the Lemoine [Des Moines] without delay . . . and execute the principal object of the expedition, in erecting a fort" to command the Mississippi.[29]

Taylor's Credit Island foes did not bother him again. Although the British continued to control Prairie du Chien throughout the ensuing fall and winter, his work was successful to the extent that neither redcoat nor redskin penetrated within striking distance of Saint Louis for the duration of the war. Implicitly following General Howard's instructions, he halted opposite the mouth of the Des Moines. And there, on a high bluff on the eastern bank of the Father of Waters, he supervised the construction of a post named in honor of his Kentucky friend, Colonel Richard M.

Johnson, whom contemporaries credited with the slaying of Tecumseh at the recent bloody battle of the Thames.

Notwithstanding the intricate planning which preceded its
erection, Fort Johnson was destined to be Brevet Major Taylor's
station no more than a few weeks. Late in October, 1814, learning
that death had come to Benjamin Howard, he was forced to burn
the fort he had so laboriously built. He had been called back to Saint
Louis to reassume temporary command of all American forces in
Missouri Territory.[30] In November, relinquishing this added responsibility to Colonel Russell, he accompanied his superior two
hundred and fifty miles up the Missouri River to strengthen a
remote settlement which Indians were threatening. When the
savage menace failed to materialize, Taylor again returned to
Saint Louis with no fighting in prospect, intent on bolstering his
credit with the War Department in Washington.[31]

## 8

For the Kentuckian, this was a new avenue of attack. Affiliated
with the Army more than six years, he had long been loath to pull
political wires for purposes of self-aggrandizement. Yet now he
nursed a grudge. And justice sided with him. Four years had
elapsed since his elevation to a captaincy, and, though flattered by
the brevet majority bestowed by President Madison, he knew that
promotion to the full line rank of major was long overdue. His
service had been satisfactory. His immediate superiors had without exception heaped encomiums upon him. Hence Taylor could
not avoid the conclusion that some outside influence must be
blocking the way. Two fellow frontier officers, Colonel William
P. Anderson and Captain W. N. Wilkinson, hated him. Of their
enmity he was certain. They had protested his every move. They
had relayed complaint after complaint against his conduct. Still
it seemed scarcely logical in this hour of national crisis that their
sound and fury would be given serious consideration by the new
chief of the War Department, Secretary James Monroe.

Colonel Anderson of the Twenty-fourth Infantry was a crotchety old woman of a soldier, the type toward which Taylor would instinctively feel and voice contempt for the duration of his military life. Hair-trigger demands in days of war, with lives of noncombatants hanging in the balance, meant little or nothing to William P. Anderson. Consumed by a strange passion for uniting his scattered command, he appeared incapable of countenancing the idea that some of his recruits might be exposed to wilderness danger under Taylor's leadership at a time when Anderson himself was frantically attempting to cement his regiment in the safe confines of Nashville, Tennessee.

Anderson's subordinate, Wilkinson, was a captain to his liking—a chicken-hearted fellow who tried to thwart Taylor at every step and quaked in mortal terror of Indian sharpshooters. With this pitiful person at one end of the line, and the pompous Colonel at the other, a stupid anti-Taylor correspondence kept the pair occupied throughout the summer and early autumn of 1814—letters flying from Anderson to Wilkinson, from Wilkinson to Anderson, and from Anderson to James Monroe himself, each missive crammed with complaints lodged against the Brevet Major.[32]

How had Taylor offended? In April, handicapped by dire lack of regulars, he had ordered Lieutenant Joseph Perkins to leave recruiting for another day, and to assist Governor William Clark in the establishment of Fort Shelby at Prairie du Chien. This was a vital move. It could not be postponed. Yet Anderson besought the War Department to countermand the order, and in September he repeated the request. "No violation more in violation of the 3d. article of the recruiting regulations could be made," the Colonel speciously insisted. "Surely you will not let those infractions pass with impunity."[33]

Having been given no satisfaction, Colonel Anderson wrote one more letter to Washington, this time in October, his dignity having been damaged beyond repair on receipt of the following report from Captain Wilkinson, amazing in its contents:

"DEAR COLO.

"Truly sorry am I to say that your Orders have again been coun-

termanded and I have been ordered with my company to a Fort
three hundred miles up the Mississippi built by Maj. Taylor[.]
Part of my company is already there. . . . When I recd your Orders
I sent an Express off to Maj Taylor who was then up the Mississippi, for that part of my company that was with him but instead
of sending them he has ordered the balance up. I am fixed and
determined not to do duty in this country[,] particularly to be put
in a place where you dare not put your head out—I shall not go up,
as I am at present much indesposed—I shall before this reaches
you send on my resignation to the War Department. . . . I was
over anxious to join the Regiment in the South when we should
have had an opportunity of gaining laurels or finding honorable
graves. . . ."[34]

So much for petty army politics. Exposed to weasel words of
this variety—half-courage, half-cowardice—Zachary Taylor was
fearful that he had lost standing in Washington. Writing from
Saint Louis on November 29, he requested specific information as
to the nature of the complaints. Concurrently, probably at Taylor's
instigation, his friends deluged the War Department with demands that he be promoted. "He deserves . . . attention, confidence
and promotion from the Administration," wrote Jonathan Jennings, a future governor of Indiana, and Richard M. Johnson, a
future vice-president of the United States, in a joint dispatch.[35]
"If an officer were in request to execute any enterprise for his Country, I never knew one I would sooner rely upon."[36] This was the
voice of General Hopkins. Representative Stephen Ormsby considered Taylor a "meritorious officer."[37] And Alexander Stuart
"saw enough to satisfy my mind that he is a most valuable
officer."[38]

Such hearty avowals of confidence bore fruit long overdue. The
Jennings-Johnson letter carried an endorsement for promotion to
the rank of major, signed by the Secretary of War. And in January, 1815, the Adjutant General assured Taylor that "no complaints have been made . . . which can affect your good reputation
with the War Department. . . . I fear you have been under a mistake, relative to promotions—you have never been superceded."[39]

As a matter of record, Taylor had been under no mistake. The proof of the pudding is found in the fact that the Major's new commission, announced in that selfsame letter from the Adjutant General, bore the date of May, 1814—more than seven months before.[40] He was lastingly right in his contention. A pinch of pressure had turned the trick.

### 9

Although Major Taylor's promotion nominally transferred him from the Seventh to the Twenty-sixth Infantry, he did not join his new regiment on the New York border. Following a two-month furlough in Kentucky, he brought his wife back to Vincennes where their second daughter had been born on March 6, 1814.[41] To this baby, whose role in American history was to be a tragic one, her parents gave the name of Sarah Knox Taylor— Sarah in honor of her paternal grandmother, Knox in recognition of Fort Knox which had served Major and Mrs. Taylor as home and fortress during years of national crisis.

Meanwhile grizzled Andrew Jackson, on the outskirts of New Orleans, had taught the English a lesson they were not likely to forget. And a young Virginian named Winfield Scott, a brigadier at twenty-seven, was reaping fame for the glorious part he played at Chippewa and Lundy's Lane. Most important of all, a peace treaty had been signed at distant Ghent. The second war with Great Britain was at an end. For the first time in history, the United States held a clear title to undisputed possession of the entire Northwest.

With the disbanding of America's wartime army, officers saw their grades reduced all along the line. Taylor traveled to Washington in an effort to retain his majority,[42] but his plea fell on deaf ears, and soon he was reduced to his pre-war status of captain in the Seventh Infantry. With the nation out of danger, and with no new wars impending, Taylor considered the times auspicious to devote his energy to private business. On June 15, 1815, when the defender of Fort Harrison was honorably discharged, he was already in Kentucky making a crop of corn.[43]

# CHAPTER IV

## The Years of Peace

### 1

IF SOLDIERING was Zachary Taylor's passion, the soil was the object of his chaste devotion. He liked to see things grow, to earn a living from them, to invest his surplus earnings in land and still more land. Reared amid rural surroundings as four generations of Taylors had been reared before him, he always would prefer the clean, fresh air of the countryside to the proscriptive atmosphere of city living. Hence the wedging of agriculture more deeply into the marrow of his make-up than banking, manufacturing, medicine or law. And hence the soldier's decision to forsake the Army for the lush scenes of his Kentucky childhood.[1]

As early as the second decade of the nineteenth century, planting in Kentucky differed from farming in Ohio or Pennsylvania or New York. In Kentucky, Negroes were plentiful. And Zachary Taylor and his brothers relied on slaves to till their fields and to harvest their crops. Although Lieutenant Colonel Richard Taylor—now a gray-haired grandfather of seventy-one—still owned and managed a majority of the family acres, each of his sons possessed land in his own right, and Zachary was no exception. If the fertility of Jefferson County farms netted the Taylors a handsome profit, nearly as important as the quality of their yield was their proximity to Louisville where mills and markets featured the growth of a coming city of the West. Pioneer had followed pioneer, family had followed family, to the Falls of the Ohio. A handsome new courthouse, paved streets, and policemen to patrol them, contrasted strangely with the swampy village of another day. Steam had been applied to transportation, and Louisville residents were now accustomed to the high-pitched whistle of the river boat, the same shrill sound that seemed so phenomenal four years earlier when Captain Nicholas Roosevelt announced the landing of the *New Orleans* on her maiden voyage from Pittsburgh down to Natchez.[2]

Jefferson County citizens, intent on carving a city out of swampland and farms out of forests, held no man in higher esteem than Richard Taylor and his sons. Nor was this a matter of thumbing genealogies or counting generations. All four boys had forsaken home fires in the War of 1812, Joseph Pannill Taylor obtaining a second lieutenant's commission at the age of seventeen, George Taylor rising from the rank of ensign to that of third lieutenant, Hancock Taylor sacrificing important tasks of a domestic nature to enlist as a quartermaster's sergeant, and Zachary Taylor emerging a full-fledged hero.[3] Springfield was noted for hospitality, a quality dear to Kentuckian hearts, and feminine charm was never lacking. Elizabeth, the Richard Taylors' eldest daughter, had married her cousin John Gibson Taylor. But Sally and Emily were still in their teens. And many a frontier Brummell came to call or court.

It was to this humming Taylor household in the friendly brick homestead that the veteran of Fort Harrison and Credit Island returned as a civilian, bringing his wife and two small children to join their relatives at Springfield. The routine of planting suited him so well that in April, 1816, he wrote to a distant kinsman: "I have comenced making corn and tobaco & am now in my own cabbin where I will always be extreamely happy to take you by the hand. . . . I can assure [you] I do not regreat the change of calling or the course I have pursued. . . ."[4] A happy scene, this picture of contentment, so perfect that the young veteran must have been strongly tempted to linger in the bosom of his family. Linger he did not, and that is significant. Love of the land gave way once again to passion for military duty. And summer found him back in the Army, restored to his wartime rank of major.[5]

## 2

Far to the north, on the western shore of Lake Michigan's blue

waters, the primitive French village of Green Bay—whither Major
Taylor was ordered—was a far cry from the expanding, thriving
river town of Louisville. Green Bay also bordered on a river,
but there the similarity ceased, for Green Bay housed inhabitants
as backward and un-American as Louisville's were progressive and
prosperous. With three exceptions the forty-seven heads of families were of French origin, ignorant peasants who hunted and
traded with the Indians and made half-hearted attempts to cultivate pitiful patches of ground around their shabby log huts.[6]

French in tradition, French in language, these underprivileged
people measured land in arpents, not in acres. A few profited from
the fur trade, but nine-tenths were lowly laborers performing
menial tasks, cohabiting with Indian "wives," and raising enormous families of half-breed boys and girls. Used to living their
own lives in their own parochial way without interference from
the general government, they had long been influenced against the
United States by British agents who succeeded in poisoning their
unformed minds with an anti-American virus. Small wonder,
then, that gloom pervaded Green Bay when four American vessels
sailed into the Fox River on August 7, 1816, transporting troops to
erect a fort and to control for the first time land which the United
States had nominally possessed for more than thirty years, but
never peopled.[7]

Major Taylor, now of the Third Infantry, found it impossible to
reach Green Bay as promptly as his brother officers. His new commission, dating from May 17, failed to arrive in Kentucky before
the month of August, and Taylor was forced to put his private
affairs in order before leaving Louisville for Detroit.[8] Here he
reported to Brevet Major General Alexander Macomb. But he did
not tarry. For soon his boat was chopping its way in the face of
wintry weather up Lake Huron to Mackinac Island, and crossing
Lake Michigan to within eighteen miles of his prospective post.
"After a series of storms and difficulties, I have got so far," Robert
Dickson, one of his companions, wrote from their camp on November 25. "We . . . found the ice a short distance from this place.
Maj. Taylor . . . , Capt. Gray, and Lieut. Hopkins came with me.

Maj. Taylor will command at LaBaye when Col. Chambers goes away, which will be early in the Spring."[9]

Together with Dickson, George Gray and Edmond Hopkins, Taylor finally attained his destination in the last week of November, finding Fort Howard under construction on the west bank of the Fox River at the southern terminus of the bay. Situated in the heart of the Indian country, Fort Howard was perhaps the most important military post in the United States. Upon its commander devolved the duty of pacifying the redskins and transforming the American Northwest into terrain safe enough for pioneers to rear their families in comparative security and to establish permanent homes. Its garrison of half a thousand, its six captains, six lieutenants and regimental band of sixteen musicians would soon be housed in "a range of barracks facing three sides of a square parade, and surrounded by a stockade of timber thirty feet high with block houses at the angles." Glistening with whitewash, it would present "a smart military appearance . . . in the midst of a grassy plain and backed by a dense forest of pine," and contribute a dash of color and gaiety to an otherwise bleak landscape.[10]

"Everything at present bears a peaceful aspect," wrote a vagabond physician named William Henry Henning, who chanced to be at Green Bay. "But how long this state of things will continue is very uncertain. Without a great deal of circumspection on the part of the Indian department, and a chain of posts always properly garrisoned[,] I have little hesitation in saying that our frontier again will witness the horrors of savage warfare. . . . The storm is murmuring at a distance, which I am fearful will, sooner or later, burst on us with all the accumulated horrors of savage vengeance."[11]

## 3

Despite Doctor Henning's pessimistic prediction, storm clouds failed to burst upon the fort. Had eventualities borne out the prophecy, another laurel might have been added to the reputation of Zachary Taylor, who succeeded Talbot Chambers in command.

In the eyes of the privates of Fort Howard, who critically observed
his stocky figure, every word and action of their thirty-two-year-
old commandant bespoke strict attention to the nation's business.
If Taylor's unusually short bow legs occasionally excited merriment, this eccentricity was usually overlooked by soldiers who
envied the well-developed chest, the massive shoulders, the lofty
forehead and the thin, tight lips of the veteran from Kentucky who
had dared repel hostile Indians under the fire of Fort Harrison.
Men of action admire men of action, and Taylor was one of these.
Not a man, perhaps, to tread the measures of the minuet with the
grace and ease demanded in the ballrooms of the East, but, to isolated regulars at faraway Fort Howard, Major Taylor looked the
leader.

4

Wisconsin antiquaries have written that Margaret Taylor, whose
devotion never faltered, again journeyed far from Kentucky com-
forts to join her husband at his post of service.[12] Since Indian troubles no longer loomed on the western horizon, the story is at least
worthy of consideration although not a single document verifies
the tradition. It is definitely known that Mrs. Taylor did not come
to Green Bay on or before October 25, 1817,[13] but history does not
tell if she arrived at a later date or whether she was accompanied
by her three small children—Ann Mackall Taylor, aged six; Sarah
Knox, barely two; and the infant Octavia, whose birth coincided
with her father's reinstatement in the Army.[14]

Joined, or not joined, by his wife and daughters, Major Taylor
installed material conveniences in his hitherto crude quarters. Fine
old china had been sent out from Louisville, and a mammoth side-
board and mahogany tables took the place of the rough-hewn
benches of Green Bay.[15] Unfamiliar as such refinements were to
the Green Bay peasantry, to the Major they seemed essential; and
his quarters provided a pleasant setting for the entertainment of
his subordinates, his friend the Indian agent, and those few settlers
who knew what to do with a knife and fork. Travelers who made

their way out to Fort Howard in that primitive era paid tribute to Taylor's hospitality. Colonel Abram Edwards, a frontier merchant prince, expressed surprise and appreciation, and another visitor, Samuel A. Storrow, gratefully acknowledged that he had been "most kindly entertained."[16]

The business of commanding Fort Howard, however, was by no means an entirely enjoyable affair. Grief aplenty was attached, and Taylor drew a man-sized measure. The typical peacetime bickering of military tyros went on around him and over his head. Nor were his gestures in the direction of justice as tactful as they might have been. By virtue of his position as the ranking officer of his regiment in the region west of Detroit, the Major assumed the right to issue orders to troops of the Third Infantry stationed at Fort Mackinac and Fort Dearborn as well as at Fort Howard. At Mackinac, Brevet Colonel John McNeil of the First Infantry disputed this assumption. General Macomb sided with McNeil, and for nine months a spirited controversy raged. Taylor was disgusted. He seriously considered challenging McNeil to a duel because of remarks attributed to that officer, and he viewed Macomb's arguments as so many small potatoes, lashing out at his commander in his most sarcastic vein. Please inform me, he asked the General with mock politeness, "if I am to report through a junior officer ... and if the command of Mackina[c] ... descends regularly from one to another in the same family without respect to rank."[17]

In this connection, the spirit if not the letter of Taylor's attitude verged on insubordination. Yet in internal garrison difficulties at Green Bay, he set his face sternly against insubordination of any kind. Discovering that the liquor supply was running low and that regular rations of the stuff could not be obtained inexpensively until spring, the Major determined to protect his soldiers against exorbitant fees. In February, 1818, he specified that for the present no whisky should be made available to officers or men, as such a purchase "was ... calculated to benefit the Speculator ... and not to benefit the Soldier."[18] A miniature Whisky Rebellion threatening, Taylor stood resolute. "When I was informed that

Lieut. McLeod [Colin McCloud] was very much dissatisfied at the order ... and ... was carrying his dissatisfaction to such lengths as was calculated to excite mutiny among the troops ..., I immediately arrested him. . . . I am informed that Lieut. McLeod, aided by the certificates of Lieut. [Turbey F.] Thomas, has preferred charges against me, for not having ... whisky purchased. . . . I hope the General will act on them. . . . I court investigation."[19]

Zachary Taylor confronted other problems during his tour of duty at Green Bay, some of no consequence whatsoever, others as significant as the threat of mutiny. He feared that the food supply would not hold out: "Unless considerable exertions are made to forward ... provisions early in the Spring, the troops here must suffer very much."[20] He found fault with Macomb's inefficiency: No muster rolls or inspection returns could be dispatched to the General "untill this post is furnished with blank forms . . . or paper."[21] He suspected that insult had been added to injury when Fort Howard's sole semi-literary private was peremptorily ordered to Detroit: "It appears [if] a clerk is wanting at H. Quarters[,] one must be selected from the company clerks of the 3d [Regiment] and ordered from the extreme part of the Department. . . . Those are acts I consider of oppression, that I conceive myself bound to oppose in a proper manner. . . ."[22]

## 5

The Major rejoiced when, after twenty-two disagreeable months on the northwestern frontier, he took advantage of a furlough in the late summer of 1818 and left Green Bay for Louisville.[23] Here he was to remain for more than a year, and, although superintendence of the recruiting service occupied much of his time, the period was not without incident. One high spot occurred on April 20, 1819, when he won promotion to the rank of lieutenant colonel of the Fourth Infantry,[24] and an even more colorful event took place in the early summer during President Monroe's visit to the southern states.

Joined in Georgia by the popular Andrew Jackson, the presidential procession had swung over the War Path to Knoxville,

GEORGE ROGERS CLARK        WILLIAM HENRY HARRISON

ALEXANDER MACOMB        THOMAS SIDNEY JESUP

FOUR ARMY MEN WHO INFLUENCED TAYLOR

The portrait of Clark is from the original painting by Matthew Jouett, in the Filson Club, Louisville. The portraits of Harrison, Jesup, and Macomb are from paintings in the possession of the War Department, Washington, photographed by the United States Army Signal Corps.

along the Cumberland Road to Nashville, and thence into Kentucky.[25] Taylor was one of the party in the Bluegrass State, and the morning of June 30, witnessed the unusual spectacle of the chief executive of the United States and two future chief executives breaking bread as fellow guests at Liberty Hall, ex-Senator John Brown's spacious residence in Frankfort. On July 1, their hostess was writing to her son Orlando, a Princeton undergraduate: "The President, *James Monroe*[,] has arrived and departed. . . . Yesterday morning he breakfasted with us, in company with General Jackson and that hero whose cool, determined and successful courage has never been rivalled in ancient or modern times, who so bravely defended Fort Harrison, Maj. Zachary Taylor. They spent the last evening at Mr. Bibb's, breakfasted this morning at the Governor's[,] and are now on their way to Colonel Richard M. Johnson's where they will dine today."[26]

There is no record of the conversation engaged in by Monroe and Jackson with the younger man whom destiny also fated to reach the White House. Nor is it known when Taylor, taking leave of his illustrious companions, retraced his steps to Jefferson County. It is presumed that he returned before July 27, when Mrs. Taylor presented him with a fourth daughter whose name was Margaret Smith Taylor and whose earthly life was to be brief.[27]

## 6

Without having served actively with the Fourth Infantry, Taylor on August 13, 1819, was transferred to the Eighth Infantry, probably at his own request.[28] The following February, accompanied by his family, he descended the Ohio and Mississippi Rivers to Bayou Sara, Louisiana, where he saw Mrs. Taylor and the children comfortably settled at the house of her sister, Mrs. Chew. The Lieutenant Colonel then continued south to New Orleans and, making his way one hundred and twenty miles northeast of Madisonville, he reached a point near the line between the state of Mississippi and the Choctaw Nation where his regiment was completing construction of the Jackson Military Road.

"You must be well aware of my unpleasant situation," he wrote to Quartermaster General Thomas S. Jesup on April 20 at Six Towns. "... The 8th is composed entirely of recruits without organization, subordination, or discipline, and without harmony among the officers. ... The opening [of] this road has been most shamefully delayed ... , & the money that will be expended in completing it, will I am fearful greatly exceed what was ever calculated on. ... That part of the Regt. immediately under my command, consists of about four hundred & sixty men, which I found under the command of Capt. [Willis] Foulk, in a state of starvation. ... They had remained about six weeks where I found them, were on half rations of bread, & in a country where nothing could be procured except beef, of the poorest kind. ..."

Having only five days' rations on hand, and a quartermaster without funds, Foulk had been content to wait for supplies. Taylor took a more realistic view of the problem. He did not wait. Sending a detachment of soldiers to Pearl River, he pledged the credit of the government to obtain meat and flour, built a storehouse at Six Towns, and at once pressed forward to open the road in the hope of advancing three miles per day and of arriving at the Gulf of Mexico within a month.[29] This hope was too sanguine, but in two months' time the work was done, and mid-June found six companies erecting quarters at Cantonment Bay Saint Louis.[30]

To Bay Saint Louis in 1820 came Ethan Allen Hitchcock, a scholarly young lieutenant who devoted his leisure hours to a study of David Hume's *History of England*. "It was about the only book that Col. Taylor had ever read," wrote Hitchcock, "and he was fond of revising his reading and then coming to my hut to talk it over."[31] Hitchcock, however, was mistaken in assuming that the *History of England* was the only serious work that Taylor had mastered. Jesup had sought the Lieutenant Colonel's views as to the future frontier policy to be pursued by the United States. In his reply, Taylor shed light on the breadth and weight of his military knowledge. "As to fortifications," he advised, "I think we are in some instances extending them farther than necessary. ... Your plan of establishing large depots in time of peace well supplied with all the munitions of war, on the great avenues leading to the frontiers, are much more important . . . than covering the whole with fortifications. . . . No countries in Europe, or the world, were so well fortified as France & the Netherlands, and yet those fortifications did not prevent the allies from overrunning the . . . former, a few years since, nor the French under Pichegrew [Charles Pichegru] subduing the latter during the French revolution; fortifications along our maratime frontier, I only deem important. . . ."[32]

In view of later criticism that Taylor harbored prejudice against West Point and West Pointers, his opinion at this time is of interest. "I am in hopes . . . ," he observed, "[that] we shall get nearly or all the officers who may be hereafter appointed, to keep up the peace establishment, from that institution. . . . There has been a few appointments recently made from the Cadets, in this Regt, that would do honor to any army—But . . . unless practice can be blended with theory, the latter will be but of little service. . . . Better to have a practical, than a theoretical soldier, if they are to possess but one qualification, but when a soldier can combine both, it gives him every advantage. . . . Such unfortunately is the passion in our country for making roads, fortifications, and building barracks . . . with soldiers . . . that a man who would make a good overseer, or negro driver, is better qualified for our service, than one who had received a first rate military education. . . . The ax, pick, saw & trowel, has become more the implement of the American soldier, than the cannon, musket or sword. . . ."[33]

Taylor did not deplore manual labor, but he thought such labor ought to be limited. The Eighth Infantry "cannot even go through its facings correctly, much less through its firings & battalion evolutions, nor is this . . . to be attributed to a want of intelligence, or industry on the part of the officers. . . ."[34] Eighteen months on the Jackson Road told part of the story, and no sooner had Cantonment Bay Saint Louis been established than Brevet Brigadier General Daniel Bissell blundered by ordering two companies to Baton Rouge to erect works there.

In Washington, Jesup and others were planning the reorganization of the Army. Taylor contributed definite proposals. His suggestions were revolutionary, calling for the elimination of one major general and staff, two brigadiers and staffs, the adjutant and inspector general, the surgeon general, two assistants, and a portion of the post surgeons "who perform little or no duty, & in some instances have embarked in private practice...." The Army ought also to dispense with the apothecary general and his two assistants, the whole of the purchasing department, and some of the military storekeepers, turning over the latter's duties to the quartermaster department. The commissary department of subsistence should be fostered, and the engineer corps put to work on a "complete & accurate survey ... of the whole of the frontier, to make maps & charts of the same, shewing the most vulnerable points, pointing out the proper routs, that troops & munitions of war could be transported ... with the greatest facility & the least expence...." The ordnance corps should be remodeled, an invalid corps established, and sick and antiquated officers forced to join it.[35] This last recommendation was to be repeated by Taylor throughout his military career. The inefficiency of superannuated generals annoyed him, and he resolved to retire from the Army before his years made him a burden. In 1820, Bissell provided the object lesson. Before the idea of an invalid corps occurred to Taylor, he thought Bissell should be "permitted to return to St. Louis, & spend the balance of his days on furlough...."[36]

## 7

Meanwhile calamities of a personal nature beset the Lieutenant Colonel. On July 8, 1820, death came in the form of "a violent bilious fever" to his "sweet intelligent" three-year-old daughter Octavia Pannill Taylor.[37] Octavia's father absented himself from Bay Saint Louis in August, and the presumption is that he went to Bayou Sara to comfort his wife. Returning to his post, he received word on September 18 that Mrs. Taylor lay dangerously ill. Setting out immediately for Bayou Sara, he held no hope of her recovery.

"At best her constitution is remarkable delicate. ... This information has nearly unmanned me, for my loss will be an irrepareable one. . . . I am confident the feminine virtues never did concentrate in a higher degree in the bosom of any woman than in hers. . . ."[38] Eventually Mrs. Taylor did recover, but the entire family was affected by the sickness. Ann and Sarah Knox gradually gained back their health, but on October 22 the baby Margaret succumbed.[39] The death of two children within four months was a dreadful blow. Taylor had considered purchasing a plantation in Louisiana, but "this has allmost determined me from even thinking of settling permanently in this country, and it is more than likely when I quit the army, that I shall return to Kentucky. . . ."[40]

Due to unsettled banking conditions in Kentucky, money matters gave Zachary Taylor cause for added concern. It is a matter of record that only his lack of an adequate income from his properties dampened his desire to retire to civilian life. "If my private affairs was not in some measure embarrassed," he confided to General Jesup on June 18, 1821, "I would not remain in the army another moment on any terms. . . ."[41] And three days earlier he had written: "If I cannot be retained with my present rank . . . , it is my wish to be placed on the list of disbanded officers. . . ."[42] This reference to a possible reduction from a lieutenant colonelcy to a majority was not without foundation. The reorganization of the Army had resulted differently from his anticipation, and Taylor would have been reduced in rank through no fault of his own if his friend Jesup had not interceded. "I was not mistaken," he wrote in gratitude to the Quartermaster General, "in attributing my retention to your friendly interference—The numerous acts of friendship I have red from you . . . will not be forgotten, & for none do I feel more greatful, than for the late stand you took in my behalf, when such evident injustice was about to be done me by the board of officers in question. . . . At the same time, I am almost sorry that you had not suffered their first intentions to have been carried into effect. . . . Disbandment . . . has no terrors, & I have no fears of succeeding tolerably well in civil life. . . ."[43]

# CHAPTER V

## GUARDING THE FRONTIER

### 1

RETAINING his rank and remaining in the army, Taylor left the Eighth Infantry in 1821. On June 1 he was assigned to the First Infantry. And on August 16 he was again transferred, this time to the Seventh Infantry,[1] the regiment which had been selected to protect western Louisiana and Arkansas Territory from lawless white adventurers and to keep order among the Indians. Reports from Fort Smith indicated that the Indian problem was especially acute. The warlike Osages violently objected to the infiltration of Delaware, Sauk, Fox, Shawnee, Iowa and Kansas tribes from the north, and committed many an outrage upon the Cherokees and Choctaws, who were in the act of taking possession of their new lands. As early as 1818, more than forty thousand Indians congregated on the Red River.[2] White pioneers were also making their toilsome way into the Southwest, where Fort Smith was the only outpost. Brevet Major General Edmund P. Gaines, the hero of Erie, commanded the Western Division of the Army. Gaines instructed Colonel Matthew Arbuckle and four companies of the Seventh Regiment to garrison Fort Smith and ordered Lieutenant Colonel Taylor to northwestern Louisiana. Taylor, who was still at Bay Saint Louis in mid-October, reached Natchitoches with four companies on November 14.[3]

With customary energy, Taylor, in November, established Fort Selden on the crest of a high bluff overlooking Bayou Pierre, upstream from the junction of the bayou with the Red River, two miles above Grand Ecore and twelve miles from Natchitoches.[4] Here he wintered with his men, whom General Gaines found in good order during his tour of inspection the following March.

"The Commanding General," Gaines wrote, "is gratified to find, that ... the companies at this place exhibit in their healthful appearance, their arms, equipment and dress, and particularly in their Battalion evolutions, the most satisfactory evidence of skill and vigilant attention on the part of the immediate commandants, as well as the company officers; and of obedience and good conduct on the part of most of the N-Commissioned Officers and private soldiers. The General congratulates the troops on the prospect of their immediately occupying an eligible position near the national boundary, where they may calculate upon the enjoyment of health and advancement in professional knowledge; and a participation in the first activity which may occur upon this important border of our country."[5]

"An eligible position near the national boundary" referred to the site of a permanent post which Gaines, advised by Taylor, had selected[6] and on March 28, 1822, ordered the latter to occupy. This site, Shields's Spring, was twenty-five miles southwest of Natchitoches atop a ridge equidistant from that sleepy town and the muddy Sabine River which was then considered the boundary between the United States and Spanish Texas. "Lt. Col. Taylor," said Gaines, "... will canton the troops in huts of a temporary kind, sufficient for their health and comfort during the ensuing summer. The huts will be built by the troops; and to facilitate their completion, tools, waggons, and teams, planks and nails will be furnished by the quartermaster department...."[7] Abandoning Fort Selden, the Lieutenant Colonel moved his companies to Shields's Spring where a log work which he named in honor of Jesup was begun under the superintendence of Captain George Birch.[8] Taylor was officially transferred back to the First Infantry on January 1, 1822,[9] but he remained with the Seventh Regiment until November, dividing his time between Cantonment Jesup and Fort Smith.[10] Military occupation of the Sabine River region resulted in none of the hostilities which General Gaines so sanguinely expected, and Taylor's tenure was uneventful. On November 9, Taylor commanded one hundred and forty-one officers and men at Cantonment Jesup, but by the end of the year he had taken

charge of Cantonment Robertson near Baton Rouge with its First
Infantry garrison of three hundred and fifteen.[11]

## 2

Except for a period during March and April when he obtained a
leave of absence, and an interval in November when he attended
a court-martial at Cantonment Jesup, Taylor continued in the
vicinity of Baton Rouge throughout 1823. On January 27 of that
year, he purchased from Byrd Buford a plantation of three hundred and eighty acres in the neighboring Parish of Feliciana near
the Mississippi line. He paid two thousand dollars down, and gave
promissory notes for four thousand dollars to be met in two equal
installments in 1824 and 1825.[12] His slaves he transported from
Kentucky. The first crop was a disappointment. "I have found it
to fall considerably short of my expectations," Taylor wrote in
January, 1824. Working "as good land as any in the country, 18
prime hands . . . made only 40 bales of cotton, which is worth at
present about 60 dollars pr bale. . . . Deducting the wages of an
overseer, & other expenses, the net proceeds will not exceed $1,500
if it will amount to that sum. . . ."[13]

Ethan Allen Hitchcock, who was one of Taylor's subalterns at
Baton Rouge, found Cantonment Robertson extremely depressing.
"Some thirty idle officers were present for a number of months," he
confided to his diary, "a majority of them dissipated men without
education. . . . The general talk was of duels—of what this one said
and that one threatened." Unable to tolerate such companions,
Hitchcock often escaped into the woods with a small volume in
his pocket "and remained a whole day, for no other purpose than
to be out of hearing of profanity, ribaldry, and blustering bragga-
docio."[14] Zachary Taylor was more fortunate than the unmarried
Hitchcock, for Mrs. Taylor and Sarah Knox were with him, and
domestic interests and planting operations occupied that portion of
his time not given over to supervising the construction of the new
barracks. Taylor wrote many letters, advising his brother Hancock
on the management of the Kentucky farms,[15] complaining to

Mrs. John Gibson Taylor that work on the Feliciana plantation "has gone on very badly,"[16] and lamenting the death of his mother, who had passed away in 1822. Taylor's eldest daughter had been spending a vacation from her Lexington school with her Aunt Elizabeth. "We was truly gratified," the Lieutenant Colonel wrote his sister, ". . . to learn that Ann was with you. . . . I well know that being among her kind and affectionate relatives . . . was a perfect treat to her. . . . I flatter myself that you were able to send her back by the time school commenced. . . . She has already lost a great deal of time. . . ."[17] The senile stubbornness of his octogenarian father was another matter of concern. Zachary wished the Revolutionary veteran might be induced to consult Hancock on affairs of business: "Indeed I should not be at all astonished . . . [if] some person or other will cheat him out of his plantation one of these days. . . . It is perhaps one of father's weakest points that he has no confidence in his children, who . . . [are] all interested in his welfare; but this should in no wise alter our deportment to him . . . , and I am truly sorry that it is not in my power to visit him frequently."[18]

Taylor's father participated actively in affairs of state, siding with the "Old Court" in the spirited Kentucky judicial controversy and acting as a presidential elector on several occasions. Now Taylor himself evinced a growing interest in politics and politicians. Due probably to President Madison's failure to interfere in his behalf when his rank was reduced in 1815, Taylor had considered that gentleman, who was his own second cousin, "perfectly callous, & unacquainted with the noble feelings of a soldier. . . ."[19] John C. Calhoun, on the other hand, possessed "the finest talents, the greatest firmness, & the most liberal views of any man in the Nation. . . ."[20] In Baton Rouge he lauded President Monroe who, thanks chiefly to John Quincy Adams and George Canning, had lately evolved the Monroe Doctrine.

"The President's message appears to be generally approved throughout the Nation. . . . The view he has taken as respects our situation in relation to Spanish America is certainly a correct one,

& I have no doubt, the nation will be prepared to go [to] any lengths in preventing the European potentates from interfering in the affairs of that country so far, as relates to ... compeling them to submit to the mother country, or to the laws of old Spain—We all no doubt feel interested for the success of the Greeks, but ... I do not believe that it would be policy for us to interfere in the convulsions of that country; the crowned heads of Europe, might complain of our interfering in the affairs of Greece, with the same propriety that we would in their intermedling with those of South America or Mexico—Fa[r]ther than humanity is concerned, & the wish we have to see every Nation free, I believe it to be very immaterial, as regards the interest of this country, whether the Crescent, or Cross prevails; This subject however appears to swallow up every other. ... In some parts of the country even the Presidential question ... appears to be merged in the cause of the Greeks, & I should not be at all surprised ... at the good citizens of N. York ... embarking in a crusade, against the Turks ... , with the same enthusiasm ... as the catholicks of Europe did during the 12th & 13th centuries, for the recovery of the holy land."[21]

## 3

When Zachary Taylor left Baton Rouge in February, 1824,[22] he became superintendent general of the Western Department's recruiting service with offices in Cincinnati and later in Louisville.[23] Except for his brother Joseph, who had rejoined the Army and was now a captain in the Third Artillery, all the living members of his immediate family dwelt in Jefferson County, Kentucky, or visited there frequently. His father still resided in the old brick homestead, Springfield, near the Ohio River. His brother Hancock, a widower, had married again and was rearing a second brood of children. His sister Emily, who was the wife of Captain John Stadler Allison and the mother of two young sons, divided her time between Louisiana and Kentucky. His sister Elizabeth, her husband and five children made their home near Springfield at Beechland. His sister Sally and his brother George, leading unhappy existences, leaned on their kinsfolk for financial and moral aid. Sally's marriage to French Strother Gray, whom Zachary described as a "worthless puppy,"[24] had turned out unfortunately. And a falling tree had injured George's back, deforming him for life.[25] Mrs. Zachary Taylor and Sarah Knox returned to Jefferson County when the Lieutenant Colonel paused there en route to Cincinnati. On April 20, 1824, Mrs. Taylor gave birth to her fifth daughter, Mary Elizabeth, who was known as "Betty" from infancy up.[26]

Save for Betty's birth and the subsequent birth of Taylor's only son, Richard, on January 27, 1826,[27] the Cincinnati-Louisville period passed without unusual incident. The superintendent general's was a responsible task and a tedious one, but it rarely required decisions of a high order since nearly all such decisions were automatically referred to Washington. For two and a half years Taylor concerned himself with compiling enlistment reports, submitting monthly returns, supervising the performance of captains and lieutenants on recruiting duty, and estimating costs of feeding, clothing, arming and transporting privates from rendezvous at New Orleans, Natchez, Saint Louis, Louisville, and Cincinnati to posts on the frontier. That he functioned efficiently is witnessed by files of yellowing letters in the Adjutant General's office,[28] but no doubt his hopes of recognition and advancement soared when at last he was ordered to leave Louisville and to sit as a member of a board of officers in the national capital.

Lieutenant Colonel Taylor reached the City of Magnificent Distances on October 3, 1826, signed the War Department register,[29] then repaired to his room at Basil Williamson's Mansion House at the northeast corner of Fourteenth Street and Pennsylvania Avenue.[30] The Washington of that day failed to awe a critical visitor. Its streets were a succession of ruts and mudholes, and Nathaniel P. Willis thought heaven "had rained naked buildings upon an open plain."[31] Unlike the drawing-room officers of the East, however, Taylor came to the capital so seldom that the city's development since 1815 must have impressed him. Congress was not in session, and neither President Adams nor Vice-President Calhoun had ended their vacations. But Taylor's cousin, Secretary of War James Barbour, had arrived from Virginia,[32] and Postmaster General John McLean, whose beautiful daughter Eveline would soon be the bride of Joseph P. Taylor, had likewise returned. On the Washington stage, actors were performing *Paul Pry,* a "new and popular comedy. . . ."[33] James Fenimore Cooper, the *National Intelligencer* noted, "has been recognized by the King of France, as consul . . . for the city of Lyons. . . ."[34] Forty-three deaths in Washington in September! One of gangrene, one of scrofula, and one "suddenly."[35] An editorial writer roundly condemned Robert Owen's communistic experiments at New Harmony, Indiana, which "are calculated to lead to the most mischievous results. . . ."[36] And the tongues never wagged faster than at the mention of the name of Andrew Jackson whose quest of the presidency dominated conversation in the homes of the fashionable and in the taverns on the Avenue.

Taylor's letters do not reveal the part he played in the social Washington of 1826. That he called on Barbour is probable, and he certainly engaged in many a prolonged discussion of the merits and demerits of America's citizen soldiery, since determination of the fate of the Militia was the purpose for which his board convened. These discussions were destined to achieve nothing. Taylor's fellow officers included four Militia generals together with Scott, Macomb, Brevet Colonel Abram Eustis, Lieutenant Colonel Enos Cutler and Captain Charles J. Nourse.[37] Scott, supported by Taylor, advocated a few minor alterations in the *status quo* and opposed the Militia's adopting more of the character of the Regular Army. Although a majority of the officers concurred in this view, the bill based on their findings was never enacted into law and in time was relegated to the limbo of congressional oblivion.

4

In Washington, Taylor availed himself of the Jesups' hospitality, and it was to the Quartermaster General that he described the wearisome land and water trip back to Kentucky after adjournment of the military board. "By traveling the whole of two nights, & the greater part of the third," he wrote from Louisville on January 29, 1827, "I reached Wheeling on thursday morning about 7 Oclock, which made me three days & five hours from Washington, during which time I was not more than two hours in bed. . . . [I] was fortunate in meeting with a small Steamboat which set out on the evening of the same day for this place, but . . . we were seven days in getting down [from Wheeling to Louisville]. . . . We . . . was frequently aground. . . . We had to break the ice the whole of the last day's run, the river being frozen entirely over. . . . [Since that time] all comunication by water has been . . . stoped above & blow the falls. . . . There has been commenceing the day after christmas thirty days of the coldest weather experienced in this country for the last thirty years. . . . This has detained me here much longer than I had wished. . . . I am in hopes the river will be navigable in a few days, if so, I shall proceed in the first Boat for N. Orleans, where I expect to find orders from Genl Gaines, which in all probability will determine my destination for the present year. . . ."[38]

Taylor departed from Louisville shortly after the penning of this letter, and reported in New Orleans before the end of February.[39] His nominal superior in the First Infantry was the same Colonel McNeil with whom he had altercated in 1818, but either design or chance kept the old antagonists apart. General Gaines, a distant relative of the Lieutenant Colonel, was a commander to his liking, and the following fourteen months passed pleasantly enough.[40] From February to June, 1827, Taylor was stationed in New Orleans. During the greater part of the summer, he transferred regimental headquarters to Baton Rouge,[41] perhaps in order to be near his Feliciana Parish plantation. Returning to New Orleans in November, he remained there until May 1, 1828,[42] when a new assignment placed him in charge of the northwesternmost post in the United States, Fort Snelling, at the junction of the Mississippi and the St. Peter's Rivers, in what one day would become the state of Minnesota.

Built by Colonel Josiah Snelling, the impetuous red-haired "Prairie Hen" whom an unknown captain named Zachary Taylor had supplanted at Fort Harrison as far back as 1812, the commandant's quarters at Fort Snelling provided more comfort than might have been expected in such an isolated outpost. Inside the diamond-shaped fortress and facing the flagstaff, the parade ground and the old round tower, the Taylor family's new home contained four rooms on the main floor and kitchens and pantries in the basement.[43] In this house Mrs. Taylor, never happier than when occupied by domestic duties, presided. And here Miss Ann Taylor, a belle of seventeen, entertained her suitor, Assistant Surgeon Robert C. Wood. To civilian eyes, Fort Snelling looked impressive. Officers thought differently. "Main points of *defence against an enemy*," ran an official inspection report, "appear in some respects sacrificed . . . to secure the . . . convenience of the troops at peace. . . . The buildings are too large, too numerous, and extending over a space entirely too great. . . ."[44] As one visitor aptly suggested, "the strong stone wall was rather erected to keep the garrison in, than the enemy out."[45]

Who was the enemy? Frontiersmen feared an Indian thrust, and not without cause. Winnebago braves, incensed at lead miners' encroachments on Winnebago lands in the Fever River region, had murdered nine settlers near Prairie du Chien in 1827 and, together with Sauk and Fox allies, had attacked a keelboat returning from Fort Snelling, killing two members of the crew. Travelers were molested, and miners forced to leave. Potawatomi chieftains had agreed to join in the border warfare, and soldiers at Fort Snelling had anticipated trouble from the Sioux. Brevet Brigadier General Henry Atkinson, with aid from Forts Snelling and Howard, had overawed the Indians and quelled the outbreak in the summer of 1827 by concentrating five hundred troops at Prairie du Chien. Yet the War Department deemed further precautionary measures necessary. Conditions warranted the transfer of other regulars to the Northwest, and it was for this reason that Lieutenant Colonel Taylor's infantrymen were shifted to Fort Snelling.[46]

5

Taylor commanded Fort Snelling from May, 1828, until the twelfth day of June, 1829.[47] Although various tribes squabbled with one another in the course of those thirteen months, the presence of the Army prevented their renewing assaults on the whites.[48] Taylor's vigilant efforts to preserve peace contributed to the comparative calm of the frontier, which he occasionally found leisure to describe in letters to relatives. "Fort Snelling," he wrote to a cousin, William Berry Taylor, ". . . stands . . . seven miles below the falls of St. Anthony. . . . Those falls are several miles in extent, the principal cascade which extends across the river, is twenty-two feet perpendicular. . . . The country is mostly prairie[,] the timber, what there is of it, being for the most part confined to the margin of the water courses; Interspersed in every direction throughout the country are a number of beautiful lakes of the purest water from one to twenty miles in circumference, similar I presume to those in the western parts of N. York, & which are abundantly stocked with every species of fish common to fresh water—The country around the falls is inhabited entirely by Indians. . . . The Buffalo have . . . disappeared. . . . Bear and dear are now very scarce. . . . The Indians subsist principally on fish, wild rice[, and] wild fowl, the latter being uncommonly plenty spring and fall— A few valuable furs are still taken . . . by the indians, which they barter with the traders for clothing, guns, ammunition[, and] traps. . . . The soil is tolerable[,] producing vegitables . . . in great perfection, particularly potatoes. . . ."[49]

Taylor's thoughts turned into other channels. His father died in January, 1829. "I need not say how much his loss has distressed us all," the son wrote to John Gibson Taylor.[50] Richard Taylor's will specified that Springfield be sold to meet demands against the estate, but the remainder of the property was divided among his children, Zachary's share being Charles Farm in Jefferson County, Kentucky. "It would have been very gratifying to me if it had been in your power . . . [to purchase] the old family establishment as Hancock did not," Zachary wrote his brother-in-law. ". . . I was very desirous that it should have remained in the family."[51] The will named Zachary as one of the executors, but he could not serve, and his brothers Hancock and Joseph qualified.

In reply to John Gibson Taylor's inquiry, Zachary expressed a willingness to sell his interest in the Goose Creek land, a fair price to be determined by Hancock or by William Berry Taylor.[52] Zachary faced a lawsuit due to other real-estate transactions. A number of years previously, he had gone on a friend's note. This securityship and crop failures cost him twenty thousand dollars.[53] Still the Kentucky financial picture was brightening. The court fight had been settled properly, Taylor thought. The currency was sound. "No country can be prosperous without an able & independent judiciary, & a sound currency, neither of which has this state been blest with for some time past," he had observed to Jesup in 1827.[54] To Taylor, now as always, concerns of a military nature never entirely overbalanced questions of investment, credit or ready cash. Zachary Taylor, soldier, was also Zachary Taylor, man of property.

When he relinquished command of Fort Snelling, Taylor moved to what was then Michigan Territory, sailing down the Mississippi to Fort Crawford at Prairie du Chien in the future state of Wisconsin. Here his principal job was to start construction of a new fort, General Gaines having condemned the old post as no longer serviceable.[55] Superseding Major Stephen W. Kearny on July 18, 1829,[56] Taylor commenced erecting barracks within a month. He did not approve the site selected. It "is an eminence in the prairie about 50, or 60 feet above the level of the river [on its eastern bank], a mile from ... [the old Fort Crawford], & one fourth of a mile from the nearest landing on the river. ... Getting wood, & perhaps water ... will always be attended with considerable difficulty; Besides which it is in the edge of a village, where every other house at least is a whiskey shop. ... Had the establishment been located on the opposite side of the Mississippi, the expenses of building ... would have been ... lessened. ... I now regret that I had not built on ... [the western shore]. Had I been aware on my arrival of the objections to the present position[,] I

THE BATTLE OF THE BAD AXE

A painting by Henry Lewis in *Das Illustrierte Mississippithal*, by George B. Douglas.

BLACK HAWK          HENRY ATKINSON

CHIEF ANTAGONISTS IN THE BLACK HAWK WAR

The portrait of Black Hawk is reproduced by permission of the Bureau of American Ethnology, Smithsonian Institution, Washington.

should certainly have done so, although the site had been fixed on, the ground purchased, & 1, or 2 hundred cartloads of stone hawled...."[57]

Companies A, D, F and G of the First Infantry, a force of ten officers and one hundred and seventy-three men, were building the barracks under the immediate direction of Brevet Major John Garland.[58] Taylor held the privates in low esteem. "The drunken materials the rank, & file of our Army are now composed of, without adequate laws to restrain them," disgusted him. He began a road to the bluff from the waterfront, but the troops' conduct irritated their commandant. The work could be done in less than a year, he complained to General Jesup, "by the labour of one half the men who will be lying in the guard house here to sober...."[59] The dreary nature of his duties and the monotony of frontier life depressed Taylor: "Since I have been stationed in this out of the way part of the world, I had nothing to write about unless it was to have given you a description of a most miserable & uninteresting country...."[60] The least uninteresting person with whom the Lieutenant Colonel was associated at this time was the post surgeon, Dr. William Beaumont. While stationed at Mackinac, Beaumont had made a highly important contribution to medical science by describing the working of the stomach of a soldier who had been shot and through whose unhealed wound the digestive processes could be observed.[61] If Beaumont made an impression on Taylor, however, the latter's known letters fail to reveal it.

## 6

Early in July, 1830, Lieutenant Colonel and Mrs. Taylor departed from Fort Crawford,[62] leaving behind in the Northwest their eldest daughter Ann, whom Doctor Wood had married the preceding September.[63] Having procured an extended furlough, Taylor spent some months in Louisville and its environs, occupying a house on the east side of First Street, near Jefferson Street, a portion of the time.[64] Financial troubles vexed him, but he disposed of a portion of his Kentucky property and on March 6, 1831, bought one hundred and thirty-seven acres in Wilkinson County, Mississippi, which were not far from his holdings in Louisiana. He made the purchase outright with a full payment of fifteen hundred dollars to Hamilton M. Orr.[65] In August, September and October of 1831, Taylor commanded the New Orleans post,[66] but most of the period he passed in Louisville where regimental returns indicate he was sick in April, 1831, and again in January and February, 1832.[67]

If Taylor was sick in body, he was equally sick in spirit. He had served twelve years in one grade without receiving the brevet and pay of a colonel which were his due. An 1812 act of Congress authorized the conferring of brevet rank on "such officers . . . who shall have served ten years in any one grade." A later act, bearing date of 1818, provided "that the officers of the army who have brevet commissions shall be entitled to receive the pay & emoluments of their brevet rank, & at no other time." In December, 1831, Taylor cited these laws in identical letters to members of the United States Senate.[68] The laws had not been repealed. They were still in effect. With a single exception, every colonel of infantry was a brevet brigadier general to boot, and that exception, Willoughby Morgan, had been brevetted lieutenant colonel before the full promotion came. James B. Many, whose lieutenant colonel's commission dated from 1821, won a brevet in 1831. Yet Taylor's commission dated from 1819, and no brevet had come his way.[69] In presenting his case to the senators, Taylor gave example after example and named names. Never prone to tolerate unfair treatment, he sought justice from President Jackson and the Senate. "I . . . only ask to be placed on an equality with other officers who have been brevetted for serving ten years in the same grade," he wrote. He did not obtain satisfaction until 1836, and history does not tell why. On April 4, 1832, however, death came to Willoughby Morgan.[70] Thereupon, by right of seniority, in his forty-eighth year, Zachary Taylor advanced to the colonelcy of the First Regiment.[71] He had traveled a long, hard road since that distant day when a green subaltern recruited green privates in a half-forgotten town called Washington, Kentucky. But now he must be up and doing. A sick chamber was no place for a soldier in time of war. And now war rumbled in the West.

# CHAPTER VI

## THE BLACK HAWK WAR

### 1

IN THE decades elapsing since its termination, the Black Hawk War has not been forgotten. It is remembered chiefly for the distinction that in no other of America's Indian campaigns did so many famous soldiers and statesmen ride and hunt, fight and kill. Zachary Taylor and Abraham Lincoln, Jefferson Davis and Albert Sidney Johnston, Robert Anderson and Winfield Scott— these names have colored the history of the struggle, quite obliterating the somber truth that the campaign was a tissue of blunders, miserably mismanaged from start to finish. This was Taylor's opinion.[1] The record proves he was right.

As is true of most wars, big or small, whether conducted in the grand manner with brigade pitted against brigade and division against division, or fought without spectacle by scattered bands in frontier forests, the primary cause of the Black Hawk War was land. In five separate treaties, solemnly signed and sealed, the Sauk and Fox tribes had ceded their property in northwestern Illinois and had agreed to move across the Missisipi as soon as white settlements would be opened.[2] In 1829 the conservative wing of the Sauk Indians and all the Foxes fulfilled this agreement,[3] but Black Hawk refused to go. Denying the legality of the cessions, he remained on the eastern bank and stirred his fellow warriors into hatred of the whites. Pioneers seized the site of the Sauk village on the Rock River, fenced Sauk fields, burned Sauk lodges, whipped Sauk squaws who dared to remonstrate. Spring after spring the braves came home from winter hunting to find more land appropriated, more property destroyed, and in the spring of 1831 they had returned to a village as desolate as Carthage.[4] When

83

the Indians retaliated against what Black Hawk told them was an invasion of their rights, white men had fled in terror. And Governor John Reynolds appealed to General Gaines for army aid.[5] Acting promptly, Gaines had concentrated regulars at Fort Armstrong, a post on the southern end of Rock Island, awing the Indians into promising that they would cross the river never to return.[6]

That was 1831. Gaines left with his troops, and only two companies garrisoned Fort Armstrong. In December of the same year, part of the Sixth Infantry was shifted from Fort Leavenworth on the Missouri to Jefferson Barracks below Saint Louis.[7] Why this detachment was not forwarded to Rock Island in March, 1832, is a mystery, as Fort Armstrong's commandant, Major John Bliss, feared another Sauk outburst and had so reported.[8] "Had the garrison of Fort Armstrong been re-enforced as [it] could, & ought to have been, with three or four companies from Jefferson Barracks the moment the Mississippi was clear of ice, which was the last of March, there would have been no indian war," Taylor was to write.[9] General Atkinson on April 8 at last set out from Jefferson Barracks with six companies of the Sixth Regiment[10] and on April 10, at the Rapids of the Des Moines, word reached him that Black Hawk's band had recrossed the Mississippi to the forbidden eastern shore.[11]

Atkinson arrived at Rock Island on the night of April 12,[12] and the next day he requested Governor Reynolds to call out the Illinois Militia.[13] Taylor, who was still in Kentucky, later believed that the General ought straightway to have pursued Black Hawk in an attempt to halt his ascent of the Rock River, "which I am under the impression he could have done. . . . Whether his doing so . . . would have prevented the war, it is impossible for anyone to say . . . , but at any rate it would have very much crippled [the Indians]. . . ."[14] The General, however, took no such steps. Instead he dispatched emissaries, whom Black Hawk defied. And then he proceeded to Fort Crawford for additional troops, and on April 19 was back at Fort Armstrong with two companies of the First Infantry.[15]

2

This portion of the campaign revealed striking dissimilarities between the leader of the Indians and the American commander. A tall and rugged son of North Carolina just under fifty years of age, Henry Atkinson had entered the Army as a captain two months after Taylor joined as a lieutenant. Serving uninterruptedly since 1808, he had fought with Jackson in Florida[16] and had led two important and hazardous expeditions into the then Far West: one up the Missouri River and a second beyond the mouth of the Yellowstone.[17] A colonel of infantry in 1814, he had won promotion to a full brigadier generalship in 1820. But in the subsequent reorganization of the Army, when Taylor thought of retiring, the number of generals had been reduced, and Atkinson dropped back to a colonelcy with the brevet of brigadier.[18] Personality, character and training pointed to his skillful direction of the Black Hawk War, yet already on two occasions he appeared to lack initiative. Militia officers, rarely partial to regular army men, were to criticize him on that ground. And Taylor, who frankly admired many of his qualities, said Atkinson "had too high an idea of the prowess of the enemy, & too little confidence in his own command. . . ."[19]

Atkinson's opponent in 1832 was an Indian of courage and dexterity. Unable to rise to the rank of chief because of lowly birth,[20] Black Hawk had amassed honors and a tribal following by dint of sheer ability and enmity toward the whites. Nearly six feet in height, spare to the point of emaciation, he counterbalanced muscular weakness with strong chin and Roman nose. Over piercing eyes rose a high, full forehead that did credit to his intellect, and his hair had been plucked from eyes to scalplock, emphasizing the contour of a skull destined to delight phrenologists.[21] Born in 1767, Black Hawk had seen four and sixty summers when Atkinson heard of his defiance.[22] Warfare was not new to him. A fighter to the manner born, at the tender age of fourteen he had slain and scalped his first Osage, and thirty-three years later he had helped Duncan and Keating defeat Taylor at Credit Island.[23] A

MAP OF BLACK HAWK WAR

By Shirley Ann Briggs in *I Am a Man: The Indian Black Hawk* by Cyrenus Cole
(State Historical Society of Iowa, Iowa City, 1938).

mediocre orator, deficient in conciliation, he was a resourceful leader in the field, a foe whose name might be used at night to frighten frontier children, one of the most gifted and treacherous Indian geniuses in the annals of the Northwest.

On April 6, Black Hawk crossed the Mississippi at the Yellow Banks below the mouth of the Rock within full view of Fort Armstrong.[24] Thus he passed his Rubicon, but not until the refusal to heed Atkinson's warning did he burn his bridges behind him. Black Hawk's force was unimpressive. As Taylor indicated, a few companies of regulars could probably have whipped it with ease there and then. The number of braves approximated five hundred.[25] Their progress up the Rock in a fleet of canoes, encumbered by women, children, baggage, corn and meat, proved slow and laborious even without armed opposition. One night they rested near Dixon's Ferry, Black Hawk supping amicably as the guest of "Father" John Dixon, a picturesque wilderness tavern keeper who estimated that Winnebago and Potawatomi allies had swelled the ranks of able-bodied warriors to a total of eight hundred.[26] Now, having advanced into Winnebago territory with the avowed intention of planting corn, on Monday, May 14, they were encamped thirty miles northeast of Dixon's Ferry in the vicinity of Old Man's Creek.

### 3

Black Hawk displayed hostility toward the white man not only by breaking his oft-repeated promise but also by endangering the life of General Atkinson's representative who came to the redskins' camp to plead the cause of peace, and escaped death only by a ruse and the skin of his teeth. Already the frontier was ablaze. In answer to Reynolds' call to arms, thirteen hundred horsemen and three hundred foot soldiers of the Illinois Militia volunteered for thirty days' service. They assembled at Beardstown and reached Rock Island on May 7,[27] the same day that Colonel Taylor, having parted with his family at Galena,[28] assumed command of the First Infantry at Fort Armstrong.[29] The militiamen formed a motley group. "They were a hard-looking set ...," wrote William Cullen Bryant, "unkempt and unshaved, wearing shirts of dark calico, and sometimes calico capotes."[30] Samuel Whiteside, who had fought under Taylor in 1814, commanded the mounted volunteers with the rank of brigadier. The Governor accompanied them. And Atkinson on May 8, the day after Taylor's arrival, swore the embryo army of sixteen hundred into the service of the United States.[31]

Now all was readiness. With keelboats laden, not a man on the sick list, and glory hunters eager for the chase, Atkinson completed last-minute preparations on Wednesday, May 9, and the next morning at daybreak, nearly five weeks since the hour of Black Hawk's overt act, the ascent of the Rock River began. Here Atkinson committed his third and most calamitous blunder. Years of frontier experience might have made him chary of the genus volunteer, causing his subjection of every militiaman, officer and private to rigid supervision under regular army eyes. This precaution he did not adopt. Aware that the untrained horsemen could move three times as swiftly as the infantry, the commander found four courses open: Either hold the mounted troops in check, or accompany them himself, or assign Taylor or another professional soldier to accompany them, or permit General Whiteside to speed them to Dixon's Ferry in advance of the regulars. Henry Atkinson chose the fourth course. To make matters worse, he issued this improvident order: "Should General Whiteside ... be of opinion that it would be prudent to come up with the enemy with as little delay as possible, he will move upon him, and either make him surrender at discretion, or coerce him into submission."[32]

Neither Whiteside nor Governor Reynolds understood the rudiments of discipline. While they rode ahead with their thirteen hundred harum-scarum farmers, storekeepers, border lawyers, and what not, abandoning a large part of their baggage and provisions on the way,[33] General Atkinson proceeded slowly by water. With him moved six companies of the Sixth Regiment of United States Regulars, and four companies of the First,[34] together with three hundred Illinois infantrymen, all under the direct command of Colonel Taylor.[35] "The troops on foot," Atkinson instructed his adjutant, Lieutenant Albert Sidney Johnston, to write, "will move in ascending the river in the following order: The First Infantry will march in front, the Sixth Infantry in the center and the Illinois Infantry in the rear. An advance guard from the First Infantry will precede the column from 400 to 1,000 yards; a flank guard from the Sixth Infantry will be thrown out from 200 to 400 yards. . . . The Illinois Infantry will . . . furnish the rear guard, which is not at any time to leave any of the boats. . . . In case of attack the troops will form to the front, the rear or upon the flank as circumstances may demand."[36]

On the alert, Atkinson and Taylor neared Marais d'Ogee on May 11, passed the village of the Prophet three days thereafter, and on Thursday, May 17, finally attained their destination, Dixon's Ferry, without having encountered a single Indian.[37] During the regulars' week-long journey, bedlam had broken loose among the volunteers. Reaching the Ferry the preceding Saturday, Whiteside had given a militia major, Isaiah Stillman, permission to spur forward with two hundred and seventy-five amateur cavalrymen "to the head of Old Man's Creek . . . for the purpose of taking cautious measures to coerce . . . [the] Indians into submission. . . ." On Monday night, the incautious Stillman had led his force into an ambush. Not more than eighty Sauks attacked him, but at the first fire the frontiersmen fled. Twelve died, at least eight of them while making an heroic stand in an attempt to cover the flight. Their two hundred and sixty-three panic-stricken comrades abandoned camp, raced helter-skelter southward. Into Dixon's Ferry they straggled, flushed and fearful, from three o'clock to daylight Tuesday morning.[38] The rumor spread along the border, taking terror with it. Black Hawk, heartened by success so signal, planned depredation after depredation. And Whiteside's force knew new confusion.

"That disgraceful affair of Stillmans ought not to have occurred. . . . The General ought to have prevented it. . . . That attack made on the indians brought on the war. . . . Had the regular troops overtaken them, at any rate in conjunction with the Militia then in the field, before any blood had been shed, they would have been removed back to the West side of the Mississippi, without there being a gun fired. . . ." So opined Atkinson's second-in-command, Colonel Zachary Taylor.[39]

4

After so inauspicious a beginning, Atkinson now took personal command of militiamen as well as regulars, straining to bulwark the volunteers' morale and to provide protection for the settlements. He and Taylor set out from Dixon's Ferry on Saturday morning, May 19, and had no sooner completed their second day's march than word came that a band of braves had murdered fifteen persons on Indian Creek.[40] On Tuesday, a messenger brought more disquieting news. Stillman's corps, left behind at the Ferry to guard food and ammunition, had deserted that post and headed for home.[41] This checked the advance of the commanding general. Someone must defend the supply base. Taking nearly all the regulars with him, Atkinson on Wednesday retraced his steps, detailing Taylor to remain with the militia as inspector general in the hope that the Colonel's presence might mend the shattered confidence of the rank and file as they rode northeastward on the trail of Black Hawk. Had Taylor been given this assignment on May 10, Stillman's rout might never have occurred.

Opportunity no longer beckoned. Non-commissioned officers and privates refused to cross the Illinois line into the northern territory. Crops at home lay idle. Families were defenseless. Politically-minded majors and colonels, hungry for votes in the autumn election, let lawlessness run riot, their followers dividing into cliques within cliques. Taylor could do nothing, and on Friday, May 25, the volunteers abandoned pursuit. Sunday and Monday, they were mustered out of service at the mouth of the Fox River opposite Ottawa.[42] The first phase of the Black Hawk War was history.

5

Seven weeks had sped since the crossing at the Yellow Banks, and upward of two thousand troops had failed to capture or defeat an Indian band less than half their number. With the hostiles' reputation spreading horror through the countryside, settlers abandoning home and farm, and outrage following massacre, no white man knew where Black Hawk might strike next. Atkinson, undismayed by the crisis, now took realistic action. On May 29 he came to Ottawa, established headquarters at Fort Johnston on the opposite shore of the Fox, and instructed Colonel Taylor to assume charge of Dixon's Ferry.[43] There Taylor erected Fort Dixon on the north side of the Rock, a log-and-sod structure designed to serve as a rendezvous for detachments of regulars and picked volunteers whom the General would send out at intervals to patrol the border while a new and larger army assembled at Fort Johnston.[44] Taylor's adjutant at the Ferry was a young West Pointer with chiseled features and handsome bearing, Second Lieutenant Jefferson Davis who had cut short a furlough to rejoin his regiment.[45]

For a solid month Fort Dixon, with Taylor in command, formed the hub of a stopgap campaign against guerrilla raids. To Taylor, patrols reported for orders. At Taylor's behest, they sallied forth. Now the tone of warfare changed. Skies were brightening. Confidence, booted and spurred, gained a firm footing in the stirrup and mounted to the saddle. At Horseshoe Bend on June 16, strapping six-foot Henry Dodge pursued seventeen Indians to the bank of the Pecantonica and exterminated the entire party. "My husband and sons are between me and the Indians," Mrs. Dodge had written. "I am safe so long as they live."[46] Other men of merit participated in the Black Hawk War: William Stephen Hamilton, son of the first Secretary of the Treasury; Nathan Boone, son of the Kentucky pioneer; Robert Anderson, who was to fire the first gun at Fort Sumter; William S. Harney, who had been Taylor's assistant inspector under Whiteside; and the unsung blacksmith, James D. Henry, heretofore a major but soon to be a brigadier. Less prominent then was lanky Abraham Lincoln, "a raw youth . . . whose quaint and pleasant talk" the poet Bryant found delightful.[47] Lincoln, formerly captain of the Sangamon County company, had revolunteered on May 27 and now served as a private under Elijah

Iles. Savages had killed six white men on the Galena road, and Atkinson dispatched Captain Iles's spy battalion to Dixon's Ferry for orders.

On the evening of June 7, Iles and Lincoln reached the Rock River. "We found Col. Taylor on the opposite side in a little fort built of prairie sod," wrote Iles. "He sent an officer in a canoe to bring me over. I said to the officer that I would come over as soon as I got my men in camp. . . . On meeting Colonel Taylor (he looked like a man born to command) he seemed a little piqued that I did not . . . camp with him. I told him we felt just as safe as if quartered in his one-horse fort; and, besides, I . . . wanted to try the mettle of my men before starting on the perilous trip I knew he would order. He said . . . that since the murder of the six men all communication with Galena had been cut off, and it might be besieged; that he wanted me to proceed to Galena . . . , and asked me what outfit I wanted. I answered nothing but coffee, side meat and bread."[48] Iles's fifty men, one of whom was Lincoln, marched to a stockade on the Apple River and on to Galena, to find the place in a state of defense but the inhabitants unmolested.

On June 17 a murder occurred on Bureau Creek. Atkinson the following day directed Major John Dement to scour the woods in that vicinity, and continue north to report to Colonel Taylor. Reaching Dixon's tavern on Friday night, June 22, after an exhausting march "through . . . swamps, high creeks and . . . pouring rains,"[49] Dement was met by Taylor who commanded the detachment to leave on the morrow in order to guard the road between the Ferry and Galena. This was no easy assignment for wet and tired troops who, resentful of discipline, were murmuring mutiny. His patience unstrung by the militia's past performance, Taylor on Saturday morning made it painfully clear that he expected obedience. Raking the volunteers fore and aft, he concluded with these words: "You are citizen-soldiers and some of you may fill high offices, or even be president some day, but never unless you do your duty. Forward! March!"

Major Dement, secretly approving the Colonel's orders, understood the militia mind.

"Sir," he said, addressing Taylor, "your allusions are . . . entirely uncalled for from a man who, with experience of the Regular Army, would entrench himself behind walls and send to the front men who had never seen service."

Then, turning to his command, he cried: "You need not obey his orders. Obey mine and follow me."[50]

With a single exception, the volunteers followed Dement to Kellogg's Grove. There a savage band got the better of them. Five Illinoisans died. But the road was kept open, and their action protected the Galena region. Soon thereafter Abraham Lincoln arrived at the scene of the skirmish, and helped to bury the five. "I remember just how those men looked as we rode up the little hill ...," he wrote. "The red light of the morning sun was streaming upon them as they lay heads towards us on the ground. And every man had a round, red spot on top of his head, about as big as a dollar where the redskins had taken his scalp. It was frightful, but it was grotesque, and the red sunlight seemed to paint everything all over. I remember that one man had on buckskin breeches."[51]

Lincoln also left a breezier version of the campaign. Poking fun at Lewis Cass's record in the War of 1812, he recalled: "In the days of the Black Hawk war I fought, bled, and came away. Speaking of General Cass's career reminds me of my own. I was not at Stillman's defeat, but I was about as near it as Cass was to Hull's surrender; and, like him, I saw the place very soon afterward. . . . I did not break my sword, for I had none to break; but I bent a musket pretty badly on one occasion. If Cass broke his sword, the idea is he broke it in desperation; I bent the musket by accident. If General Cass went in advance of me in picking huckleberries, I guess I surpassed him in charges upon the wild onions. If he saw any live, fighting Indians, it was more than I did; but I had a good many bloody struggles with the mosquitoes, and although I never fainted from the loss of blood, I can truly say I was often very hungry."[52]

## 6

Abraham Lincoln viewed the war light-heartedly, boxing, racing, wrestling with carefree companions.[53] Even Jefferson Davis and his fellow West Point graduates fished and hunted squirrels in the vicinity of Dixon's Ferry.[54] That Zachary Taylor participated in such pleasures is highly doubtful, his principal diversion being the purchase of a shirt pattern and other merchandise for six dollars and fifty cents at "Father" Dixon's store.[55] The human toll of the campaign was no laughing matter. Two hundred men, women and children had met death along the border, and, though many a savage warrior paid the penalty, Black Hawk's arrogance had not been nicked.

Now the final push began. At ten o'clock on Monday morning, June 25, Atkinson took command of Fort Dixon, whence he moved up the Rock River to Stillman's battleground the following Friday.[56] His field force, bolstered by re-enforcements from the Second and Sixth Regiments, comprised four hundred and fifty regulars and two thousand volunteers.[57] Alterations in the personnel had brought new faces to the front, Brigadier Generals Alexander Posey, Milton K. Alexander, and James D. Henry leading the militiamen, and Colonel Dodge riding at the head of a band of rangers, while Colonel Taylor of the regulars was subordinate to Brevet Brigadier General Hugh Brady. On Saturday, four miles were made; on Sunday, seven. It was not until late on the night of Tuesday, July 3, that the advance division halted at Lake Koshkonong, a large body of water formed by the widening of the Rock.[58] By Wednesday, the entire army was in camp.

Here delay succeeded delay. Black Hawk, his ranks reduced, provisions low, and non-combatants hindering the movements of his warriors, was somewhere in the vicinity. But Atkinson failed to find him. It was clear that the savages could not flee eastward without being boxed on the sands of Lake Michigan. Dodge reported no fresh trails in the southwest. Therefore, by elimination, the northwest it must be. A speedy pursuit was paramount. Yet the General did not act. Stationary on Thursday and Friday, he limited Saturday's march to four miserable miles and on Sunday fell back to the mouth of the Whitewater to establish a base and to await artillery. On Monday, Governor Reynolds, disgusted by Atkinson's dilatory policy, abandoned the chase and returned to

Illinois. On Tuesday, Atkinson mustered out of service many volunteers, including Captain Jacob M. Early's company of which Private Lincoln was a member, and the same day he sent Alexander and Henry to Fort Winnebago at the Fox-Wisconsin portage to procure supplies.[59] This last decision, haphazardly enough, proved the turning point of the Black Hawk War.

To Fort Winnebago came the rumor that Black Hawk was on the Rock River. Alexander, obeying Atkinson's orders, elected to ignore the report and returned to the Whitewater. Henry and Colonel Dodge were of a different mind. They hastened to the Rock, but found no signs of Indians. But after dark on Wednesday, July 18, they chanced to cross a broad, fresh trail. This discovery spurred them on, and three days later under Henry's able generalship the volunteers defeated Black Hawk in the decisive battle of Wisconsin Heights. Sixty-eight redskins were killed. Only one frontiersman died. And on the following Tuesday the slowly advancing regulars, whom Atkinson, Brady and Taylor led, received the news of victory.[60]

Jefferson Davis had served under General Henry at Wisconsin Heights. Shortly before his death, he recollected: "We were one day pursuing the Indians, when we came close to the Wisconsin River. Reaching the river bank, the Indians made so determined a stand, and fought with such desperation, that they held us in check. . . . The squaws tore bark from the trees, with which they made little shallops, in which they floated their papooses and other impedimenta across to an island, also swimming over the ponies. As soon as this was accomplished, half of the warriors plunged in and swam across, each holding his gun in one hand over his head, and swimming with the other. . . . [Reaching] the opposite bank, they also opened fire upon us, under cover of which the other half slipped down the bank and swam over in like manner. This was the most brilliant exhibition of military tactics that I ever witnessed—a feat of most consummate management and bravery, in the face of an enemy of greatly superior numbers. . . . Had it been performed by white men, it would have been immortalized as one of the most splendid achievements in military history."[61]

If, as Lieutenant Davis thought, Black Hawk was the hero of the white man's first important triumph, James D. Henry surely shared the honors of the day. Meanwhile Zachary Taylor, who early in the war toiled to keep Whiteside's troops in line and later dominated the Fort Dixon scene, had yet to face the fire of the enemy. The Indians' retreat was now a rout. On July 27 and 28, the pursuing army crossed the Wisconsin at Helena. And Atkinson had ordered the steamboat *Warrior* up the Mississippi from Prairie du Chien.[62] For all his courage, the Battle of Wisconsin Heights broke Black Hawk's spirit. For weeks his followers had subsisted on berries, bark, roots, and the flesh of their drooping ponies. All were famished, many wounded. Wednesday, August 1, found the remnant of the savage band on the Mississippi's eastern bank near the mouth of the Bad Axe. There the *Warrior* met them. Three quick rounds of canister plowed a path of carnage in their ranks, and twenty-three fell dead.[63]

That night Atkinson's soldiers, nearing the prey, slept on their arms. Thursday morning, August 2, before dawn streaked the summer sky, they were roused from slumber. At sunrise they were marching on. Black Hawk now deployed a score of braves to stand out in full view high above his camp and lure the army up the Mississippi, to the end that the main body of the Sauks might effect an escape below. Born of desperation, this stratagem was brilliant. It almost worked. Atkinson, deceived completely by the ruse, led all the regulars and three-quarters of the volunteers precisely where the enemy wanted them to go. Mounted militiamen, under Posey and Alexander, rode on the extreme right. In the center, infantrymen of the First, Second and Sixth Regiments advanced under Brady and Taylor. Dodge's command and part of James D. Henry's force skirted the river on the left, while General Henry himself remained in the rear to guard the baggage.

Chance played directly into Henry's hands. No sooner were Colonel Taylor and the others out of sight than the giant blacksmith's scouts breathlessly brought the news that the fugitives' main

JEFFERSON DAVIS

From a miniature in the possession of Davis' great-granddaughter, Mrs. Gerald W. Bennett
of Colorado Springs, Colorado.

trail led down, not up, the river. Henry spurred three hundred followers forward to the south, and dismounted at the base of a lofty bluff which bordered on the bottoms. Here he formed his men on foot, and charged the Indians. From tree to tree at bayonet's point the savages fell back, women and children in their midst, with little mercy shown. It was death on land or death in the water, and many a warrior dropped that August day, and many a non-combatant drowned in the muddy Mississippi.

A few braves begged for quarter, but others, targets for the troops, swam furiously toward the farther shore. Now Taylor's regulars reached the scene. Too late to lead in the assault, they joined in the pursuit, Taylor wading through breast-deep water across a broad slough to a willow-covered island. Raking it with musketry, he either shot or drove away every Indian seeking shelter there. Three hours of bloodshed, and the massacre ended, and with it ended the Black Hawk War.[64] In the Battle of the Bad Axe, twenty-four white men had been killed or wounded. More than one hundred and fifty savages were slain on the field, and an equal number drowned. Of the thousand-odd who had crossed the Mississippi on April 6 at the Yellow Banks, less than three hundred recrossed on August 2 at the Bad Axe, and half of these were later scalped by hostile Sioux.[65] Fifty Indians surrendered. To this number, at Prairie du Chien on August 27, was added the crestfallen figure of Black Hawk himself, who had escaped to the western shore in safety, only to be captured by treacherous Winnebago allies.[66]

## 8

After the final battle, Colonel Taylor accompanied General Atkinson aboard the *Warrior* to Fort Crawford, arriving Saturday evening, August 4. There he found Mrs. Taylor and Sarah Knox awaiting him, and the following day he formally assumed command of the post.[67] On Thursday, General Winfield Scott reached Fort Crawford from Galena. Sent out from the Atlantic seaboard to supersede Atkinson, he had met a deadly enemy en route in the form of Asiatic cholera. His soldiers were stricken on the Great Lakes, but the hero of Lundy's Lane had not been harmed and had come posthaste with a staff of three to the theater of operations. Upon finding the Black Hawk War over, Scott proposed to negotiate treaties with the various tribes and on August 10, together with Atkinson and most of the regulars, he went down the Mississippi to Fort Armstrong where the chiefs were invited to assemble.[68] Before his departure, Scott gave Taylor instructions concerning the disposition of Black Hawk and other captives.

"The great chief of the warriors told me to take the prisoners when you should bring them, and send them to Rock Island to him," Taylor informed the Winnebagoes. "I will take them and keep them safe, but I will use them well. . . . I tell you again I will take the prisoners. I will keep them safe, but I will do them no harm. I will deliver them to the great chief of the warriors, and he will . . . use them in such a manner as shall be ordered by your great father, the President."[69]

Second Lieutenant Robert Anderson was the officer whom the Colonel first selected to convey Black Hawk down the river. Anderson fell ill, and the duty devolved on Second Lieutenant Davis. The "young war chief . . . treated us all with much kindness," the sixty-five-year-old Sauk gratefully remembered. "He is a good and brave young chief, with whose conduct I was much pleased."[70]

## 9

As Black Hawk descended the Mississippi past Fort Armstrong where cholera was raging, and on to disease-free Jefferson Barracks, Zachary Taylor remained at Fort Crawford with his garrison, his family, and his thoughts. The recent war failed to meet with his approval. Three million dollars had been needlessly spent, one thousand lives needlessly sacrificed. "There has been an error somewhere," the Colonel wrote, "but how or by whom it has been committed it is not for me to say, & my only wish now is . . . that we may profit by past blunders. . . ."[71] Toward the overcautious Atkinson, he was charity itself: "I differed with him in some important points as to our operations (for the enemy ought to have been destroyed before they crossed the Ouisconsin) yet I never spared myself for a moment, & exerted every faculty both body, & mind to sustain him. . . ." When President Jackson did not censure Atkinson, Old Hickory's decision delighted Taylor: "I am truly gratified to learn that the executive has approbated the Genls conduct, which I know has relieved him from the greatest possible anxiety. . . ."[72] Yet Atkinson on the Rock could be compared neither to Harrison on the Wabash nor to Jackson on the Coosa. Colonel Taylor's commendation, if qualified, was charitable indeed.

Upon Taylor himself, the second war of his career had bestowed a minimum of glory. Having served from first to last of a strenuous three-month campaign and acquitted himself as ably as in the War of 1812, he hoped for a brevet of brigadier—a hope not to be realized for several years to come.[73] Settling down at Fort Crawford for a long tour of duty, he found the region undergoing a rapid transformation. The Black Hawk War constituted the final conflict with the Indians in the old Northwest, and in the eyes of the Sauks and Foxes it established lasting proof of white supremacy. Because of it, migration of the Winnebago, Potawatomi, Chippewa and Ottawa tribes was to gain momentum, and settlers from the East were to populate the country of savages now dispossessed.[74] Within six years of the Battle of the Bad Axe, both Wisconsin and Iowa would become territories; within sixteen years, they would become states. Just as he had protected Indiana and Illinois from Indian forays and had made a substantial contribution to the settlement of the Southwest, in like manner Zachary Taylor had aided in opening and developing the northwestern lands. Forty-seven years of age, blessed with financial security, a devoted wife and happy, growing children, Taylor now looked forward to another period of peace.

# CHAPTER VII

## SARAH KNOX TAYLOR AND JEFFERSON DAVIS

### 1

IF FREEDOM from armed conflict was to be Zachary Taylor's portion in the months immediately following the Battle of the Bad Axe, peace of mind and peace of spirit would never be more elusive. The years 1832 and 1833 marked the inception of the most heart-rending personal tragedy of Taylor's life, and the most vivid romance with which his name is interwoven. For it was then, sometime after August 5, 1832, that the courtship of Lieutenant Jefferson Davis first found favor in the hazel eyes of the Colonel's second daughter.

Sarah Knox Taylor was eighteen years old, a gay and gracious girl whose slim figure was crowned by a mass of brown wavy hair. Contemporaries considered her hands and feet unusually exquisite, but facially she resembled her father, especially "as to her forehead which[,] though indicating strength and courage, moral and physical in a man, was not particularly becoming to a woman. She had her father's splendid hazel eye and strong even teeth, and her mother's domestic traits and aimiability."[1] Born in picturesque Vincennes during the second war with England, Miss Taylor had been educated by Thomas Elliott in Jefferson County, Kentucky, and at the Pickett School in hilly Cincinnati while her father was stationed on the frontier.[2] She rejoined her parents during the Lieutenant Colonel's extended furlough in 1831, lived with them at their town house in Louisville and became "the best dancer in the state of Kentucky"[3] under the direction of "Professor" Patrick, fashionable master of the art, who was blacker than the ace of spades. As her charm and wit developed, the number of her beaux increased. And now she saw more of her mother and father, whom long periods of separation had transformed into semi-strangers. Filial devotion, however, never entirely absorbed the young lady's self-reliance, and independence ever was a dominating trait.[4]

The subaltern from Mississippi, to whom Sarah Knox Taylor became engaged, was destined to fill a dramatic role in the annals of America. Born in Kentucky in 1808, Jefferson Davis was six years his sweetheart's senior, tall, slender, straight as an arrow, handsome and reserved.[5] Taken to Mississippi while yet an infant, he had spent his first sixteen years in the state of his nativity and the state of his adoption, and three years as an undergraduate at Transylvania University in Lexington had preceded his West Point cadetship. To the theory of war, Davis had added the practical experience of army life. Short tours of duty at Jefferson Barracks and Fort Crawford in 1828 and 1829 were followed by a longer period at Fort Winnebago.[6] Action in the Black Hawk War gave the Mississippian his first whiff of battle smoke,[7] and later he read law while stationed at Fort Crawford.[8] Clearly the Lieutenant was a worthy suitor, popular in the drawing room, respected in the barracks. But from the very outset, Colonel Taylor looked upon the match with undisguised disfavor.

## 2

Taylor at first bore no grudge toward Davis as an individual. He simply sought to protect his daughter from the hardships endured by army wives,[9] and that he considered a valid reason for opposition. Mrs. Taylor's frontier sacrifices were graven on his memory, and already Mrs. Wood had twice undergone the rigors of childbirth amid the monotonous wilderness surroundings of Fort Snelling.

"I will be damned if another daughter of mine shall marry into the Army," the Colonel exclaimed to Major Stephen Watts Kearny. "I know enough of the family life of officers. I scarcely know my own children or they me. I have no personal objections to Lieutenant Davis."[10]

As the courtship continued, Taylor's objection shifted to personal grounds. The specific cause of friction is lost in a maze of frontier folklore, but the story persists that trouble began when Colonel Taylor, Brevet Major Thomas F. Smith, Lieutenant Davis and an anonymous fourth officer were detailed to compose a court-martial. According to this account, the fourth officer, recently arrived at Prairie du Chien, had left behind his dress uniform which military etiquette prescribed for court service. When the officer asked his fellow judges to excuse this infraction of the regulations, Taylor is said to have voted in the negative, and Smith and Davis in the affirmative. Whereupon the Colonel supposedly swore that "no man who votes with Tom Smith shall marry my daughter."[11]

An even more fantastic tradition is found in a description of an Indian wedding, which Taylor and Davis attended. "Among the wedding party was a young squaw of great personal attraction, who danced in her Indian style with much grace. Lieutenant Davis became fascinated with her charms, and danced with her in almost every set. He would do many remarkable things, sometimes changing the order of the dance to suit his fancy. When quadrilles were danced, he would change into a waltz, so he could have his arms around the waist of the young squaw; then again, freeing himself from her, he would dance with all his might, causing his tall form to jerk and wiggle as it swayed to and fro; sometimes jumping up and down in quick succession, and yelling at the top of his voice, in imitation of the Indians at the door. Colonel Taylor and Captain Smith took no part in the dance, but sat in one corner of the room, looking on, and almost splitting their sides with laughter. . . . The young squaw, feeling herself insulted in the presence of the company became indignant, and informed her brother of it. Her brother, a tall, athletic Indian, was very angry . . . and felt determined to punish the offender. Being quite drunk, his brain frenzied by anger and whiskey, he went up to Lieutenant Davis, and in bad English accused him of insulting his sister, at the same time pulling his nose. Davis, who never lacked courage, pushed the Indian from him, and drew forth a pistol. The Indian, with a fiendish smile, drew from its scabbard a long scalping-knife, and was prepared to meet his antagonist in a deadly combat. The dance stopped, the women screamed, and all was confusion and alarm; everyone expected to see the death of one or both. . . . But in an instant Colonel Taylor sprang between the combatants, and thereby prevented the effusion of blood."[12]

Davis' conduct at the dance was hardly of a sort to command the respect of a prospective father-in-law. Although neither the Lieutenant's conduct then, nor the Colonel's oath, at the court-martial, is well enough substantiated to warrant unqualified acceptance, nevertheless a rift did exist, and in the course of time it widened to serious proportions. Davis continued to advance his suit. And Miss Taylor, despite the disapproval of both her parents, resolutely refused to break the engagement.

"The time will come," she told her father, "when you will see as I do all his rare qualities."[13]

## 3

Zachary Taylor, more skeptical than ever, adhered to his decision. Davis, now forbidden to enter the home of his beloved, seriously considered challenging his commandant to a duel, only to be dissuaded by Captain Samuel McRee, whom he had invited to act as his second. With the connivance of friends, the couple managed to keep the spark alive. "Miss Mary Street, Knox Taylor's devoted friend, and her admirer, Lieutenant George Wilson, were in a like situation. General Street objected, as Colonel Taylor had done, to his daughter's marriage to an army officer. The young people finally made an arrangement satisfactory to the four. Davis and Wilson each called at the home where he had no intentions, and when Davis called at General Street's he found Miss Taylor there also; and Wilson would find Miss Street at Colonel Taylor's."[14] Jefferson Davis and Sarah Knox Taylor arranged other meetings through the kindness of Mrs. McRee, who invited the subaltern to call at her tent on evenings when his sweetheart also was a guest. When Sarah Knox took her little sister and brother on walks away from the fort, Davis joined them by appointment, "and the children would be told . . . that they might play a little while as the lovers talked."[15]

On March 4, 1833, Davis was promoted to a first lieutenancy in the First Regiment of Dragoons. Ordered to Kentucky on recruiting duty, he later removed to Fort Gibson in the Southwest to remain for two full years.[16] During his absence Miss Taylor divided her time between Prairie du Chien and Kentucky, where she visited relatives. In the heart of each the flame still burned, as the following letter shows:

"Fort Gibson, December 16, 1834.

*"To Miss Sarah K. Taylor*
   *"Prairie du Chien*

" 'Tis strange how superstitions sometimes affect us, but stranger still what aids chance sometimes bring to support our superstitions. Dreams, my dear Sarah, we will agree, are our weakest thoughts, and yet by my dreams I have been lately almost crazed, for they were of you, and the sleeping imagination painted you, not as I felt you, not such as I could live and see you, for you seemed a sacrifice to your parents' desire, the bride of a wretch that your pride and sense equally compelled you to despise. A creature here, telling the news of the day in St. Louis, said you were about to be married to a Doctor McLarin, a poor devil, who served with the battalion of rangers. Possibly you may have seen him. But last night the vision was changed. You were at the house of an uncle in Kentucky. Captain McCree was walking with you. When I met you he left you and you told me of your father and of yourself, almost the same that I have read in your letter to-night. Kind, dear letter; I have kissed it often and it has driven away mad notions from my brain.

"Sarah, whatever I may be hereafter, neglected by you I should have been worse than nothing, and if the few good qualities I possess shall, under your smiles yield fruit, it shall be yours, as the grain is the husbandman's. It has been a source productive of regret with me that our union must separate you from your earliest and best friends. I am prepared to expect all that intellect and dignified pride brings. The question, as it has occurred to you, is truly startling. Your own answer is the most gratifying to me; is that which I should have expected from you, for you are the first with whom I ever sought to cast my fortune, so you are the last from whom I would expect desertion. When I wrote to you I supposed you did not intend soon to return to Kentucky. I approve entirely of a preference to a meeting elsewhere than at Prairie du Chien, and your desire to avoid any embarrassments which might widen the breach made already cannot be greater than my own. Did I know when you would be at St. Louis I could meet you there. At all events, we will meet in Kentucky. Shall we not meet soon, Sarah, to part no more? Oh I long to lay my head upon that breast which beats in unison with my own, to turn from the sickening sights of worldly duplicity and look in those eyes, so eloquent of purity and love.

"Do you remember the heart's-ease you gave me? It is as bright as ever. How very gravely you ask leave to ask me any question without apology. Miss Bullitt did not give me a guard for a watch, but if she had do you suppose I would have given it to Captain McCree? But I'll tell you what she did give me—a most beautiful and lengthy lecture on my and your dreams once upon an evening at a fair in Louisville. You can, and I have left you to guess what, besides a resistibility to your charms, constituted my offense.

"Pray, what manner of message could La Belle Florine have sent you concerning me? I hope no attempt to destroy harmony. I laughed at her demonstration against the attachment of dragoons, but that, between you and I, is not fair gains; it is robbing to make another poor. But, no, she is too discerning to attempt a thing so difficult and in which success would be valueless. Miss Elizabeth, one very handsome lady—Oh Knox, what did you put that semicolon between 'handsome' and 'lady' for. I hope you find in the society of the Prairie enough to amuse, if not to please. The griefs over which we weep are not those to be dreaded; it is the little pains, the constant falling of the drops of care, which wear away the heart.

"Since I wrote you we abandoned the position in the Creek nation and are constructing quarters at Fort Gibson. My lines, like the beggar's day, are dwindling to the shortest span.

"Write to me immediately, my dear Sarah, my betrothed; no formality between us. *Adieu ma chere, tres chere amie.*

"JEFF"[17]

According to various traditions, all erroneous, Davis and Miss Taylor eloped from Prairie du Chien, Wisconsin; Vincennes, Indiana; Fort Smith, Arkansas; Saint Louis, Missouri; Baton Rouge, Louisiana, and Galena, Illinois. They did nothing of the sort. Davis sent in his resignation from the Army to take effect June 30, 1835, obtained a leave of absence for the month of June, and set out to join his fiancée at the residence of her Aunt Elizabeth, Beechland, near Louisville, Kentucky.

At Beechland on the morning of her wedding day, Sarah Knox Taylor penned this loving letter to her mother, who had remained with her father at Fort Crawford:

"Louisville, June 17, 1835.

"You will be surprised, no doubt, my dear mother, to hear of my being married so soon; When I wrote to you last I had no idea of leaving here before fall; but hearing the part of the country to which I am going is quite healthy I have concluded to go down this summer and will leave here this afternoon at 4 o'clock; will be married as you advised in my bonnet and traveling dress. I am very much gratified that sister Ann is here. At this time having one member of the family present, I shall not feel so entirely destitute of friends—But you, my dearest Mother, I know will still retain some feelings of affection for a child who has been so unfortunate as to form a connection without the sanction of her parents, but who will always feel the deepest affection for them whatever may be their feelings toward her. Say to my dear father I have received his kind and affectionate letter, and thank him for the liberal supply of money sent me. Sister will tell you all that you wish to know about me. I will write as soon as I get down and as often as my mother may wish to hear from me, and do, my kind ma, write. I shall feel so much disappointed and mortified if you do not. I send a bonnet by sister, the best I could get. I tried to get you some cherries to preserve, but could not. Sally has kindly offered to make your preserves this summer. Farewell, my dear mother; give my best love to pa and Dick.

"Believe me always, your affectionate daughter,

"Knox"[18]

4

To Mrs. John Gibson Taylor's two-story, green-shuttered white frame house in Jefferson County,[19] not far from Springfield, members of the Taylor family came in mid-afternoon to witness the wedding for which Jefferson Davis and Sarah Knox Taylor had waited many months.[20] Mary Louise Taylor, aged eleven at the time, was later to recall that the guests included Dr. and Mrs. Wood, brother-in-law and sister of the bride; Hancock Taylor, the Colonel's elder brother, who gave the bride away; her Aunt Elizabeth, whose home it was; and Sally Strother Taylor and Nicholas M. L. Taylor, Knox's cousins, who attended as maid of honor and best man.[21] The Reverend Christopher Ashe, rector of Christ Church, read the Episcopal service in the east parlor, after which "everybody cried but Davis, and the Taylor children thought this most peculiar." While cake and wine were dispensed in the west parlor,[22] relatives admired Knox's simple costume, "a dark traveling dress with a small hat to match." The bridegroom wore "a long-tail cutaway coat, brocaded waistcoat, breeches tight-fitting and held under the instep with a strap...."[23]

5

Bride and bridegroom left Louisville that night, taking a river packet to Warren County, Mississippi, where they visited Jefferson's elder brother, Joseph E. Davis, at the latter's Hurricane Plantation. Soon they moved to their own plantation, Brierfield, which was near Hurricane and lay in Palmyra Island in the Mississippi— a present from Joseph to Jefferson in lieu of Jefferson's interest in their father's Negroes.[24]

It was here, on August 11, that Zachary Taylor's daughter wrote her last extant letter and addressed it to "my dearest mother": "I have just received your affectionate letter forwarded to me from Louisville; you may readily imagine the pleasure it afforded me to hear from you. . . . Have you been much annoyed with visitors this year? do tell me who you have been obliged to entertain. How often, my dear Mother, I wish I could look in upon you. I imagine so often I can see you moving about attending to your domestic concerns,—down in the cellar skiming the milk or going to feed the chickens. . . . Tell Dick I have a beautiful colt, prettier than his I expect; when did you hear from dear little Betty? Give my love to Dr. [Wood]; Mr. Davis sends his best respects to you. did you receive the letter he wrote you from St. Louis? My love to Pa and Dick. . . . Remember me most affectionately to Sister and the Doc. Kiss the children. . . . Do not make yourself uneasy about me[;] the country is quite healthy."[25]

But the country was not healthy enough. Neither Jefferson nor Sarah Davis was acclimated, and, the fever season approaching, they forsook Brierfield to spend the last part of their honeymoon at the plantation of the groom's sister, Mrs. Luther Smith, Locust Grove, in West Feliciana Parish, Louisiana.[26]

Here both contracted malaria. Too sick to be told of his wife's dangerous condition, Jefferson Davis heard her singing "Fairy Bells," a song associated with the days when he had wooed and won her. He crawled from his bed, stumbled into her room, and reached her side to see her die unconscious. It was the fifteenth day of September, less than three months since their wedding afternoon.[27]

## 6

Sarah Knox Davis was laid to rest in the Smith family cemetery adjoining Locust Grove, and there she has slept for more than a century.[28] The effect of her passing upon her father and mother can only be imagined, for no known record tells the story of their grief. The youthful widower failed to recover from his own illness for many months, journeying to Cuba and to the eastern part of the United States to recuperate. And the loss of his wife affected him so deeply that he became a recluse for eight years, avoiding society altogether, confining himself to the management of his estate, and studying assiduously in his library in the company of his gifted brother and surrounded by his books.[29]

It was a new Jefferson Davis, who at last emerged from the ivory tower to participate in the political arena on the side of his beloved Southland, and the tragic death of Sarah Knox Taylor was assuredly an important factor in transforming an able but not unusually ambitious soldier-planter into the foremost champion of the rights of the states. No account of the Brothers' War can be complete without giving Zachary Taylor's daughter some credit for this intellectual rebirth of Jefferson Davis. She influenced him profoundly. When the anchorite of Brierfield became successively Representative in Congress, Colonel of Volunteers, United States Senator, Secretary of War, and President of the Confederacy, the memory of that vivacious girl would be with him always.

# CHAPTER VIII

## LIFE AT FORT CRAWFORD

### 1

WITH the exception of sixty-eight days in the fall of 1834 when he availed himself of a furlough, Zachary Taylor commanded Fort Crawford at Prairie du Chien uninterruptedly from August 5, 1832, until November 16, 1836.[1] Caleb Atwater of Ohio, who acted as an Indian commissioner at Fort Crawford, considered the post too remote and too cheerless to warrant prolonged periods of service there. No officer, he believed, should be compelled to remain more than ten years in the Indian country. Citing the case of the Taylors, he noted that men and women accustomed to the "most polished and refined society" were being forced to educate their "worthy and most interesting . . . children" far from the advantages of civilization.

"The situation of delicate females, belonging to some of the best families in the nation, reared in tenderness, amidst all the luxuries and refinements of polished society, now living in a fort" elicited Atwater's sympathy and admiration.[2] During Taylor's absence in the Black Hawk campaign, Mrs. Taylor had been denied even the comparative comfort of the commandant's quarters.[3] With the Colonel's return, however, she moved into her own house, a two-story frame dwelling, thirty feet by twenty-six, with a tiny wing on the south side and a kitchen and wine cellar in the basement.[4] Here she attended to her domestic concerns, skimming the milk, going out to feed the chickens, and supervising the Negro servants, Will and Sally, who had accompanied her from Louisville.[5] "She was a most kind and thorough-bred Southern lady," thought John H. Bliss, who visited the Taylors in 1832.[6] That she was a loving wife and mother is attested on every hand. And her husband paid

110

the most cherished of tributes when he wrote: "The feminine virtues never did concentrate in a higher degree in the bosom of any woman than in hers...."[7]

## 2

While Mrs. Taylor presided over the Fort Crawford household, the Colonel attended to a multiplicity of duties. Never a hard taskmaster, he imposed no unreasonable burdens on his men, but he did demand discipline, and he knew how to enforce it. Construction of the new fort necessitated "quarrying stone in the nearby bluffs, cutting pine logs on the distant Chippewa, sawing lumber on Yellow River, getting out shingles and squared pickets, [and] burning lime at the coulée across the Mississippi. . . ."[8] Taylor saw all these details faithfully performed, gardens cultivated in spring and summer, hay made for the horses and cattle, and wood chopped to feed the roaring fires during long, cold winter months. In 1834, the number of officers stationed at Prairie du Chien ranged from eight to thirteen, the number of non-commissioned officers and privates from one hundred and ninety-one to two hundred and fifty-seven. Taylor commanded ten officers and two hundred and twelve soldiers the following year, detaching three companies to build a road from Fort Crawford to Fort Winnebago in May, June, July and August. The first Wisconsin territorial census, that of 1836, reveals "the presence of two hundred and sixty officers and men at Fort Crawford, thirteen women, twenty-three children, and seventeen slaves of both sexes."[9]

What was the routine at this frontier post? What filled the hours from dawn till after dusk? "At dawn the trumpeters ... took their stations, and the ringing tones of *reveille* called the sleeping garrison. . . . The rolls of the companies were called in front of the quarters; then the quarters were put in order; the ground in front swept; and the horses fed and watered. After sick call had sounded those who were ill in the barracks were taken to the hospital. Following a second roll-call breakfast was served at nine o'clock. Then came the various tasks of the day under the supervision of a mem-

ber of the garrison designated as 'officer of the day.' A detail known
as the 'General Fatigue' swept the parade ground; or if the guard-
house held enough prisoners . . . , they fell heir to this disagreeable
task. Sentinels were posted, and details formed to do the work for
that day. At three o'clock in the afternoon a third roll-call was
followed by dinner. Half an hour before sunset the trumpeters
called the garrison for dress parade. Drills and maneuvers were
practiced, and orders were read. Following dress parade, companies were dismissed, arms were placed in the armracks, and the
horses were bedded for the night. Another roll-call was followed
by tattoo, candles were extinguished, and the troops settled down
in their quarters for the night."[10]

Their uniforms, food, fuel, shelter and arms provided gratis by
the government, privates received a cash allowance of six dollars a
month. Although intoxication irritated and concerned Colonel
Taylor, resulting in the creation of the Fort Crawford Temperance
Society with the commandant's approval, not all the soldiers'
money went to the taverns of the town. Candy, raisins and spices,
tobacco, soap and needles, odds and ends to suit the most exacting
taste, could be purchased from the sutler. The sutler in turn do-
nated a portion of his profit to the "post fund," a primitive form
of social security which supported widows and orphans, the post
school, and the post library.[11]

The officers had a library and reading room of their own, where
standard scientific, historical and mathematical works might be
procured.[12] Taylor's friends later averred that the Colonel made
abundant use of books on the Fort Crawford shelves, and all his
life he enjoyed reading newspapers. His chief interest lay in news
of a military nature, but he also managed to keep abreast of the
political tide. A worshiper at the shrine of James Monroe, he had
been favorably disposed toward the Jackson Administration early
in 1829 but now vehemently sympathized with the opposition.[13]
Constitutionally eligible to cast his ballot in eight presidential elec-
tions between 1808 and 1836, he never took advantage of the privi-
lege.[14] This failure to fulfill the first function of a citizen may be
attributed to the fact that duty frequently led him far from his

## ANN MACKALL TAYLOR

Eldest daughter of Zachary Taylor, wife of Dr. Robert Crooke Wood. From a
daguerreotype, a photograph of which is in the collection of her grandson,
Trist Wood, of New Orleans.

legal residence, and possibly to his personal conviction that the arena of politics was no place for a soldier.

### 3

If Taylor's Virginia birth, Kentucky youth, and Louisiana interests established his status as a son of the South, it must be remembered that the western Virginia of 1785, the Kentucky of 1800, and the Louisiana of 1820 were scarcely less western than southern. If Taylor lacked the political sixth sense which set Andrew Jackson in a niche apart, he closely resembled the master of the Hermitage in slaveholding, southwestern, and soldierly associations. Like Jackson, he harbored no sectional prejudice. His disinclination to live in the Northwest failed to jaundice his view of northern people, and he frequently observed that the farms of the free states bred the finest soldiers in the land. The probability that Taylor's long service in Wisconsin, Minnesota, Missouri, Illinois, and Indiana contributed materially to his unswerving nationalism cannot be bulwarked by documentation. But the record shows that, in thought and in emotion, neither state nor local pride diluted his devotion to the country as a whole. From early manhood to the last earthly hour, Taylor's patriotic breadth never narrowed.

Zachary Taylor avowed profound respect for Christianity, its ministers and priests. Contrary to the widespread assumption that he joined the Episcopal Church, and despite the fact that Mrs. Taylor, the Taylor children, and many of his forebears were Episcopalians, he never became a communicant.[15] During the Fort Crawford period, the Reverend Richard F. Cadle held regular religious services on Sundays.[16] These were well attended by men and officers, Mrs. Julia E. Stevens, a pious visitor from the East, finding the latter "gentlemanly and Christian" and stressing the civilities shown her by the Colonel.[17] Taylor was not a natural "joiner." He was never initiated into the mysteries of Masonry.[18] Conservative by instinct, and a venerator of the established economic order, he was an individualist in religious and fraternal matters as well as in politics.

Fort Crawford's commandant displayed more than perfunctory interest in the post school, which came under his supervision. In 1832 his daughter Betty was eight years old, his son Dick was six, and the Colonel was eager to give them the sort of education which he had been denied. Joseph T. Mills taught the children in 1834, and later the Reverend Mr. Cadle served as instructor as well as chaplain of the post. Dick was with his parents as late as 1835 and probably remained into the following year, but Taylor subsequently placed Betty in a boarding school at Philadelphia, and his only son studied in Kentucky. Both eventually became fluent linguists, conversant with literature and history, and Richard Taylor would one day write *Destruction and Reconstruction,* a creditable memoir of the Civil War. In 1845 their father was to advise Betty to study French with her brother, "which would contribute so much to your minds. . . . You and he should . . . read alternately aloud after tea in the history of England or Shakespear's plays, till near bedtime, to conclude with a chapter in the Bible."[19] At Fort Crawford, naturally, less advanced subjects composed the curriculum, and there were other boys and girls with whom to play. "Bessie and Dick . . . were about my own age," recalled John H. Bliss, a comrade of their childhood, "and . . . we became excellent friends. . . . I was awfully sorry to part with Dick, and to show the strongest evidence of my regard, named one of my squirrels after him. . . ."[20]

4

In addition to supervising the education of the white children, Colonel Taylor was entrusted with the erection of a school for the Winnebago Indians who still resided in the vicinity of Prairie du Chien. Agent Joseph Montfort Street, whom Taylor liked and trusted, let the contract for the school buildings at a site on the Yellow River about ten miles from Fort Crawford, and the Colonel directed their construction. In his dealings with the aborigines, on this occasion and on many others, Taylor was uniformly fair and firm. Intent upon protecting their rights, he had in 1830 forced white squatters out of the Indians' lead mines which they were exploiting, and in 1832 and 1833 he dispatched First Lieutenant John J. Abercrombie and Second Lieutenants Wilson, Davis, and Erasmus F. Covington to the diggings when the miners put in a reappearance. In November, 1834, when Taylor was absent on leave, a band of Sauks and Foxes murdered ten Winnebago braves and some women and children. The following May, his mediation effected a truce.[21] In 1836, when settlers feared a savage outbreak northeast of Fort Crawford, Taylor led three companies to Fort Winnebago, and the uprising did not materialize.[22]

Apart from independent whisky sellers, the special target of Taylor's detestation was the American Fur Company. Whereas Taylor's word was law at Fort Crawford, the company's local representative, Joseph Rolette, dominated the village. Known as "King" Rolette, he had achieved no little notoriety in September, 1830, by acquiring within twenty-four hours twenty-three hundred dollars received by the Winnebagoes as an annuity from the government.[23] Villagers feared Rolette worse than death, wrote John H. Fonda.[24] The company's president, John Jacob Astor, issued medals "similar to those of the . . . President of the United States, for circulation among the Indian tribes. . . ."[25] Rolette and his kind not only warred with rival traders, "but set their faces sternly against . . . the formation of . . . farms for the . . . [Indians], as game rapidly decreased. No[,] the Indians must hunt for their gain, and their gain alone."[26] Years of proximity to such sharp practices impelled Taylor to lay down this principle: "Take the American Fur Company in the aggregate, and they are the greatest scoundrels the world ever knew."[27]

His own integrity beyond reproach, Zachary Taylor was quick to decry questionable transactions on the part of others. His own mien exceedingly modest, his manners those of a planter or farmer rather than of a martinet, he was overeager to detect sham, flummery, ostentation in his fellow men. Winfield Scott, who knew him well but whose opinion was probably conditioned by at least a tinge of jealous rivalry, described him as "quite ignorant" and "bigoted in his ignorance." Taylor's simplicity "was childlike," Scott continued, "and with innumerable prejudices—amusing and

incorrigible—well suited to the tender age. Thus if a man, however respectable, chanced to wear a coat of an unusual color, or his
hat a little on one side of the head;—or an officer to leave the corner of his handkerchief dangling from an outside pocket—in any
such case, this critic held the offender to be a coxcomb—perhaps,
something worse, whom he would not, to use his oft-repeated
phrase, 'touch with a pair of tongs.' Any allusion to literature
much beyond good old Dilworth's Spelling Book, on the part of
one wearing a sword, was evidence, with the same judge, of utter
unfitness for heavy marchings and combats. In short, few men
have ever had a more comfortable, labor-saving contempt for learning of every kind. Yet this ... soldier ... had the true basis of a
great character:—pure, uncorrupted morals, combined with in-
domitable courage. Kind-hearted, sincere, and hospitable in a
plain way, he had no vice but prejudice, many friends, and left
behind him not an enemy in the world. ..."[28]

In this connection Scott's own foibles should be taken into account. A vain man, Scott was proud of his person. He loved ostentation. He delighted in display. "Not even the gorgeously bediz-
ened marshals of Napoleon wore their plumes, sashes, aiguilettes,
and glittering uniforms with more complacency than did this re-
publican soldier," Scott's reliable biographer has written.[29] Scott's
second specification likewise demands inquiry, for Taylor's advice
to his children, his letters to Jesup throughout the 1820s, and his
later correspondence with Doctor Wood point to contempt for ignorance rather than contempt for learning. Prejudice he did possess to an unfortunate degree. But in 1834 Captain Hitchcock, one
of the best educated West Pointers of the period, considered Taylor
"a faithful officer" who "has probably rendered as much personal
service as any officer in the army."[30]

## 5

Whatever other traits might be attributed to Taylor, he was and
would always remain an essentially simple person, free from con-
ceit and not deficient in humor. One day "all the soldiers were

mustered for dress parade. Taylor came sauntering in from his quarters, and running his eye along the front rank, observed a large stout German recruit out of line. The German was a raw recruit anxious to do his duty, but did not understand the English language. So when the order was given to 'dress,' the soldier remained as before. Col. Taylor remarked this, and thinking it a willful neglect on the soldier's part, walked up to him and after one or two trials, got hold of his ears and shook the fellow severely. This treatment was called 'Wooling,' a favorite mode of punishment with Taylor, but the German not knowing how to appreciate it, nor why it was inflicted on him, had no sooner got his head free than drawing back, he struck Taylor a blow that felled him to the ground like a log. This was mutiny, and the officers would have cut him down, if Taylor had not ... [risen] up and said, 'let that man alone, he will make a good soldier.' "[31]

The Colonel's habits, clothes, opinions, tastes reflected the sort of man he was—plain, without pretense, almost painfully straightforward. His only vice, if such it can be called, was chewing tobacco. In an age when overindulgence in alcohol was usual, he did not drink;[32] neither did he smoke, probably out of deference to Mrs. Taylor, whom smoke made actively ill.[33] At nine o'clock in the evening, Taylor went to bed. It was his custom to rise at daybreak, to breakfast before six o'clock, to stroll down to the bank of whatever river he happened to be near, and, if a steamboat had come up in the night, to converse with the captain and the passengers, who usually sized him up as a well-to-do farmer. "What's the news from Washington? How's the Louisville tobacco crop! Are the levees holding in Louisiana?" Questions such as these characterized his conversation. Agricultural information, in particular, was welcome to Taylor. But on more than one occasion politics intruded.

"Colonel Taylor immediately told me to make his house my home till I should arrange my quarters," recorded Captain Hitchcock, who arrived at Prairie du Chien on the Saint Louis boat one April morning. "This courtesy is evidence of kindness which in this case has been made more apparent by the manner. He is full of spleen against a variety of the measures of the government, and, having been a Jackson man and being now an Anti, he is, like most converts, rather warm. . . . He began reading to me what he called 'a little note to a member of Congress.' It ran . . . through three sheets of letter paper closely written. He is very long-winded and by writing so voluminously must have defeated his own efforts."[34]

"We were received at . . . [Taylor's] quarters most hospitably, and made perfectly at home," wrote John H. Bliss. ". . . As a boy, I was very fond of him. He was a large, strongly built man, rather quiet and deliberate in movement and conversation, and with the same disregard of dress and 'the pride, pomp and circumstance of glorious war' which was so conspicuous in General Grant. . . . [He was] a perfect specimen of the Kentuckian."[35]

Bliss and Hitchcock were not alone in stressing Taylor's hospitality. The word "hospitable" recurs time and time again in the journals of American and foreign visitors to the fort. An Englishman, Charles J. Latrobe, met with "that warmth of welcome which makes the traveller feel at once at home" and found "as warmhearted a set of fine young fellows, and as staunch and brave an old Colonel as you would wish to see."[36] His compatriot, Charles Augustus Murray, carried away a similar impression. "A plate was laid for me at the commanding officer's table, and another gentleman, in whose quarters I lodged, actually insisted upon my occupying his bed while he slept on a sofa fitted up with a buffalo robe."[37] Henry Merrell referred to the town as "Prairie of de d—d dog," but "thought it delightful. . . ."[38] "I made many acquaintances," he recalled, "among them Colonel Zachary Taylor. . . ." Charles Fenno Hoffman, the New York author, spent several months at Fort Crawford. His *A Winter in the West* discloses a graphic picture.

The troops, Hoffman wrote, were housed "in very handsome barracks, built by the soldiers themselves of cut stone; the buildings being arranged in the form of a square, and enclosing an area large enough for a battalion to drill in. The parade is nicely graveled, and a colonnade, which extends round three sides of the parade, gives a cheerful aspect to the whole. . . . The place as it now stands, would be easily tenable against hordes of Indians, should they be mad enough to assail it. . . . There is a small but well-chosen library belonging to the post, and several of the companies have quite good miscellaneous libraries of their own,—a fact exceedingly creditable to the private soldiers. The amusements of the place so far as society is concerned, are of course, limited. . . . The officers sometimes amuse themselves in getting up what is called a gumbo ball, which from the descriptions . . . must be a kind of harlequinade. . . . Sporting, however,—when the resources of the library are exhausted, or a pipe of kinnekinic ceases to charm,—is the great source of amusement at Prairie du Chien. The grouse now keep in large packs near the garrison; snipe, too, I am told, are abundant when in season, and of ducks I am assured it is easy to kill a canoe-load, when they begin to fly along the Mississippi. Elk, bear, and wolves are the game of those who are more ambitious in their sport, and choose to go farther to seek it. The meat of the first I have not yet tasted, but I made a capital dinner yesterday from a sirloin of the second, at the commandant's quarters. Bruin was served up in handsome style, and some old wine from Colonel T.'s hospitable cellar relished in this latitude."[39]

## 6

Late in 1836, Taylor's association with Fort Crawford was interrupted. On November 16 he turned the post over to Captain William R. Jouett, and a fortnight thereafter assumed command of Jefferson Barracks.[40] In the absence of General Atkinson, Taylor's new assignment placed him temporarily in charge of the right wing of the Western Department with full authority under General Gaines over the entire Northwest. Six months of this dual responsibility brought Taylor little opportunity for distinction, though in September, 1837, he demonstrated commendable foresight by urging the establishment of temporary, rather than permanent, posts when the frontier should be extended.[41] Indian scares in Wisconsin Territory came with the late winter and spring of that year. Taylor and his subordinates took precautionary steps, and the storm subsided.[42] At this time his planting operations in the deep South worried the Colonel, and both he and Mrs. Taylor grew increasingly lonely. Their eldest daughter, Ann Wood, was not with them. Their second daughter, Sarah Knox Davis, was dead. Both Betty and Dick were away at school. It was a father and a planter as well as a soldier who addressed to Adjutant General Roger Jones this characteristic letter:

"HEAD QUARTERS RIGHT WING WESTN. DEPT.
JEFFERSON BARRACKS Mo., March 19th 1837.

"SIR,

"Circumstances compel me reluctantly to ask of the General Commanding the Army through you, a leave of absence for six months to take effect when relieved in Command of this place, and the Right Wing Western Department . . . , for the purpose of visiting my Children who are at school in Philadelphia and Kentucky, and who have been absent from us for . . . several years, as well as to enable me to go to the States of Louisiana and Mississippi for the purpose of looking into the situation of my private affairs. . . . I deem it entirely unnecessary to urge or set forth my claims with a view to a favourable result of my application, on account of service, the Posts I have been at, or the length of time which has intervened since I have had such an indulgence, as the documents on file in your Office ought to govern in all such cases. An early decision on the case is respectfully requested as it may have some bearing on my future arrangements. . . . At the same time I wish it distinctly understood should there be difficulties between the Whites and Indians on the frontier of the State of Missouri or the Territory of Wisconsin[,] I would not take advantage of a leave of absence if granted until such difficulties were brought to a close, which must be by the end of Autumn.

"Very Respectfully
"Your Obt. Servt,

"Brigr Genl. R. Jones
Adjt. Genl. U.S. Army
Washington City
  D.C."

"Z. TAYLOR—COL,
"1st Regt, U.S. Infy,
"Comdg—[43]

His application promptly approved in Washington, Zachary Taylor no doubt would 'have set out for the East and South shortly after May 1, 1837, had it not been for Governor Dodge's fear of further Indian raids in Wisconsin. Taylor considered Dodge's fear unfounded, and the future proved the Colonel correct. Nevertheless, on May 8, Taylor informed Jones: "I shall ... return forthwith to Fort Crawford ... , where I shall continue until all apprehensions ... subside; and should they occur will be ready to contribute my mite in restoring peace in that quarter, after which I will avail myself of the leave of absence granted me."[44] He started up the Mississippi from Jefferson Barracks on May 19, supplanted Brevet Major Gustavus Loomis in command of Fort Crawford on May 30 and stayed there through the month of June.[45]

Meanwhile events in Florida Territory were shaping the Colonel's destiny in such a way that the cherished leave of absence would long remain a thing of ink and paper. Part of the Fifth Infantry arrived at Prairie du Chien on July 7, and Taylor received instructions to transfer the First Infantry from Forts Crawford and Snelling to Jefferson Barracks, "where I have just learned the Regiment is to halt some time previous to proceeding to the South."[46] On July 18, Taylor bade a last farewell to the isolated post where he had seen more service than in any other single place. He reached the Barracks two days later at the head of six companies, and was joined by the four Fort Snelling companies under Lieutenant Colonel William Davenport within thirty-six hours.[47] Now the northwestern period belonged to the past. Again the call to arms was sounding, and soon the scene would shift to the swamps and Everglades of Florida.[48]

# CHAPTER IX

## FLORIDA GLORY

### 1

NEARLY nineteen months before Colonel Taylor began his broken journey from Prairie du Chien to Tampa Bay, savage warriors under Osceola had shed the red blood of white men on Florida soil. December 28, 1835, was a day of such shocking slaughter as seldom Huguenot or Spanish don or "Old Hickory" Jackson had seen in the land of sun and flowers that once belonged to Spain.[1] Climaxing a decade of misrepresentation and misunderstanding between Washington and the Indians, it marked the inception of the longest, costliest and bloodiest Indian war in United States history. To congressmen at the capital, this war would mean an appropriation of thirty million dollars; to fifteen hundred soldiers, death; to Zachary Taylor, a tortuous path to glory, and the brevet of brigadier.

Tribes of Muskhogean stock had made their home in Florida for upward of a century, all of them identified with Alabama or Georgia Creeks.[2] Some now were known as Seminoles, some as Mikasukis, others as Apalaches, still others as Tallahassees. Antedating these savages in Florida were the so-called Spanish Indians: the Calusas, supposedly of Choctaw origin; and the Tequestas, whom tradition says came to continental America from the near-by Bahama Islands. Most important to Taylor were the Mikasukis and the Seminoles, and from the latter the conflict had already taken the name of the Second Seminole War.

Florida had been United States territory since 1821. Soon after its acquisition, thirty-one chiefs and headmen had agreed to move their relatives and followers from productive land in the vicinity of the Apalachicola and Suwanee Rivers to central and southern

122

sections of the peninsula.[3] Finding this region unpromising from the standpoint of cultivation, many a rash brave ignored treaty provisions, encroaching on northern districts, indulging in depredations, burning, slaying, terrorizing. Negroes complicated the already tangled situation. Having escaped from Georgia and Florida plantations, these hunted creatures merged and intermarried with the Indians, whom they recognized as nominal masters but frequently dominated.[4] Some of the white men who raided Indian encampments in search of runaway slaves were law-abiding citizens despoiled of rightful property by the Seminoles. Others were lawless adventurers, professional plunderers who debauched the redskins with alcohol, pillaging Indian towns and stealing blacks to whom they held a tenuous claim or none at all.

2

With the arrival of additional white settlers in the border country, the federal government determined to rid Florida of its Indian population. At Payne's Landing in 1832 a group of prominent hereditary leaders promised to migrate west of the Mississippi provided that a delegation should visit the western lands, report favorably on removal, and have its report ratified by the Indian rank and file. This delegation included Jumper, John Blunt, Charley Emathla, and Holahte Emathla. In 1833, at Fort Gibson in the Southwest, although lacking authorization, the four chiefs signed a treaty which purportedly committed every Indian in Florida to removal within a three-year period.[5] Subsequently the rank and file repudiated this treaty, but President Andrew Jackson regarded it as law. In order to enforce it, the War Department dispatched Brevet Brigadier General Duncan L. Clinch with ten companies of regular troops to co-operate with territorial authorities and with Indian Agent Wiley Thompson, and to bring about emigration.[6] The Indians refused to budge.

The Treaty of Fort Gibson was the straw that broke the camel's back. Like white planters of cotton, corn, and sugar—whom not a few Indians regarded as interlopers—the Seminoles and Mikasukis had borne much and had not complained. Now they rebelled. Led by a fiery young warrior, Osceola by name, they spat defiance at the United States. And on that fateful day, December 28, 1835, they not only ambushed and massacred one hundred and seven of the one hundred and ten officers and men in the command of Brevet Major Francis Langhorne Dade, six miles north of the Withlacoochee River, but also slew Agent Thompson and four comrades at Fort King.[7]

"You have guns," Osceola informed Clinch in a dramatically frank letter, "and so have we—you have powder and lead, and so have we—you have men, and so have we—your men will fight, and so will ours, till the last drop of the Seminole's blood has moistened the dust of his hunting ground."[8]

Thus the gauntlet fell. The battle hour struck.

3

From December, 1835, until November, 1837, when Zachary Taylor would take the field, four of Taylor's superior officers commanded forces in Florida. Three days after the Dade Massacre, General Clinch came to grips with the foe in a hot little engagement at the ford of the Withlacoochee.[9] Winfield Scott superseded Clinch in February, 1836, but met with less success in bringing the elusive Indians to battle.

Dividing his troops into three columns, Scott attempted to encircle the great "Cove," trap Osceola, and force him to fight. Feasible in theory and workable on any other terrain, this elaborate plan in practice was conditioned by the topography of Florida's swampy and inaccessible interior and by the presence on the peninsula of Scott's detested rival, Edmund P. Gaines. Scott considered Gaines insane. Gaines called Scott traitorous and compared him to Benedict Arnold. Between two such implacable and petulant gentlemen, co-operation was impossible. Gaines left Florida in March, having accomplished nothing. Scott, his plan an utter failure, followed in May.[10] In December, 1836, after an interval when Governor Richard Keith Call commanded, Brevet Major

General Jesup left the quartermaster department in the hands of a subordinate and assumed charge of the Florida operations.[11]

During three months of strenuous pursuit, Jesup and his men thrice skirmished with the Indians and thrice emerged victorious. Penetrating deep into the dismal swampland, they destroyed enemy property wherever they could find it and convinced the Seminoles that indefinite aggression might result in slow starvation at best and slaughter at worst. Accordingly, the Indian leaders altered their strategy. They sued for peace. Agreeing to emigrate, Jumper, Alligator, and Micanopy came in to Fort Brooke at Tampa Bay. Sam Jones and even Osceola intimated surrender. Impressed by what he saw and more impressed by what he heard, Jesup let down his guard. Dismissing volunteer soldiers, he scattered his regulars and relaxed precautions. He felt certain that the war was at an end.

Jesup's action was premature. Clothed and fed by the Army, Indians at Tampa Bay employed one pretext after another to excuse their allies' prolonged absence from the point of embarkation, while the absentees busily planted corn and prepared for further fighting. Soon the jig was up. The beans were spilled. Osceola kidnaped the peace-loving Micanopy from the rendezvous. Other friendly Indians vanished overnight. And confusion once more reigned along the border.[12]

Thomas Sidney Jesup, his illusions shattered by failure to forestall enemy subreption, resolved now to meet the Indians on their chosen ground—the ground of duplicity. Lashed by ridicule, castigated by a thousand pens, the General found his force too depleted to renew the struggle in the spring of 1837. Biding his time, Jesup waited until autumn. Then, by one pretext or another, ignoring flags of truce and violating first principles of civilized warfare, he took into custody not only Micanopy and other savages to the number of two hundred but also the dreaded Osceola.[13] So it was that, when Colonel Taylor landed at Tampa Bay from New Orleans in the autumn of 1837, the master spirit of the war had been removed from the scene of hostilities by foul means rather than by fair.

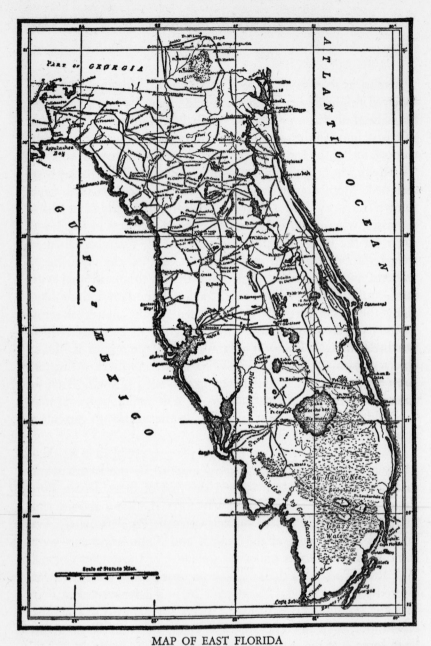

MAP OF EAST FLORIDA

Reduced from the Map compiled by Captain John Mackay and Lieutenant J. E. Blake and published by order of the Senate of the United States, for Drake's Book of the Indians, 1840.

4

Almost as soon as he set foot in Florida, Taylor made what he believed might be his last will and testament.[14] In view of dangers ahead, it was a prudent step to take. A desperate American offensive hung in the offing, for, with Osceola in chains, belligerent compatriots of the Indian leader determined to avenge his capture. To Taylor, the brunt of this campaign's direction had already been assigned. Momentarily he expected the signal to sally forth from known territory into the maze of Middle Florida's trackless morasses, where Seminole warriors lurked muskets in hand and eager for the kill. Patiently he supervised the disembarkation of troops, the breaking and loading of pack-mules, the repairing of wagons, and the equipment of more than a thousand men with guns, ammunition, clothing, and food. Of the labyrinthine land along the Kissimmee River, and down on the shores of semi-legendary Lake Okeechobee, Taylor learned all he could, which was little enough. He became familiar with the names of Indian chiefs remaining in the field—Wild Cat, Sam Jones, Alligator, Jumper. In their traits and habits he schooled himself. And, in accordance with Jesup's instructions, he sent native scouts out into the wilderness in an effort to persuade the enemy to capitulate before the offensive should begin.[15]

It was part and parcel of Taylor's plan to establish a series of garrisoned depots along the line of march. By the fourth week in November, he had provisioned the first of these depots, Fort Fraser on Pease Creek, with nearly forty thousand rations and more than twelve hundred bushels of corn. Approximately five hundred infantrymen of the Fourth and Sixth Regiments were completing its defenses under the guidance of Lieutenant Colonel William S. Foster. "I shall . . . lose no time at that place," Taylor assured Jesup on Sunday, November 26, in a letter written at Fort Brooke, "but shall move forthwith with 25 or 30 days rations to the Kissimmee, or in any other direction I may ascertain the enemy to lie in force, & as far as practicable to bring him to battle, by which time or before, I hope to have the pleasure of meeting with you, or of receiving your instructions as to my future operations."[16]

On the morrow, November 27, Taylor left Tampa Bay with a baggage train of eighty wagons and one hundred and ninety-one members of the First Infantry under Lieutenant Colonel William Davenport. The forty-mile route due east to Pease Creek was a poor excuse for a military road, but the Colonel made the journey in two days, attaining his immediate destination at ten o'clock on Wednesday morning. Having stocked Fort Fraser with supplies, he assigned a strong detail to guard them. A slow twenty-five-mile march to the Kissimmee followed, with pioneers and pontoniers building bridges and laying causeways along the unmarked trail. Reaching the western bank of the river on the afternoon of December 3, Taylor selected a suitable site for the erection of a bridge and, on the opposite side, constructed the second of his series of depots which he called Fort Gardiner.[17] Here he halted two full weeks to comply with instructions from General Jesup, who had dispatched an express from his headquarters at Picolata on the St. Johns River with word that the hostiles were seriously contemplating surrender.[18] When his superior officer's optimism vanished, the Colonel ordered part of his force forward to the south on Tuesday, December 19, and himself departed with the balance on the following morning.[19]

Exclusive of the detachments left behind at Fort Fraser and and Fort Gardiner, Zachary Taylor's brigade of the "Army South of the Withlacoochee" numbered one thousand and sixty-seven officers and men, of whom seven hundred and twenty-seven were regulars. Davenport's First Infantry comprised one hundred and ninety-seven privates and non-commissioned officers; Foster's Fourth Infantry, two hundred and seventy-four; Lieutenant Colonel Alexander R. Thompson's Sixth Infantry, two hundred and twenty-one; Captain John Munroe's Fourth Artillery, thirty-five. All the volunteers were citizens of the state of Missouri, and all were mounted. One hundred and eighty composed Colonel Richard Gentry's regiment, the remainder acting as scouts or "spies" under the leadership of Major Alexander G. Morgan. Thirty pioneers, thirteen pontoniers, and seventy Delaware Indians completed Taylor's command. The Colonel's brother, Captain Joseph P. Taylor, accompanied the expedition as a supernumerary.[20]

## 5

Taylor's army was moving down the west bank of the Kissimmee in a southeasterly direction late Wednesday evening, December 20, when Jumper came in and surrendered. Heartened by this omen of success, Taylor on Thursday pressed forward on the double quick. At ten o'clock that night, his scouts reported Alligator's recent presence in the vicinity. Sleepless, the Colonel advanced at midnight with half the mounted men, met the remainder ten miles to the south, crossed Istokpoga Outlet, and took possession of Alligator's camp.[21] Here he found several non-combatants, among them an old Seminole who repeated the scouts' story that Alligator intended to follow Jumper's example. Alligator had the reputation of being a shrewd leader. A writer for the Pensacola *Gazette* had described him as "worth all the Indians I have met."[22] And Zachary Taylor, who knew Indian nature, was not impressed by the old Seminole's report. "If Alligator is sincere, he will surrender at once," was the gist of Taylor's statement to the intermediary; and the ford of the Kissimmee, eleven miles below, was designated as a meeting place. After the intermediary's departure, Taylor awaited the regulars' arrival and then proceeded with his entire command to the appointed rendezvous, where he arrived the same night.[23] In less than sixty hours he had brought his brigade safely through sixty miles of wilderness never before explored by white men.

Less than twenty miles now separated Taylor from the entrance of the Kissimmee into Lake Okeechobee, the largest body of inland water south of the Great Lakes and east of the Mississippi. Ahead of him (handicapped by lack of adequate guides, he knew neither their exact location nor their number) the united warriors of Sam Jones, Wild Cat, and Alligator lay in wait. An evasive message from Alligator, which was what he anticipated, fixed Taylor's decision to pursue the Indians swiftly and ruthlessly, regardless of the cost. Only a bloody struggle could convince the redskins of the whites' determination to carry the campaign forward to success. Laying out a small stockade where he was, the American commander deposited all his heavy baggage at that site, Fort Basinger. Then, instructing Munroe and the Fourth Artillery to garrison the post, he parted company with eighty-five sick and disabled infantrymen, the pontoniers and pioneers who were no longer needed, and many of the friendly Indians who balked at battle. His force now reduced to eight hundred and thirty-four able-bodied troops, plus a handful of Delawares, Taylor on Saturday set out on the last lap of his incursion.[24]

Early Sunday morning, Taylor found Alligator's latest position. Slaughtered cattle lay upon the ground, but the enemy had fled. Advancing farther, the scouts surprised a small Indian encampment and captured four warriors, who were impressed as guides and said the Mikasukis were ten or twelve miles distant. In the afternoon, the troops plodded through undergrowth, and reached the edge of an extremely dense cypress swamp. Taylor deployed his army, anticipating action, but no action was forthcoming. Another Indian, caught by the whites, confirmed his fellow captives' statements. And, as the sun went down upon the scene, the Colonel gave the order to halt and pass the night. The soldiers slept on their arms with the enemy six miles away.

Daylight of Monday, December 25, saw the brigade once more sweeping southward on a five-mile march to the border of another swamp. Here Taylor came upon a third Seminole camp, its smoking fires and unconsumed beef bearing telltale evidence of hurried abandonment. Again the Colonel prepared his men for battle. Again no enemy appeared. The Americans crossed over to enter a broad prairie on the north shore of Lake Okeechobee, where cattle and ponies grazed oblivious of the impending struggle. Here a youthful Indian, taken into custody, "pointed out a dense hammock on our right, about a mile distant, in which he said the hostiles were situated and waiting to give us battle."[25]

"At this place," wrote Taylor, "the final disposition was made to attack them, which was in two lines; the volunteers under Gentry and Morgan's spies to form the first line in extended order, who were instructed to enter the hammock, and in the event of being attacked and hard pressed, were to fall back in the rear of the regular troops, out of reach of the enemy's fire; the second line was composed of the 4th and 6th infantry, who were instructed to sustain the volunteers, the 1st infantry being held in reserve."[26]

## 6

Advancing four hundred yards across the prairie at high noon on Christmas Day, the aggressors neared as wide a swamp as any they had penetrated, its surface covered with a thick growth of saw grass which stretched to the enemy's intrenched position three-quarters of a mile away. Extending to the left as far as eye could see, and bounded on the right by a deep creek, this swamp presented a hazard of no mean proportions. Unhesitatingly, Zachary Taylor determined to send his soldiers plunging ahead over the spongy soil. There was no other course to take. Here horses could make no headway, and he bade the volunteers dismount. Leaving the animals with the baggage and a guard, he detached Captain George W. Allen and two companies of mounted infantrymen to scour the region on the right, with instructions to return to the baggage in the event that no Indians appeared in that direction.[27]

As Allen wheeled and cantered toward the creek, the volunteers led the main body of troops across the formidable swamp, sloughing through knee-deep water with unsure footing underneath. Facing them were approximately three hundred and eighty Indians, one hundred and eighty under Sam Jones on the Americans' left, one hundred and twenty under Alligator at the center, and eighty commanded by Wild Cat on the right.[28] Hidden behind a screen of palmettos, enveloped in moss-covered foliage, the well-armed aborigines withheld their fire until Gentry was only twenty yards away. Then, each Indian deliberately selecting a target, Alligator gave the signal and they poured a galling volley into the Missourians' ranks. The onslaught did its work. A score of whites fell wounded, Colonel Gentry mortally. And the same ball which struck him shattered the wrist of his son, who was serving as sergeant major. The volunteers stood their ground long enough to return the fire, but soon the loss of their leader created pandemonium. Ignoring Gentry's heroic example, his followers fled in confusion, deaf to the entreaties of Joseph P. Taylor and other officers to re-form their line in the regulars' rear.[29]

Zachary Taylor's regulars were made of sterner stuff. They had pushed steadily onward behind the volunteers, quickened the charge when the first line faltered and now courageously were matching ball for ball. The Sixth Infantry, under Thompson, advancing on the right, received a murderous fire from Wild Cat and Alligator, who stood firm behind their camouflaged entrenchment. Exposed and defenseless, the whites by twos and threes were killed or wounded. With a single lucky exception, every officer was hit, together with the sergeant major, four orderly sergeants, and more than sixty privates.

Captain Joseph Van Swearingen, leading his company, was shot in the neck. Turning back to obtain treatment, he fell flat on his face, expiring instantly.

A ball pierced the stout heart of Lieutenant Francis J. Brooke.

Lieutenant John P. Center perished on the spot from a shot in the head.

Thompson himself, thrice wounded, died as he cried: "Keep steady, men. Charge the hammock. Remember the regiment to which you belong."

As the remainder of the Sixth dropped back to close ranks preparatory to renewing the attack, six companies of the Fourth Regiment under Lieutenant Colonel Foster were finding fortune on their side. Although Taylor did not know it at the time, Sam Jones had fled precipitately at the outbreak of the battle. Alligator rallied nearly all his followers, but the Mikasukis lacked the desperate bravery of the Seminoles. Gaining the hammock in good order from the left, Foster's force was joined by a segment of the Sixth and by a few Missourians who came up from the rear.

Taylor himself, directing operations from the prairie in full view of the enemy, now learned that Captain Allen was flanking from the right. The time to put on pressure had arrived, and the Colonel instructed Davenport to lead the reserve regulars on a similar flanking movement from the left. The instant that the fresh First Infantry swung into position, the redskins fired a final round and then retreated, Alligator in their midst. The battle of Okeechobee now became a rout, the men of Davenport and Foster sweeping all the Indians before them "until near night, and until these troops were nearly exhausted, and the enemy driven in all directions."[30]

"The action was a severe one," Taylor reported to the Adjutant General. It "continued from half-past twelve until after three P.M. ... We suffered much, having twenty-six killed and one hundred and twelve wounded, among whom are some of our most valuable officers. The hostiles probably suffered, all things considered, equally with ourselves, they having left ten dead on the ground, besides, doubtless, carrying off many more, as is customary with them when practicable."[31]

## 7

Tuesday, December 26, was devoted to constructing litters for the wounded, and burying the dead. "Here ... I experienced one of the most trying scenes of my life," wrote Taylor, "and he who could have looked on it with indifference, his nerves must have been very differently organized from my own. ..." Further pursuit was impossible. One-eighth of the brigade lay injured, and the food supply was dangerously low. Having transformed the primary purpose of the campaign into substantial achievement, the footsore and heavy-eyed troops retraced their steps. The Colonel detailed a small detachment to garrison Fort Basinger. He himself, together with the First Infantry, halted at Fort Gardiner on December 31. The Fourth continued west as far as Fort Fraser, while the Sixth Regiment and the Missouri Volunteers conducted their injured comrades into Fort Brooke at Tampa Bay.

From Fort Gardiner, on January 4, 1838, Zachary Taylor issued his official report.

In six weeks, he recorded, "this column ... penetrated one hundred and fifty miles into the enemy's country, opened roads, and constructed bridges and causeways ... on the greater portion of the route; established two depots, and the necessary defenses for the same; and finally overtook, and beat the enemy in his strongest position. The results have been the capture of thirty of the hostiles; the ... surrendering of more than one hundred and fifty Indians and negroes ... ; the capturing and driving out of the country six hundred head of cattle, upwards of one hundred head of horses; besides obtaining a thorough knowledge of the country through which we operated, a greater portion of which was entirely unknown, except to the enemy."[32]

Had this been a personal letter, Taylor might have written more. The march to and from Lake Okeechobee, and the action there, held peculiar significance for the Colonel. Never before in twenty-eight years of military duty had he commanded so many soldiers at a single time, in battle or out. Never had he participated in so bloody an encounter. Never, save in 1812, did his responsibilities assume such proportions.

Just as a youthful captain had received the title of brevet major in recognition of his gallantry at Fort Harrison, so now a grizzled colonel with a wealth of experience would soon be brevetted brigadier general for distinguished services at Okeechobee. That struggle, the most spectacular of the Second Seminole War, was in some respects the most far-reaching in its results. Together with Colonel Persifor F. Smith's expedition along the Caloosahatchee River, and Jesup's activities in the north and east, it convinced the Indians that their adversaries were not afraid to fight. And never again, from that sanguinary Christmas afternoon of 1837 until the war's conclusion, would either the Mikasukis or the Seminoles dare to join in a pitched battle.

From January through April, hostilities continued unabated. Taylor occupied positions in the forefront of pursuit, but he did not again come under fire. "I . . . calculate," he wrote at Fort Basinger on March 20, "that during the next month we will have to retire from this part of Florida. . . . It is possible that we may be required to keep the field against the Mickasukies & Tallehassees to the north until May, when we . . . ought to go into Summer quarters. . . ."[33] During the eight-month period from September to May, one thousand, nine hundred and fifty-five Indians and Negroes either were captured or gave themselves up, of whom four hundred and eighty-four constituted Taylor's contribution.[34] Despite these exertions, many Indians refused to budge. And Jesup gave Secretary of War Joel R. Poinsett his "decided opinion" that "in regard to the Seminoles, we have committed the error of attempting to remove them when their lands were not required for agricultural purposes. . . . The prospect of terminating the war in any reasonable time is any thing but flattering. . . . Unless immediate immigration [emigration] be abandoned [,] the war will continue for years to come, and at constantly accumulating expense."[35]

Previously, the same officer had written: "This is the first instance in our history in which we have attempted to transfer Indians from one wilderness to another. On all other occasions the white population has been pressing and crowding them out, before we have attempted to remove them. To rid the country of them you must exterminate them. Is the Government prepared for such a measure? If so, resort must be had to the bloodhound and the northern Indian. . . ."[36]

With pessimistic valedictories such as these, General Jesup on May 15 turned over the command of all the troops in Florida to General Taylor, who established headquarters for the "Army of the South" at Tampa Bay.[37]

## 8

Early in June, the new commander set out from Fort Brooke on an inspection tour of the interior, journeyed northward to Forts King, Micanopy, and Heileman, and crossed the Georgia border into the Okefenokee Swamp. He returned to Tampa late in July and described his progress and problems in a letter to Hancock Taylor the following month.

"[I] have returned to this place after an absence of six weeks. Most of this time I was daily on horseback, which, in the tropical sun, and with the worst [water] imaginable for drinking, made the fatigue and privations of no ordinary character. The Indians are now broken up in small parties and scattered over this immense country, secreting themselves in their almost impenatratable swamps and hammocks. . . . Had they towns, or even habitations, to defend, or could we force them to join battle with us, the war would be brought to a close in a very short time. Unfortunately for us, the enemy have determined to use their legs instead of their arms, leaving the climate to battle for them. . . . If nature has made them fleeter of foot than the white man, and given them a country where they leave no tracks when they fly, it is our misfortune, and not our fault. The war may yet continue for many years, unless the Government should employ bloodhounds to aid the troops to ferret them out. Their hammocks are sunken or overflowed lands scattered at short intervals over the whole country, which is covered with bushes and vines of various kinds so thick that you cannot see five steps ahead and interspersed with lakes and impassable swamps.

"I last April received unsolicited the appointment of Brigadier-General, at the same time being assigned to the command in Florida. . . . I had . . . [made] up my mind to leave the country last spring, or as soon as the campaign was brought to a close, and, if any objections were made to my doing so, to have retired to civil life. I wish I may not have cause to regret changing that determination, but I was unexpectedly placed in such a situation that I could not well have acted otherwise. I can assure you that my days, or dreams, of ambition, if they ever existed, are passed; both age and inclination admonish me to sigh for ease, quiet and retirement on a snug little farm of a hundred or two acres in a healthy climate. Take the greater portion of this territory that I have been over, and it is certainly the most miserable country I have ever seen. Even should we succeed in driving out the Indians, it would not be settled in all probability by the whites for several centuries."[38]

Little could be accomplished during the scorching summer of

1838, when General Taylor visited the territorial capital at Talla-hassee in the later part of August.[39] October found him carrying on with accustomed vigor, and, having persuaded approximately two hundred and twenty Apalache Indians to emigrate, he arrived at the Apalachicola River on October 12 to superintend their embarkation; seventeen days thereafter, they sailed from Pensacola for New Orleans.

Taylor next turned his attention to preparations for the winter campaign. Leaving six companies to patrol the region from Talla-hassee to Deadman's Bay, the General rode overland to Fort Harlee in the north central section of the peninsula to consult Colonel David E. Twiggs and other subordinates. All northeastern Florida, as far down the coast as New Smyrna, he placed under the super-vision of Twiggs's ten companies of the Fourth Artillery, six com-panies of the Second Dragoons, and two companies of the Florida Militia. He ordered Brevet Colonel Davenport to scour the district between the Suwanee and the Withlacoochee with five companies of the First Infantry and one company of the Second Dragoons. Lieutenant Colonel John Greene's eleven infantry companies received a similar assignment in south central Florida, while the four companies of infantry and one of dragoons led by Major Gustavus Loomis were instructed to co-operate with General Charles Floyd's mounted Georgians in the vicinity of the Oke-fenokee Swamp. After issuing these and other orders, Taylor returned cross-country to Fort Brooke and thence to Fort Clinch on the Withlacoochee.[40]

From Fort Clinch, Zachary Taylor headed north toward Dead-man's Bay, to reach Fort Frank Brooke on December 18. Here he assumed command of Brevet Major Thomas Noell's troops in addition to his own three companies, and the combined force of seven companies brushed through the swamps adjacent to the Steinhatchee, Fenholloway, and Econfina Rivers without once encountering the enemy. Then assigning Greene to carry on in that quarter, the General left for Tampa by the roundabout route of Forts King and Mellon, where he was met by the rather discour-aging report from Twiggs, Davenport, and Brevet Colonel Alex-ander C. W. Fanning that each had thoroughly covered his allotted territory but none of the three had succeeded in drawing the Indians into battle. At Tampa, information of a quite different character arrived in the shape of a letter from Poinsett who gave full approval to a new type of campaign conceived and suggested by Taylor himself. This was heartening news indeed.

Poinsett's letter authorized Taylor to depart from the discredited policy of attempting to drive the savages from their forest fastnesses by sending soldiers marching in columns from swamp to swamp or from coast to coast. Acting on his own initiative, he set about dividing the entire peninsula into an indeterminate number of districts, each twenty miles square and each containing a fort or stockade erected at a strategic point and garrisoned by twenty or thirty men. Taylor held the commander of every post responsible for combing his district on alternate days, scouring the hammocks for signs of the enemy. Carried to a logical conclusion, this practical plan would almost certainly have driven all the Indians into the soldiers' hands, there being nowhere else for them to go except into the Atlantic Ocean or the Gulf of Mexico. In his annual report to the Adjutant General, Taylor reported proudly: "Besides what has been done around the Okeefenoke . . . , it will be observed that fifty-three new posts have been established, eight hundred and forty-eight miles of wagon-road, and three thousand six hundred and forty-three feet of causeway and bridges opened and constructed. . . . Every hammock and swamp between Fort Mellon and Tallahassee, quite across the country, has been thoroughly searched. . . ."[41]

This program was advancing rapidly on both sides of the Suwanee,[42] with full indication of success, when it was suddenly and mistakenly terminated by Major General Macomb who arrived in Florida in the spring of 1839 and, on April 30, joined Zachary Taylor at Fort King.

## 9

A veteran of the Canadian frontier, whose rank had risen rapidly during the War of 1812, Alexander Macomb now occupied the enviable post of general-in-chief of the Army. Taylor had disliked him and distrusted his judgment since the Fort Howard days, but now circumstances compelled the junior officer to bow to the opinion of a man who patently lacked the sort of experience needed to deal realistically with warring tribes. Macomb primarily was an office general. He had spent most of his career in easy eastern berths, flattered by sycophants and smiled upon in the drawing rooms of the socially elect. Now he proved himself no match for tricky Seminoles, for whom Taylor's policy of extending the olive branch while brandishing the sword was perfectly suited.

In peremptory fashion, General Macomb ordered hostilities to halt. Tossing Taylor's workable plan of systematic aggression into the discard, he induced some of the Seminoles and Mikasukis to promise to move into southern Florida and leave the white man's settlements unmolested.[43] That these promises might be broken does not seem to have occurred to the optimistic bureaucrat. "There is every reason," he wrote to Poinsett, "to believe that when the Indians remaining in Florida shall learn the prosperous condition of their brethren in Arkansas, they will, at no distant period, ask ... to join them."[44] Breathing this unctuous benediction, the ill-advised Macomb returned to Washington, leaving Taylor to reap a tragic aftermath.

Almost at once, the Indians inaugurated a new reign of terror. "Trains, express-men, and travellers, were assailed on the highway; plantations were attacked, and the occupants again fled. . . . A general alarm prevailed. . . . Lieutenant-Colonel Harney, in execution of the arrangement made by General Macomb, proceeded to Charlotte's Harbor, to establish . . . [a] trading-house. . . . He was attacked in a most treacherous manner, and [part of] his command murdered in their beds."[45] Nearly beside himself with anger and disgust, General Taylor at least had the satisfaction of knowing that the whirlwind he reaped was not of his own sowing. His own system of districts and central posts having been shelved, Taylor resumed the repudiated policy of dispatching columns back and forth between scattered seaboard forts.

Capturing a few savages, plunging into the no-man's-land of the interior, regularly inspecting defenses throughout the territory, Taylor was criticized in the House of Representatives for approving the importation of bloodhounds from Cuba, although his object in using dogs was "to ascertain where the Indians can be found, not to worry them."[46] In November, 1839, the Secretary of War gave credit where credit was due. The Florida operations, Poinsett announced, had been "conducted with vigor and ability under that zealous and indefatigable officer, brigadier general Taylor, who accomplished all that could be expected with the very limited means at his command...."[47] At Tampa, the same month, Taylor fell a victim to "the fever ... which confined me to my bed for near two weeks[,] when so many was dying around me who I could render no service nor even pay a friendly visit.... But after taking a large quantity of active medicine[,] principally callomel, and living altogether on hot drinks the disease was subdued, but left me very much debilitated."[48]

If the General occasionally became embroiled in controversies with volunteer officers, his relations with regular army subordinates remained amazingly harmonious from beginning to end of his Florida service. In addition to support lent by loyal friends, Taylor was grateful for the presence in the territory of three members of his own family. Captain Joseph P. Taylor had seen battle action at Lake Okeechobee. Dr. Robert C. Wood was now acting as his father-in-law's staff physician. And even Mrs. Zachary Taylor crossed the Gulf from New Orleans to join her husband at Fort Brooke. Writing from the Steinhatchee on January 11, 1840, Taylor told his surviving younger brother: "I recd. a letter from Peggy the 25th ulto, all well at Tampa, but very dull there; I do not expect to return to that place before the last of March or first of April by which time I trust to so arrange matters as to give security as far as it can be done to the people of Florida, when I shall ask for a leave of absence to visit Dick ..., to bring Betty home, and put my private affairs in order."[49]

Eager to escape Florida's subtropical summers and intolerable swamps, General Taylor twice sought to be relieved of his command. His second request met with the reluctant consent of the

War Department, and on May 6, 1840, he thankfully turned over the troops to Brevet Brigadier General Walker K. Armistead.[50]

"My days . . . of ambition . . . are passed," Taylor had written.

Ambitious or not, he had enhanced a growing reputation for initiative, ability, and devotion to detail. At last he was a general, in brevet grade at least. His service in Florida extended over a longer period than that of Clinch, Scott, Gaines, Jesup, or Macomb. More than any other officer, he had explored, mapped, and opened up the future winter playground of a nation. And, although the conflict would continue until 1843 and would be resumed sporadically from 1849 to 1857, he had contributed more substantially than any other individual in shaping it toward a successful termination.

Two and one-half years with the "Army of the South," albeit aggravating and laborious, were not lacking in compensation. In any well-rounded history of the Second Seminole War, the name of Zachary Taylor would be written large.

# CHAPTER X

## ARKANSAS INTERLUDE

### 1

AMONG Margaret Taylor's acquaintances at Fort Brooke was Mrs. William Davenport of Philadelphia, whose husband commanded the First Infantry at the Battle of Okeechobee. While yet in Florida the Davenports invited the Taylors to visit the Quaker City, where Betty Taylor was enrolled in a private boarding school. From Tampa Bay in May, 1840, General and Mrs. Taylor took the steamer *Salmond* to Pensacola—where friends commented on the General's poor health—and on to New Orleans which they reached on the nineteenth of the month.[1] Thence they traveled leisurely to Washington, tarrying at Baton Rouge and Louisville en route and arriving at the capital on the tenth of July.[2] In Washington Taylor conferred with War Department officials regarding the conduct of the war, then continued to Philadelphia where he and his wife were entertained by the Davenports and reunited with their daughter. Betty accompanied her parents through upstate New York as far north as Niagara Falls, then turned with them toward Kentucky, passing through western Pennsylvania on the way.

The trip did wonders for Taylor's undermined physique. And on September 19, in Louisville, he wrote to the Adjutant General: "I find my health has so much improved during my recent travels ... I consider it proper I should report for duty other than for duty in Florida, not conceiving my constitution sufficiently braced to go through the fatigue & privations encountered by me while in that country. . . . I should be pleased to be assigned to duty in Louisiana[,] my station to be at Baton Rouge or N. Orleans for the present at least. . . ."[3]

Still at Louisville on November 4, Zachary Taylor wrote to

142

Jesup: "I shall leave for the South in the course of [the] next week...."[4] On November 20, he assumed command of the Baton Rouge post, immediately north of the city of that name.[5] His new situation delighted him. Mrs. Taylor was near enough to members of the Smith family to warrant an exchange of visits, and across the river at Pointe Coupée lived Mr. and Mrs. William Taylor, whom the General found especially congenial. Most important of all, he appreciated his proximity to the cotton fields of West Feliciana Parish and Wilkinson County. The commandant's duties at Baton Rouge were light, and Taylor seized the opportunity to give personal attention to his planting interests.

In addition to the purchases of 1823 and 1831, the General in 1838 had authorized the cash payment of one thousand, nine hundred and sixty-five dollars for one hundred and sixty-three acres in West Feliciana Parish, lying to the south and west of his other lands.[6] Now he prepared to dispose of all this property, with an eye to buying the Cypress Grove Plantation in Jefferson County, Mississippi, and extending his operations on an even wider scale. At this time, too, debts were troubling Taylor. Many years earlier he had endorsed the notes of a friend who, dying insolvent, left him bound for certain liabilities.[7] He hoped to straighten out the maze of financial intricacies confronting him, before being transferred to another post. He looked forward to putting "my private affairs ... in such train as would in a few years ... enable me to retire from the army without being dependent on any one, or the country; age & infirmity ... admonishes me that I ought soon to retire, nor do I wish to continue a day longer than I am qualified for the active duties of the field."[8]

## 2

Another matter annoyed Taylor and demanded his attention during the post-Florida period. This was an unpleasant corollary to the Battle of Okeechobee, the result of an official report in which the General had informed the War Department that the Misssouri volunteers "acted as well, or even better, than troops of that description usually do; they received and returned the enemy's fire with spirit for some time, when they broke and retired, with the exception of Capt. [Cornelius] Gill[i]am and a few of his company, and Lt. [John C.] Blakey, also with a few men, who joined the Regulars, and acted with them until the close of the battle, but not until they had suffered severely. . . . The Volunteers . . . , having fallen back to the baggage, could not again be formed and brought up to the hammock in anything like order; but a number of them crossed over individually, and aided in carrying the wounded across the swamp to the hammock, among whom were Capt. [John] Curd and several other officers, whose names I do not now recollect."[9] In the same report Taylor referred to Colonel Richard Gentry as a "gallant commander," adding that Gentry's loss was "much regretted by the army, and will be doubtless by all who knew him, as his State did not contain a braver man or a better citizen." Later, in February, 1838, when many of the Missourians were honorably discharged, Taylor thanked them for their "zeal and devotion" and assured the citizen-soldiers that "the Colonel Commanding . . . separates from them with deep regret, but will recur with much satisfaction to events in which he has been operating with them."[10]

There is no indication in Zachary Taylor's papers that he considered his treatment of the Missouri men as anything but scrupulously fair. Still the fact that he charged them with falling back in disorder not only galled the volunteers, but caused their representatives in Congress and in the General Assembly to raise a hue and cry. At Jefferson City, the legislators adopted resolutions of so unusual a nature that they warrant reproduction. It was resolved:

"That the conduct of the Missouri Volunteers and Spies was such as could only be expected from good soldiers and brave men;

"That so much of Col. Taylor's report which charges that the Missouri Volunteers and Spies mostly broke and fell back to the baggage, and that the repeated efforts of his staff could not rally them, is proved to be unfounded, not to say intentionally false, and that so much of said report which states that the Regular troops were joined by Capt. Gill[i]am and Lt. Blakey with a few men, but

MARY ELIZABETH TAYLOR

The "Betty" of the letters. Youngest daughter of the General. Later the wife of William W. S. Bliss, and mistress of the White House. A miniature, artist unknown. Reproduced from a copy in the collection of Trist Wood of New Orleans.

not until they had suffered severely, is incorrect in this—that Gill[i]am and Blakey were in advance of the Regular troops during most of the fight, and never in the rear;

"That so much of said report which states that the Volunteers and Spies behaved themselves as well or better than troops of that description usually do, is not so much a compliment to them, as a slander upon citizen-soldiers generally;

"That Col. Taylor in his report has done manifest injustice to the Volunteers and Spies, and that said report was not founded upon facts as they occurred;

"That a commanding officer who wantonly misrepresented the conduct of men who gallantly sustained him in battle, is unworthy a commission in the Army of the United States."[11]

Politicians aggravated the controversy in Washington and out. Thomas H. Benton launched a vehement denunciation of Taylor's conduct on the floor of the United States Senate. The Secretary of War answered Benton, and the latter seemed satisfied. Yet from other quarters the censure continued.[12]

Taylor was disgusted, but he kept his head. With characteristic crispness, he explained his position: "I stated things simply as they occurred, solely with the view of showing the govt, & people, the difference between instructed and uninstructed troops; Besides the regulars performed all the drudgery of opening roads, making bridges, blockhouses & putting up pickets as well as for the most part fighting the battle. . . . I should have been faithless to my profession, as well as to them, had I not given them credit for what they had performed under the most trying circumstances." Charging "these people" with emptying "the vials of their wrath on my devoted head . . . in such a way as to excite a current of unjudicial feelings against me in Missouri . . . ," Taylor "looked calmly on until they had done their worst. . . ." Then, for the sake of clarification, he requested to be placed on trial by a court of inquiry "at . . . Saint Louis, or any other point in the state, where those who felt themselves agrieved could attend, state their wrongs, & have them redressed if any had been done them. . . ."[13] In Washington, the Van Buren Administration sustained the General. Checkmated, the disgruntled Missourians could only hold their peace. No court convened, but for the duration of his life there would remain an undercurrent of anti-Taylor sentiment in Missouri.

3

An effective antidote for harsh Missouri criticism was administered to General Taylor by the people of Little Rock, Arkansas, where he lingered briefly on June 27, 1841, in passing from Baton Rouge to Fort Gibson, west of Arkansas. At Little Rock, Taylor was invited to a public dinner in his honor. Circumstances compelled him to decline, but not without appreciation. "The warm reception & kind treatment I met with from the most respectable & intelligent portion of the inhabitants of the city of Little Rock ... without regard to party or for party purposes ... ," he admitted to Hitchcock, "was truly gratifying, as much so as it was unexpected; more especially coming as it did from gentlemen with whom I had not[,] with one or two exceptions, the slightest personal acquaintance. ..."[14]

Fort Gibson had long been the station of Brevet Brigadier General Matthew Arbuckle, whom Taylor now superseded as commander of the Second Department of the Western Division. Situated on the Grand River three miles from the Arkansas in what today is eastern Oklahoma, it was one of the five southwestern outposts which Taylor had been called to superintend. Fort Wayne was farther north, near the Arkansas border. East of Fort Gibson was Fort Smith. And three hundred miles dues south from Fort Smith was Fort Towson, on the Red River near the Kiamichi. The fifth post, on the western border of Louisiana, was Fort Jesup on which an energetic lieutenant colonel named Zachary Taylor had begun construction in 1822. The Second Department embraced all the territory south of the thirty-seventh degree of north latitude, from the Mississippi to the frontier, and included the present states of Oklahoma, Arkansas, Louisiana, and southern Missouri. Within this region were located the five civilized tribes of Indians—the Creek, Chickasaw, Choctaw, Seminole, and Cherokee.[15] It was

Taylor's duty to provide for the proper distribution of troops throughout the department, to protect the border settlements, and to supervise the Indians. Such an assignment called for tact and discipline in equal portions.

Fort Gibson, unhealthily situated, had come to be known as "the graveyard of the army." Disease flourished there. Its buildings were dilapidated.[16] And, as he pointed out to Major Hitchcock, General Taylor found "a scarcity of quarters for the comfortable accommodations of the officers...." After a thorough inspection of the post, the General moved the departmental headquarters to a well-shaded eminence called Camp Belknap, one mile from Fort Smith.[17] At the same time, he indicated his willingness to "go to Fort Gibson at any moment should I deem the public service benefitted by doing so, or should the dept, prefer my being there, as I have but little choice as a residence between the two posts...."[18]

From Camp Belknap, Taylor watched the development of the new establishment at Fort Smith with pronounced disapproval. "The plan ... is highly objectionable," he wrote, "& if carried out will cost three times as much ... [as] there was any necessity for; the buildings ... are to be enclosed with a thick stone wall fifteen feet high, with two large bastions, & the like number of immense stone blockhouses at the angles, which ... will cost ... more than one hundred thousand dollars; a more useless expenditure of money & labor was never made by this or any other people.... The sooner it is arrested the better."[19]

4

Fort Smith was a superfluous post, erected to please the citizens of Arkansas who might profit from the presence of soldiers in their midst. Toward the construction of necessary works on the actual frontier, Taylor took a radically different attitude. In particular, he favored the establishment of a fort on the False Washita River in the southwestern section of Indian Territory to protect peaceful Chickasaw Indians from the wild tribes of the plains, and to discourage Texan adventurers from committing depredations in the

Chickasaw Nation. On July 21, 1841, he urged the War Department to sanction such a plan.[20] On August 14, instructions were issued in Washington. And on September 25 the General left Camp Belknap to select a proper site.[21]

Accompanied by a military escort, Taylor traveled by way of Fort Gibson and Fort Towson and ascended the False Washita eighteen or twenty miles above its mouth. On his return to Camp Belknap, he expressed approval of the location which Captain Benjamin D. Moore had recommended to the Adjutant General earlier in the year: "It is situated on a high well-timbered ridge, with an extensive rolling prairie on the east, and within one mile and a half of the Washita, and from seventeen to twenty miles from Red River, and about one hundred miles above Fort Towson. An abundant supply of Building Materials, fuel and Hay can be obtained near this point, for use of the garrison. . . . Whenever boats can ascend Red River as high as the mouth of the Washita it will be navigable or can easily be rendered so as high as the point selected for a military post."[22] In compliance with an order from the capital, Taylor on April 14, 1842, commanded Captain George A. H. Blake to build summer quarters at Fort Washita,[23] which not only marked an important advance of the military frontier but even after the Mexican War would remain a boon to the march of civilization in the West.

If the Chickasaws had suffered from lack of protection, the Cherokees suffered from an overdose. As the frontier advanced, Fort Wayne became almost as superfluous as Fort Smith, and the Adjutant General ordered the post abandoned. Under Taylor's instructions, evacuation took place on May 26, 1842, and the garrison marched to a site on the Marmiton River where the soldiers were employed in erecting a second new establishment called Fort Scott.[24] Here savage Osage Indians could be held in check, and the Potawatomi protected from the Pawnee and the Sauk.

This was a logical move, but the people of Maysville, Arkansas, objected to the loss of trade involved in the removal of regulars to Fort Scott. In January, 1843, and again in July, they demanded that Fort Wayne be reoccupied so as to guard against the possibility of

a Cherokee uprising.[25] Taylor stood firm. Declaring that the
Arkansas citizens were motivated solely by selfish business considerations, he wrote the War Department that notwithstanding the
reports sent to Washington there existed no rumor of danger in the
Cherokee Nation.[26] The design of such false reports was plainly to
bring back the regulars to Fort Wayne, where whisky dispensers
might cater to the vices of the troops.

"I am . . . decidedly opposed to the re-establishment of Fort
Wayne, or the creation of any new Post within the Cherokee country," Taylor insisted. ". . . I would respectfully recommend that all
'citizens of Arkansas,' or others, making representations of probable Cherokee excitements, and expressing apprehensions of a
domestic war in that nation, may be referred to the commanding
General of this Department, who is responsible for the security of
the frontier, and who will not fail, on proper applications, and
probable grounds of danger, to take the most efficient measures to
preserve the peace. Such a reference would save the War Department much trouble, and would satisfy the applicants, were they
really sincere in their representations."[27]

Washington authorities heeded the General's counsel. Fort
Wayne was not re-established, and the "probable Cherokee excitements" never materialized.

At about the same time, for some strange reason, the War Department proposed to abandon Fort Washita. Taylor would have
none of it. The Chickasaws protested loudly, but it was the General who saved the day. "I am clearly in favor of retaining the position on the False Washita," he advised. And he cited his reasons:
"It bears immediately upon the numerous predatory bands who live
by the chase, who here approach nearest to the Chickasaw, and
against whom the latter nation, by every consideration of humanity
and policy, is entitled to our protection. The establishment of the
post has invited many Chickasaws to move into the desirable portion of their country commanded by it, who were before deterred
by the plundering expeditions of the wild bands referred to. Some
of the bands in the neighborhood, Delawares, Shawnees, &c. have
once been removed from the Chickasaw lands by military force,

and the same wholesome restraint is still needed to keep them in their proper places. In the event of any operations on Upper Red river, or of negotiations with any of the wandering tribes in that quarter, the position would be invaluable as a Depot and point of reference. Being opposite the extreme settlements on the Texas side of the Red river, it incidentally extends to them, the same protection afforded to the Chickasaws, as above cited. It acts as a check on any of our own Indians disposed to cross into Texas for mischievous purposes. . . . These considerations combine to give Fort Washita no small importance. Perhaps no Post on the frontier exerts a more salutary influence, and my opinion in this respect is confirmed by all intelligent officers with whom I have conversed."[28]

As in the case of Fort Wayne, Taylor's opinion ultimately determined the fate of Fort Washita. Fort Washita was retained. And the border country benefited.

## 5

Zachary Taylor had reason to understand the temper of the Indians. In May, 1842, accompanied by Brevet Captain William W. S. Bliss and Indian Agent William Armstrong, he attended a "Grand Council" called to assemble on the Deep Fork of the Canadian River near the site of Eufaula, Oklahoma. Designed to promote good will between the civilized Indians and their savage neighbors, the council comprised representatives of "Creeks, Choctaws, Chickasaws, Seminoles, Shawnees, Delaware, Peankashaws, Kickapoos, Quapaws, Kichis[,] Witchetaws, Pawnees, Osages, Caddoes, Towockenes, & Senecas. There were also present . . . a number of Cherokees, making persons from seventeen tribes."[29]

A correspondent of the *Arkansas Intelligencer* described the encampment, which was two miles in circumference, filled with fires, lodgings, and persons of the lodgers. "The woods and prairies, for three or four miles, were crowded by horses 'hobbled' and feeding upon the rich succulent herbage. . . . On Wednesday [May 15] the council met; the Choctaws, Chickasaws, and Caddoes sitting in front of the Creek chiefs, whose post was in the center of an outer side of the council-house. There was a vast concourse in the imperturbable gravity and decorum belonging rightly to an Indian council. The civilized tribes now arose en masse, and passing behind the chiefs' seats, formed in single file, headed by Gen. Rolly McIntosh, who was followed by Gen. Taylor, U. S. Army. . . . These coming round on the opposite side, gave to the other tribes a genial shaking of the hands, bestowed on each individual but a single shake. After them came the Shawnees and Delawares, in like manner going round and shaking hands. When these tribes had thus paid their salutation, Gen. Chilley McIntosh arose and welcomed his white brethren."[30]

Zachary Taylor addressed the gathering through interpreters and urged the Indians to maintain the peace. He interviewed representatives of the wild tribes, and from them learned that a number of white children taken captive in Texas were now in the custody of the Comanches. He promised a ransom, and in the course of the next two years the children were released. Taylor's other noteworthy achievement at the council ground was his success in inducing the Kichai, Kiowa, Tawakoni and Wichita Indians to go to Fort Gibson in order to receive presents and renew their allegiance to the United States Government.[31] The General remained two days at the Deep Fork, and reported: "None but the most friendly feelings were exhibited toward the United States, and . . . all seemed animated with a desire to cultivate peaceable relations with our Government and with each other."[32]

From the council ground, Taylor rode to Fort Gibson and then proceeded to Fort Washita, finding summer quarters already under construction at that westernmost post. He was pleased to note the progress made by the soldiers of Captain Blake's command, but did not overlook the need of additional doctors in the Second Department. At Fort Towson, on May 31, he dispatched a letter to the Adjutant General. "Though nearly 800 strong," he wrote, "the 6th Infantry brought but one medical officer with it, and the new post . . . requires an Asst. Surgeon. . . . I respectfully request that additional medical officers be ordered to the Department, if consistent with the wants of the service elsewhere."[33] This communication was fairly typical of Taylor's correspondence in Arkansas and in Indian Territory. The years had brought duties of a highly responsible nature, but details relating to the well-being of his troops were with him still.

To be sure, the General's burdens were lightened by Captain Bliss, the engaging young officer who had served him as aide-de-camp at the "Grand Council." Courtly, polished, master of six languages, and credited with reading knowledge of thirteen, Bliss was one of the most brilliant scholars ever to grace the American Army. He had entered the Military Academy at West Point as a lad of thirteen, had been graduated at seventeen, and already his amazing range of information incorporated the philosophy of Kant and the poetry of Goethe as well as technicalities of military strategy and a first-hand study of the habits of the Cherokees.[34] The Captain was less than thirty years of age when he became General Taylor's assistant adjutant general, yet the commander's confidence was not misplaced. With Bliss at his elbow, Taylor could count on "trustworthy information, honest and competent advice, a friendly hand to supplement or subtract, and a skillful pen to report, explain and, if necessary, discreetly color the facts."[35]

"Perfect Bliss" was the nickname given the man who was destined to become Zachary Taylor's *alter ego.*

6

Bliss was with Taylor in June, 1843, when the latter attended the second "Grand Council" held during his superintendency of Indian Territory. This time, eighteen tribes of western Indians met at Tahlequah. "As far as I can learn their object," one of the official agents reported, "it is to renew old customs and friendships and to enact some international laws for the government of each and all. There are some three or four thousand persons daily in attendance. Their deliberations, and the company present, are quiet and orderly."[36] General Taylor was present at the council. The spirit of its sponsors impressed him so deeply that he assured the Adjutant General: "Its results can be no other than beneficial, as well to the red man as to us. Pacific relations will be established and confirmed among different tribes—and the wilder ones, having ocular evidence of the advantages enjoyed by the more civilized will be more ready to follow their example. International relations will be adopted for the preservation of property and perpetuation of fellowship and peace."[37]

Notwithstanding the peaceful promise of Tahlequah, a mid-August election disturbance in the Cherokee Nation resulted in the murder of one man and injuries to two others. Taylor, who had returned from Fort Towson to Camp Belknap and Fort Smith in June, set out for Fort Gibson at the head of a small detachment as soon as news of the trouble reached him. On this occasion the Cherokee authorities arrested the offenders almost at once, and, when it became apparent that they were ready to administer justice and inflict the proper punishment, the General retraced his steps to his headquarters.[38] In September, 1843, a band of white desperadoes committed four murders within the borders of the same nation. This time Taylor assigned a company of dragoons to track down the killers.[39] During this period, supposedly reputable Arkansas settlers stirred up trouble among their Indian neighbors in the hope of selling contraband goods or dispensing liquor within reach of the soldiers. After one particularly flagrant violation of the aborigines' rights, Taylor wrote: "I have little doubt . . . that the present case is connected with the systematic efforts . . . [of] certain citizens of Arkansas, to revive . . . a political excitement in the Cherokee Nation[,] in the internal affairs of which they have no legitimate interest whatsoever."[40] As had been the case in Illinois and more recently in Florida, Zachary Taylor in the Southwest was by no means blind to the Indians' point of view.

Added responsibility in Arkansas and west of Arkansas did not cause Taylor to lose the essential simplicity of manner which distinguished him from other senior officers, who too often confused the dignity of rank with the pompous stiffness of a martinet. Much of the time he wore civilian clothes, his taste running to jean trousers, undress coats without insignia, and broad-brimmed palmetto hats. Rough in appearance, unassuming in conversation, he talked in terms of crops and field hands and river freshets rather than of arms or military evolutions. On more than one occasion, strangers mistook him for a frontier farmer.

The story is told of two young brevet second lieutenants, fresh from West Point and faultlessly attired, who encountered a plain-spoken, heavy-set man on their first morning at Fort Smith.

"Good morning, old fellow!" they called out.

"Good morning."

"How's crops?"

"Purty good."

"Come on, take a drink with us."

The old man joined them, though presumably he did not indulge. And the subalterns amused themselves at his expense, never guessing the identity of their companion.

Finally, when the "farmer" rose to take leave of the young lieutenants, one of them said: "Give our love to the old woman and the gals."

Later the same day, immaculate in full dress, the youths called to pay their respects to General Taylor—their commanding officer. At headquarters they found the "farmer" of the morning.

Concealing his amusement at their evident chagrin, the General gravely acknowledged his subordinates' salute. Then, presenting them to Mrs. Taylor and to his daughter Betty, who was by this time a popular and most attractive young lady in her late teens, he remarked casually:

"Here are the old woman and the gal."[41]

### 7

One reason why Zachary Taylor played the role of farmer so flawlessly is found in the fact that, throughout his life and especially when he was stationed in Arkansas in the interlude between wars, he devoted virtually as much attention to plantation details as to Army management. Thrice during the Fort Smith period he took advantage of furloughs to visit the rich Mississippi River bottom lands where his money was invested.[42]

The first of these trips occurred in November and December, 1841, when the weightiest financial transaction of his career led the General to Wilkinson County, Mississippi, to West Feliciana Parish, Louisiana, and to New Orleans. On December 15, Henry H. Wall made a full cash payment of two thousand and sixty-two dollars and fifty cents for the Wilkinson County property which Taylor had purchased from Hamilton M. Orr in 1831.[43] Two days later, Wall agreed to pay the rather large sum of seven thousand, seven hundred and ten dollars for the Byrd Buford property in West Feliciana Parish which had been Taylor's since 1823. At the same time, John Wicker purchased for one thousand, six hundred and thirty-three dollars and fifty cents the hundred and sixty-three acres which Taylor had acquired in 1838. Both men gave promissory notes. Both sums were payable in equal installments on the first day of January, 1843, 1844 and 1845.[44]

Next, General Taylor went to New Orleans where his banker, Maunsel White, agreed to endorse six vendor lien notes of varying amounts and maturities, totaling thirty-five thousand dollars. On April 21, 1842, Taylor gave these notes and sixty thousand dollars in cash to John Hagan, senior, for the latter's deed to eighty-one slaves and the nineteen hundred and twenty-three acre Cypress Grove Plantation, ten miles below the town of Rodney on the eastern bank of the Mississippi River.[45] This was the most expensive purchase that Taylor had ever made, and one to cause him no end of trouble for the duration of his life. An extract from one of his letters to Joseph P. Taylor, written June 17, 1843, suggests the degree of grief and worry suffered by the General even at that early date: "My affairs of a private character have been going backwards for the last two years in succession, & particularly so the present year. . . . The large purchase I made on said river in the winter of 41 has proved a most unfortunate one, & I fear owing [to] this circumstance, that I will . . . find my affairs in a very embarrassed situation so much so, that it will take several years of great industry, & economy to get them once more in a healthy state. . . ."[46]

# CHAPTER XI

## Storm Clouds Over Mexico

### 1

In the spring of 1844, at the age of fifty-nine, Zachary Taylor was a relatively unknown brevet brigadier general concerned as much with plantation problems as with affairs of a military nature. Less than five years in the future, by a strange twist of destiny, events over whose origin he exercised no control would catapult him to a pinnacle of fame and power. At a time of life when many men quit their vocations and fade into the limbo, Taylor exchanged the obscurity of the frontier for the preliminaries of a war which was to add an enormous expanse to the territory of the United States and to elevate an unpretending soldier who had never voted never voted to the most prized civil office within the gift of the American people.

As far back as 1836, when Taylor was still stationed at Fort Crawford, a gallant little Texas army under General Sam Houston had routed the Mexican forces of Antonio López de Santa Anna on a fateful day at the battlefield of San Jacinto. Texas was now an independent republic, governed by ambitious leaders of American birth and recognized by England, France and the United States but not by Mexico which still claimed Texas for her own. Rich in resources and vast in territory, Texas was regarded with covetous eyes by far-sighted American statesmen who considered it a promising field for expansion, exploitation, and slavery extension. Texas itself had long sought admission into the United States, and its proximity to the Second and particularly to the First Military Department gave a new importance to the southwestern frontier. This was due to the fact that, in the event of annexation, an armed conflict between Mexico and the United States might readily result.

156

Therefore, when General Taylor on April 23, 1844, was ordered to take command of the First Department with headquarters at Fort Jesup, Louisiana,[1] the transfer constituted a mark of confidence on the part of the authorities in Washington. Why the War Department assigned this important duty to Taylor in preference to a number of other veteran officers has never been brought to light to the satisfaction of the historians, although it is recorded that Andrew Jackson, in retirement at the Hermitage, had formed a high opinion of Taylor and later advised President-elect Polk: "If we get into a war with England, Gen. Taylor is the man to lead our armies."[2] Taylor's record, his experience in three wars, and his long service in the Southwest combined to make him a logical person for the assignment. In any event the order was transmitted, together with confidential instructions: "You will take prompt measures, in the first instance by a confidential officer and subsequently by the ordinary mail or special expresses, as you may deem necessary, to put yourself in communication with the President of Texas, in order to inform him of your present position and force, and to learn and to transmit to this office (all confidentially) whether any and what external dangers threaten that Government or its people."[3]

## 2

Zachary Taylor arrived at Fort Jesup on June 17, 1844, and assumed command.[4] The following day he sent Captain Lloyd J. Beall of the Second Dragoons to advise President Houston that there were at Fort Jesup "about a thousand effective men, consisting of seven companies of the 2nd regiment of Dragoons & eight companies of each of two regiments of Infantry, the 3d and 4th. Capt. Beall has instructions to await your convenience before returning to these Head Quarters and will bear any communication you may think proper to make for the information of my Government."[5] The anticipated annexation did not materialize at that time, but the border was kept open, and President John Tyler dispatched Andrew J. Donelson to Texas "with authority to com-

municate with Taylor" in case a military movement should prove
necessary. On October 10, the General received instructions to be
ready to advance "at short notice to any point in the United States
or Texas." He completed preparations for the march, but again the
looked-for final instructions failed to come.[6]

While Taylor was marking time in 1844 and 1845, approximately
twelve hundred regulars loafed away the summer, fall and winter
at Fort Jesup and at Camp Salubrity and Camp Wilkins near by.
Among the younger officers were three whose names would stand
out on the pages of American military history: Second Lieutenant
Don Carlos Buell and Brevet Second Lieutenants James Longstreet
and Ulysses Simpson Grant. Years later, as an old man, impoverished, renowned, and a victim of cancer, Grant would set down
the story of his stay at Camp Salubrity: "At first, officers and men
occupied ordinary tents. As the summer heat increased[,] these
were covered with sheds to break the rays of the sun. The summer
was whiled away in social enjoyments among the officers, in visiting those stationed at, and near Fort Jesup . . . , the planters on the
Red River, and the citizens at Natchitoches and Grand Ecore."[7]

Lieutenant Grant's letters, however, are more vivid than ex-
President Grant's reminiscences: "There were five days races at
Natchitoches. I was there every day and bet low, generally lost. . . .
[One of my comrades] undertook to play brag at our camp and
soon succeeded in ridding himself of twenty dollars, all in quarters.
The game of brag is kept up as lively as ever. I continued to play
some . . . and won considerable, but for some time back I have not
played and probably will never play again—no resolution,
though!"[8]


### 3


In November, 1844, the possibility of battle action assumed increased proportions with the election of James K. Polk to the
American presidency. Promising to annex Texas, Polk eked out a
narrow victory over Henry Clay, the Whig candidate, who had unwisely committed his party against expansion. Polk was to enter

the White House on March 4, 1845, and it appeared inevitable that imperialistic aims would at once dominate the foreign policy of the United States.[9]

For a time the identity of the enemy remained undetermined. Polk had also promised to occupy all Oregon, the English and American titles to which were equally sound, but powerful Great Britain was not expected to stand idly by if Polk should carry out his threat regarding Oregon. True, Mexico herself was in no conciliatory mood. The Mexican minister to Washington had announced that his government must consider annexation tantamount to a declaration of war.[10] But Mexico was weak, and Great Britain was strong, and the die was finally cast three days prior to Polk's inauguration when Tyler signed a congressional resolution for the annexation of Texas. Polk's northwestern plank was relegated to the scrap heap, Secretary of State James Buchanan and the British Foreign Office dividing Oregon along the forty-ninth parallel to Puget Sound.[11] In the Southwest trouble was expected. And, on May 28, Secretary of War William L. Marcy penned a pregnant message to General Taylor: "So soon as the Texas Congress shall have given its consent to annexation, and a convention shall assemble and accept the terms offered in the resolution of Congress, Texas will then be regarded by the executive government here so far a part of the United States as to be entitled ... to defense and protection from foreign invasion and Indian incursions. The troops under your command will be placed and kept in readiness to perform that duty."[12]

Secretary of the Navy George Bancroft, acting as secretary of war in Marcy's absence, dispatched more explicit instructions to Taylor on June 15. On June 29 the express rider who bore them galloped down the road from Natchitoches in time to reach Fort Jesup before dusk. Informed that Texas' ratification would probably occur on July 4, Taylor was ordered to station his force at an American port of his own selection, where the troops might embark for a point "on or near the Rio Grande" as soon as the General learned that Texas formally was in the Union.

"Bliss read the orders to me last evening hastily," Lieutenant

Colonel Hitchcock wrote on the morning of June 30. "I have scarcely slept a wink, thinking of the needful preparations."[13]

Zachary Taylor's state of mind can readily be imagined. A major war on foreign soil seemed not only possible but indeed quite probable; and he, the forgotten commander of forgotten frontier outposts, would lead the American army!

4

Taylor's plans had long been formulated. Although Bancroft suggested the mouth of the Sabine River as a rendezvous for the foot soldiers, Taylor selected New Orleans where quarters were ample and provisions plentiful. Eight companies of the Fourth Infantry left Grand Ecore July 2, and reached the Jackson Barracks on July 4. Hitchcock's Third Infantry followed on July 7, and arrived on July 10 at the Crescent City where they were housed in the Lower Cotton Press. Colonel Twiggs's seven companies of the Second Dragoons were to ride overland directly to San Antonio de Bexar from Fort Jesup, and Taylor remained there to see them off. As soon as the news of Texan ratification arrived, the horsemen set out on their hard trip west. And General Taylor was free to join the infantry regiments in New Orleans.[14]

During the General's last journey south aboard a river steamer, he had spied a fellow passenger who looked familiar. The man was Jefferson Davis, now in his middle thirties, a member of Congress from Mississippi, and no longer a recluse. Davis was bound for Natchez, where he was to take Miss Varina Howell as his second wife. No trace of animosity marred the manner of either gentleman as the father-in-law met the son-in-law who had been a fellow sufferer in the greatest personal tragedy of both their lives. Grasping Davis' hand, Taylor greeted him warmly and in the friendliest spirit wished him all possible happiness in the new marital venture.[15] Jefferson Davis never forgot Zachary Taylor's change of heart. From the chance meeting on the river packet, there sprang a mutual admiration which neither future political differences nor an ancient grudge could ever erase.

ARMY OF OCCUPATION AT CORPUS CHRISTI, TEXAS

After a drawing by Captain Daniel Powers Whiting in October, 1845.

Now another incident illumined Taylor's passage down the Mississippi. The story is told of a nameless traveler, young in years, who went to the clerk's office for a stateroom. "The clerk informed him that all were taken, and that he would have to content himself with an upper berth. The gentleman assented, and after seeing his name duly entered, he walked into the cabin, when it struck him he would find out who occupied the lower berth of his stateroom; stepping into the clerk's office, he read—'Lower, Z. Taylor, Baton Rouge.' 'Is this Brigadier-general Taylor, of the United States army?' said he to the clerk: 'I ask, because I have some curiosity to know who is my room-mate, and, more particularly, if it is General Taylor.' The clerk satisfied him that such was the fact, when our traveller entered into conversation with the old veteran. Our friend was a planter, and old Zach appeared, by his conversation, to have beaten his sword into a ploughshare; for he talked about planting, and the crops, and the civil government of our country, and appeared to be as ignorant of our army as if he had never seen it. At a reasonable bedtime, old Zach retired. After a while our traveller went into the state-room, and, to his surprise, found the broad mattress of the lower berth unoccupied—and looking, he discovered General Taylor sleeping in the upper berth. The young man, surprised, regretted what he conceived to be a mistake, and in the morning expressed his regrets at what had happened. 'Pooh, pooh!' said the old general, laughing, 'don't you know I am not the youngest, and more used to hard fare than you are!' "[16]

## 5

On reaching New Orleans July 15, Taylor found representatives of the commissary and quartermaster departments busy chartering steamboats and laying in supplies. One week later, everything was in readiness for the departure of the Third Infantry, with the Fourth Infantry and First Lieutenant Braxton Bragg's single company of the Third Artillery prepared to follow as soon as possible. An hour before midnight on July 22, Hitchcock formed his troops in the street between the yards of the Cotton Press. Wheeled into column, they tramped toward the waterfront to the beat of the regimental quickstep.

"The moon was just rising as we marched out, gilding the domes and house-tops, and caused our bayonets to glisten in the mellow light. The deep shadows on one side of the street, and bright moonlight upon the other, the solemn quiet of the sleeping city, disturbed so harshly by the martial music of the column, formed a scene which touched one's feelings, and will not easily be forgotten."[17]

General Taylor and his staff joined the regiment at the levee, where all boarded the steamboat *Alabama*. On July 23 at three o'clock in the morning the *Alabama* left her moorings. By noon she had crossed the bar at the Southwest Pass and "was gallantly and rapidly cutting her way over the Gulf, barely ruffled by the soft breeze."[18]

The *Alabama's* destination was the hamlet of Corpus Christi, Texas, at the southern bank of the Nueces River on Corpus Christi Bay.

Why Corpus Christi?

Because the War Department's vague instructions to move "on or near the Rio Grande" placed the burden of selecting a base on Taylor's shoulders, and the General determined to advance no farther without specific orders directing him to take the step.

Because the title to the region between the Nueces and the Rio Grande was obscured in half a century of controversy. Neither Polk nor Taylor possessed accurate information on the topography of the land south of Corpus Christi. And Taylor sought an opportunity to reconnoiter.

Because a Mexican assault was rumored, and Taylor wished to augment his unimpressive Army of Occupation before continuing into the disputed territory.

Because Corpus Christi was healthy. A plentiful supply of drinking water could be obtained. Fish and game abounded. And the summer temperature was ideal.[19]

Sandbars prevented the *Alabama* from steaming directly into

Corpus Christi Bay, and on July 25 the ship dropped anchor twenty-five miles north of the hamlet. That day and the next, high winds and angry seas prevailed. But on July 26 Taylor and three companies landed on St. Joseph's Island, and the other soldiers followed.[20]

In contrast to sultry New Orleans, officers and men found the island delightful. Only General Taylor and his immediate subordinates were beset with worry in connection with removal to the mainland. The troops made many a capital meal off the pompano and redfish, wild turkey, geese, and mallard duck, and the potatoes and melons which grew luxuriantly in the sandy island soil.

All the time, Taylor impatiently awaited the arrival of a lighter which had been ordered from New Orleans. It finally appeared. But the attempt to cross the flats was ludicrous, to say the least. On July 29, the General and Hitchcock, with two companies, tried to reach Corpus Christi only to run aground five miles from St. Joseph's. "There we stayed all day and all night," Hitchcock wrote, "but we at last landed some men and provisions on a raft. Another night passed. It was still found impossible to cross the flats[,] and General Taylor directed the quartermaster to hire all the fishing boats that had gathered around us . . . , and transfer the men and cargo to them. I undertook to tell him that the troops could be very comfortable on St. Joseph's Island till a high southwest wind should give us high water on the flats; but he would not listen to me and was exceedingly impatient to have the companies off. We finally were got on board of seven small boats. . . ."[21] At last, leaving the barge on the morning of July 31, the soldiers reached Corpus Christi at sundown.

6

From August, 1845, to March, 1846, the Army of Occupation remained encamped on the beach at Corpus Christi. New arrivals swelled its ranks to an aggregate of three thousand, nine hundred and twenty-two. Brevet Brigadier General William J. Worth commanded the First Brigade, which comprised the Eighth Infantry and twelve companies of artillery.[22] Worth was "of average height but noticeably strong, with a trim figure and a strikingly martial air."[23] An officer in the Regular Army since 1813, he had distinguished himself at Chippewa and at Niagara and had fought against the Seminoles. Grant was to characterize him as "nervous, impatient and restless on the march, or when important or responsible duty confronted him."[24] Another future hero of the Civil War, Second Lieutenant George Gordon Meade, wrote that Worth "has the great misfortune of being most rash and impetuous, and of constantly doing things which cooler reflection causes him to repent. This infirmity . . . renders him unfit to command, but on the field of battle, under another, his gallantry and bravery are well known and most conspicuous."[25]

Colonel Twiggs, who headed the dragoons, was a noted disciplinarian. It was said that he could get more work out of his men than anyone else in the Army. He, too, had seen service in the War of 1812 and had been subordinate to Taylor in Florida. "His robust and capacious body, powerful shoulders, bull-neck, heavy, cherry-red face, and nearly six feet of erect stature represented physical energy at its maximum. With bristling white hair and, when the regulations did not interfere, a thick white beard, he seemed like a kind of slow-clad volcano, a human Ætna, pouring forth a red-hot flood of orders and objurations from his crater of a mouth; and he was vastly enjoyed by the rough soldiers even when, as they said, he 'cursed them right out of their boots.' "[26]

Other units at Corpus Christi included the Fifth and Seventh Infantry, composing the Second Brigade which Lieutenant Colonel James S. McIntosh led; four companies of Horse Artillery; the Third Brigade, comprising the Third and Fourth Infantry, under Colonel William Whistler; two companies of Louisiana Volunteers, whom Taylor sent home on November 4 when their term of enlistment expired; and a party of well-mounted Texas Rangers under Colonel John C. Hays, whom Taylor mustered into service on his own initiative.[27]

This was a rather formidable force, but its fighting ability had not been tested, and much depended upon the leadership furnished by Zachary Taylor. No one doubted his courage, but Hitchcock privately criticized his direction of affairs. "What a pretty figure we cut here ...," the hypercritical West Pointer wrote. "Neither General Taylor nor Colonel Whistler ... could form ... [the army] into line! Even Colonel Twiggs could put the troops into line only 'after a fashion' of his own. As for manoeuvring, not one of them can move a step in it. Egotism or no egotism, I am the only field officer on the ground who could change a single position ... according to any but a militia mode."[28]

Meade, however, considered Taylor a competent commander. The routine consisted of "nothing but drill and parades, and your ears are filled all day with drumming and fifeing."[29] When a grand review took place in mid-September, Captain William S. Henry found the display "quite creditable." "We all felt that a more efficient army, for its size, was never brought into the field."[30] "Our army is well drilled and disciplined," First Lieutenant Richard E. Cochrane wrote. "Our command is very healthy and with such a body of troops as we have here it is surprising that so few are sick. . . . Brig. Gen. Taylor is in command . . . and I do not think we could have a better general."[31]

Colonel James Love of Galveston, who visited Corpus Christi, commented on the influence of the Texas Rangers on the regular troops. "They are teaching the United States officers and soldiers how to ride," Love informed Taylor's comrade of the Black Hawk War days, Albert Sidney Johnston. "The feats of horsemanship of our frontier-men are most extraordinary. I saw one of them pick up from the ground three dollars, each fifty yards apart, at full speed, and pass under the horse's neck at a pace not much short of full speed."[32]

## 7

From Washington General Taylor received a warning that the American army might be attacked at Corpus Christi by General Francisco Mejía, who was rumored to be augmenting the Mexican force at Matamoros on the southern bank of the Rio Grande.

Taylor did not ignore the possibility. Through Henry Lawrence Kinney, an adventurous Texas "colonel" who conducted a trading post at Corpus Christi, he obtained reports of the movements of Mexicans in and around Matamoros.[33] Colonel Kinney's spy, Chapita, considered a Mexican advance most improbable and at the same time outlined a route for Taylor to take if and when the order should come to advance southwestward.

Hitchcock, who ought to have known, considered Taylor ignorant of the region south of Corpus Christi. The accusation was unfounded. Chapita supplied the General with invaluable information. And Taylor dispatched several expeditions under Lieutenant Meade and his associates of the Topographical Engineers to explore the Nueces as far as San Patricio, and also the Laguna Madre—a coastwise water passage terminating at Point Isabel near the mouth of the Rio Grande.[34] As 1845 came to a close, Zachary Taylor possessed enough data to insure a relatively safe advance. And a clear majority of the officers who left records of their opinions on the subject were convinced of the General's ability to master any strictly military problem which might arise in the vicinity.

In another connection, however, Taylor was patently culpable. Here Hitchcock might have concentrated his fire with more effect, for even in an age when medical science was still in its infancy sanitary conditions could scarcely have been more primitive than they were in the Corpus Christi camp. That Taylor tolerated an almost complete lack of sanitation certainly did him little credit. Few soldiers died from disease, but the record shows that diarrhea and dysentery kept an average of ten per cent of the officers and thirteen per cent of the men bedridden throughout the late autumn and winter months. Actually, in November and December at least, the number of those affected was even larger. "The whole Army . . . might be considered a vast hospital . . . ," Surgeon John B. Porter noted. "Hundreds were affected who were never entered on sick report."[35] When gambling houses and drinking establishments sprang up mushroom-like in Corpus Christi, some of the soldiers indulged in excesses and squandered their pay.[36] Fair-minded contemporaries charged Taylor with failure to enforce discipline, and the accusation seems to have been well-founded although it is not easy to reconcile the General's latter-day laxity with his almost Puritanical anti-alcohol and anti-gambling zeal of the Prairie du Chien period.

Taylor had other troubles. It was common gossip in camp that he had again seriously considered retirement from active service, in which event both Worth and Twiggs hoped to take his vacated place at the head of the Army of Occupation. A rather undignified controversy ensued between the aspirants for the succession, Worth insisting that his brevet grade entitled him to priority while Twiggs viewed his own seniority in the lineal rank of colonel as the sole determining factor. As matters turned out Taylor's resignation remained a thing of pure conjecture, but as long as the controversy lasted Corpus Christi was in an uproar. Twiggs's position was supported by nearly every officer on the ground, including Taylor who had the good judgment and good taste to refrain from taking a personal part in the dispute.[37]

At about this time Taylor became embroiled in a controversy of his own, his antagonist being General Jesup, whom he blamed for the inefficiency of the military quartermasters. The old friends, intimate for more than a quarter of a century, were friends no longer. Either Jesup and his immediate aids or his subordinates in Texas and New Orleans were at fault; his department was painfully slow in supplying the equipment which Taylor repeatedly requisitioned. At first the army needed tents—any tents. The tents finally came after a series of discouragingly long delays, but they were of inferior texture and leaked like sieves whenever rain fell.[38] Nor was this all. The quartermaster department's unwillingness or inability to co-operate with Taylor would be one of the most harassing aspects of the General's work during the months to come.

Thomas S. Jesup, however, could not be held responsible for the scarcity of wood—an almost equal handicap, or for the troops' failure to boil their drinking water which added to their miseries. And only nature could atone for the weather, which had at first been pleasant and later tolerable but now turned steadily worse.

Even Lieutenant Meade complained. "It is a fine climate in summer," Meade wrote to his wife, "but now, when the winds are from the north, and cutting cold, it is the most disagreeable and trying I ever was in."[39] Small wonder the delicious eggnogs, served by the General at headquarters on New Year's Day, 1846, met with the approbation of his brother officers!

"One of the principal diseases now among the officers . . . is homesickness," Taylor confessed to his daughter. He himself was not immune. "Since I have been here my time has passed rapidly, having constant employment; the scene too has been quite an imposing one; what with instruction, mounting guards, reviews, etc., with between three and four thousand men, & two hundred and fifty officers, with five bands & excellent music, has made the time pass tolerably rapidly; but all the pomp & parade of such things are lost on me; I now sigh for peace & quiet with my family around me. . . . My health since I have been in this country has never been better."[40]

## 8

While Zachary Taylor awaited developments at Corpus Christi, President Polk's attempt to settle his government's differences with Mexico through diplomatic channels was meeting with dismal failure. His efforts were complicated not only by Mexico's opposition to annexation but also by her further statement that Texas' southwestern boundary was the Nueces River, the state of Tamaulipas supposedly extending beyond the Rio Grande to Corpus Christi. This was Mexico's strongest argument, and, viewed from a strictly impartial standpoint, the weight of evidence in this one case seems to have been on her side.[41]

James K. Polk, however, had powerful bargaining weapons of his own. For years Mexico's treatment of American nationals, imprisoning them without provocation, robbing and even murdering them on Mexican soil, had been notorious. American vessels had been seized, American goods destroyed, American emissaries insulted. Although American citizens had submitted claims for eight million dollars in lieu of confiscated property and a joint commission headed by a neutral umpire had requested Mexico to pay one-quarter of that sum, the money had not been produced, nor had assurances been given. On that score alone the United States would have been justified in declaring war, but she had done nothing of the sort. Mexico's attitude was radically different. Disregarding the fact that England, France and Belgium had long since recognized Texan independence, she stubbornly insisted that Texas still belonged to the mother country and that annexation constituted theft.[42]

Notwithstanding all this and notwithstanding the termination of the Mexican mission in Washington, the withdrawal of Mexican consuls from American cities, the mobilization of Mexico's fighting force, and the furtive attempts of Mexican officials to induce France and England to form a triple alliance against the United States,[43] the Polk Administration did everything in its power to promote peace except to renounce annexation and to concede that the Nueces marked the Texas-Tamaulipas boundary.

Undeterred by previous rebuffs, the President empowered John Slidell of Louisiana to negotiate with the Mexican Government, instructing him to pay as much as forty million dollars for a favorable solution of the boundary dispute.[44] Part of that sum was to be used for purchasing California if Mexico were found willing to consider the sale. Another part was to be discounted because of the American claims, which would then be met in full by the United States Government.

Mexico exercised only nominal control over California, and no control at all over Texas. Her treasury was bankrupt; her people were impoverished. Her only talking point worthy of attention was the Nueces boundary. Considered from every angle, James K. Polk's offer was as handsome as could be imagined under the circumstances. Mexico might well have received it with outstretched arms and an itching palm. But this she did not do. Twice in 1845 the Mexican officials refused to discuss terms with Slidell. And in January, 1846, word reached the White House that the negotiator would be rejected for a third and final time. Diplomacy having failed, the President determined to protect the boundary which his country claimed.

On January 13, Secretary of War Marcy sent to General Taylor the most dramatic order of the veteran's long career: "Advance and occupy, with the troops under your command, positions on or near the east bank of the Rio del Norte [Rio Grande], as soon as it can conveniently be done with reference to the season and the routes by which your movements must be made."[45]

# CHAPTER XII

## ADVANCE TO THE RIO GRANDE

### 1

SECRETARY MARCY's instructions did not call for an immediate advance, and it was not until the second week in March, 1846, that Zachary Taylor finally set out from Corpus Christi for the Rio Grande. The delay was occasioned by the commander's fear that recent torrential rains might have made an overland march impracticable. But when a reconnoitering party returned with word that the one hundred and ninety-six mile journey from the Nueces to the Arroyo Colorado could be readily effected,[1] Taylor's apprehension vanished. And last-minute preparations were at once under way.

Taylor quartered the few soldiers who were still too ill to be removed in a hospital on St. Joseph's Island.[2] He assigned Brevet Major John Munroe to transport the rest of the sick by sea to Point Isabel, together with a company of artillery, a siege train, a field battery, and all excess baggage.[3] Inspector General Sylvester Churchill held the final review.[4] And on Sunday, March 8, Taylor reported to Washington that the cavalry and Brevet Major Samuel Ringgold's light artillery, "the whole under the command of Colonel Twiggs, took up the line of march this morning. . . ."[5]

General Worth's First Brigade, accompanied by Lieutenant James Duncan's battery, moved forward on Monday. On Tuesday, McIntosh's Second Brigade followed. And Wednesday found Taylor and his personal staff, including Bliss, together with Whistler's Third Brigade and Bragg's battery, bidding farewell to the now-deserted village of Corpus Christi.[6]

"The roads are in good order," Taylor wrote, "the weather fine, and the troops in excellent condition for service."[7]

2

The region through which the General's army plodded was a scenic treat. Clumps of wild oak lent romance to the landscape, and prickly pear and mesquite dotted the plain. Captain Henry sketched a delightful glimpse of the Spanish bayonet and the flowering acacia.[8] The spiderwort, the phlox, the lupine, and the primrose bloomed on the prairie.[9] "The first night out we encamped at a beautiful place covered with blue flowers like the hyacinth."[10] Rabbits, antelope and wild boar were plentiful. And the sight of squadrons of waterfowl on the lagoons and lakes grew familiar to the men as they marched along.

"To the *eye* the whole country was beautiful; nothing can exceed in beauty the islands and clumps of oak stretching out in every diversity of form over a gently undulating country; but when you come to the *feet* it is a very different matter; it is deep, deep sand, of the heaviest description, and perfectly unproductive, barely supporting a very thin growth of grass. . . . There is the greatest scarcity of fresh water, whose . . . clear surface only aggravates without giving relief. . . . The men suffered a great deal from the heat and dust, and were glad . . . to find themselves in camp."[11]

"Officers and men . . . had their lips and noses nearly raw from the sun and winds," wrote Samuel G. French, "and could not put a cup of coffee to their lips until it was cold. I wore an immense sombrero. . . . On the route I was often told: 'When Gen. Taylor comes up you will be put in arrest for wearing that hat.' . . . When the general commanding overtook us . . . , I went over to call on him . . . and found him in front of his tent sitting on a camp stool eating breakfast. His table was the lid of the mess chest. His nose was white from the peeling off of the skin, and his lips raw. As I came up he saluted me with: 'Good morning, lieutenant; sensible man to wear a hat.' So I was commended instead of being censured for making myself comfortable."[12]

Before the General departed from Corpus Christi, he had issued

an order which was translated into Spanish for distribution in the
Mexican communities of Matamoros, Mier and Camargo. It was
clearly pacific and to the point:

"The army of occupation of Texas being now about to take a
position upon the left bank of the Rio Grande, under the orders of
the Executive of the United States, the general-in-chief desires to
express the hope that the movement will be advantageous to all
concerned; and with the object of attaining this laudable end, he
has ordered all under his command to observe, with the most scru-
pulous respect, the rights of all the inhabitants who may be found
in peaceful prosecution of their respective occupations, as well on
the left as on the right side of the Rio Grande. Under no pretext,
nor in any way, will any interference be allowed with the civil
rights or religious privileges of the inhabitants; but the utmost respect for them will be maintained."[13]

As Captain Henry predicted, the tone of this pronouncement
"could not fail to produce a good effect" upon the citizens of the
border communities.[14] Mexico's military men, on the other hand,
were in too black a mood to be conciliated. And their attitude became apparent as soon as the Americans reached the shallow inlet
known as the Arroyo Colorado.

For as the Americans approached the arroyo from the northeast,
General Mejía led a detachment of Mexican cavalry from Matamoros to its southwestern bank. There he stationed his horsemen
so skillfully that the mere handful created the illusion of a formidable array. And Mejía greeted Taylor with a ringing message
that the crossing of the Colorado by United States troops would be
regarded as an act of war and as such would be resisted.[15]

Taylor waved aside the warning.

"We will cross immediately," he gave the Mexicans to understand, "and if a single man of you shows his face after my men
enter the river, I will open an artillery fire on him."[16]

With Ringgold's battery drawn up at Taylor's side, portfires
lighted, to cover the passage, Worth and Captain Charles F. Smith

led four companies down the twenty-foot embankment and across the inlet to the farther shore.

Momentarily a bloody engagement appeared to be impending. Actually Taylor had called Mejía's bluff, and the distant clouds of dust which soon were seen bore evidence of the Mexicans' flight.

Francisco Mejía's ruse had failed.

And the moral victory was Taylor's.[17]

### 3

After the crossing of the Arroyo Colorado, General Taylor kept his entire army together until Tuesday, March 24, when he came to the "wet weather" road which linked Point Isabel with Matamoros. Here he divided his force. He placed General Worth in charge of the infantry brigades with instructions to march slowly in the direction of Matamoros, and himself rode toward the coast at the head of the cavalry. At Point Isabel he found the transports from Corpus Christi in the harbor, and here he ordered Munroe to fortify a depot for supplies.[18]

Without pausing to see that this order was carried out Taylor turned back whence he had come and, rejoining Worth on the way, rode thirty-three miles inland to a point on the left bank of the Rio Grande opposite Matamoros.

"Hundreds of citizens were assembled on the Mexican side of the river to witness the approach of our troops," wrote an eyewitness, Captain Philip N. Barbour. ". . . The four columns of the Army filed in front of the town, within range of the Mexican batteries, and took position in a plowed field on the bank . . . without molestation of any sort. . . . In about an hour a flagstaff was procured and General Taylor ordered the 'Stars and Stripes' to be run up which was done in a prompt and spirited manner while a band of music struck up our national air."[19]

Taylor's initial act on reaching the Rio Grande was to assure Mejía that his was an essentially pacific mission, designed to protect American property. Deputizing Worth to confer with the

Mexican second-in-command, Rómolo Díaz de la Vega, he volunteered to "announce formally the purpose of our advance to the
Rio Grande, and afford an opportunity to establish friendly relations, if practicable."[20]

This offer was renewed from time to time during the next two
weeks, but on each occasion Mejía maintained that the presence of
United States soldiers on what Mexico considered Mexican soil
automatically created a state of war. Mejía was superseded by
General Pedro de Ampudia. And on Sunday, April 12, the latter
assumed the same position, demanding that Taylor retrace his
steps within twenty-four hours and "retire to the other bank of the
Nueces river, while our governments are regulating the pending
question in relation to Texas."[21] Taylor replied firmly but courte-
ously that he could not think of leaving. And for the second time
since his departure from Corpus Christi a Mexican threat to resort
to force failed to materialize.

Long before Ampudia's arrival at Matamoros, the Americans
had been preparing for the worst. On Thursday, April 2, they
broke ground for a battery facing the Mexican battery at El Paso
Real on the Mexican bank, and on the following Saturday four
eighteen-pound siege guns were brought there from Point Isabel.[22]

Early the next week these guns were removed to the six-sided
fortress which had been going up at a strategic position directly
opposite Matamoros under the superintendence of Captain Joseph
K. F. Mansfield.[23] This was Fort Texas, a hastily constructed work
but stronger than any of Ampudia's defenses and large enough to
hold four hundred soldiers.

Lieutenant Meade was pleased with the prospects. As early as
April 15 he wrote: "We . . . have such superiority in artillery, that
it is impossible for them with any force to drive us from here."[24]
Several other officers, including Hitchcock, did not share Meade's
confidence. General Taylor felt gratified at what was being done,[25]
but took additional measures of a precautionary nature, requesting
the American naval squadron at anchor in the Gulf to bottle up the
Rio Grande and prevent Mexican supplies from reaching Mata-

moros.[26] He also sent messengers to the governors of Louisiana and Texas, asking the former for five thousand volunteers and the latter for three thousand.[27] For war was but a step away.

4

A step away? Already war had come, though not in name. Already Mexican irregulars were staging guerrilla raids, killing unwary Americans, spiriting others away. On Friday, April 10, Colonel Truman Cross rashly ventured beyond the bounds of Taylor's camp; he never lived to tell the tale.[28] A week thereafter almost to the day, Second Lieutenant Theodoric H. Porter was engaged in a reconnoitering expedition when he met with a similar fate at the hands of the banditti.[29]

These casualties warned Taylor of trouble ahead. And on Saturday, April 25, learning that a large body of Mexicans had crossed the Rio Grande to the Fort Texas side, he assigned Captain Seth B. Thornton to spy on their activities. Accompanied by a detachment of dragoons, Thornton unwittingly rode straight into a trap where he found himself surrounded by sixteen hundred Mexicans. Part of his command was slain on the spot. The remainder, including their leader who was knocked insensible from his horse, were compelled to surrender.[30]

This encounter differed from the forays in which Cross and Porter died. For here the antagonists were no freebooters. They were government officers and government soldiers, officially representing the Mexican military and acting under orders issued by the new commander at Matamoros, Mariano Arista, who had taken Ampudia's place.

In effect, the Thornton affair was a declaration of war. There could be no mistaking it. "Hostilities may now be considered as commenced," Zachary Taylor informed his superiors in Washington.[31] And on the five days immediately following the assault he bent every effort to improve the defenses of Fort Texas.

There remained the problem of Point Isabel. Wisely or unwisely, Taylor had put thirty-three miles between the main body

"OLD ROUGH
AND READY"

*From an original daguer-*
*reotype no longer in ex-*
*istence, formerly in the*
*collection of Mrs. Jouett*
*Taylor Cannon of Frank-*
*fort, Kentucky*

WINFIELD SCOTT                    WILLIAM LEARNED MARCY

JAMES KNOX POLK

TAYLOR AND HIS SUPERIORS

The portrait of President Polk is from a daguerreotype by Brady, that of Secretary of War
Marcy from an engraving by J. C. Buttre based on a daguerreotype by Whitehurst.

of his men and the supply depot on the coast. Captain Samuel H. Walker of the Texas Rangers now brought word that Mexicans were crossing the river below Matamoros by the thousands, and the natural assumption was that Arista hoped to cut off the Americans from the supply base.[32] General Taylor may have delayed too long. Now he acted quickly. And on Friday, May 1, he set out at the head of some two thousand troops in the direction of Point Isabel.[33] Major Jacob Brown was left behind at Fort Texas with the Seventh Infantry, four eighteen pounders, and Bragg's battery at his disposal. "Hold out as long as you can," was the gist of the General's instructions to him.

5

Taylor constructed Fort Texas strong enough to withstand the most spirited attack of which the enemy was capable. Nevertheless, when the booming sound of cannon from the direction of Matamoros reached his ears at Point Isabel, he sent the valiant Captain Walker to find out how Brown was faring. The fieldwork was besieged, but Walker gained admittance. Then, riding back to Taylor's side on Tuesday, May 5, he assured the General that all was well.[34] Already Captain Charles A. May of the Second Dragoons had scouted the Mexican army, finding it assembled less than twenty miles inland from Point Isabel in command of the road. Walker, who passed Arista's force on his way back from Fort Texas, verified May's report. And Taylor was more certain than before that a bloody battle was impending.[35]

Still he did not return to Fort Texas at once. The fortifications at Point Isabel were weak, and from Saturday, May 2, until Wednesday, May 6, he strengthened them. At the same time he loaded wagons with provisions for Brown's beleaguered command. Several of his subordinates urged him to leave the supply train at the coast until after the fighting, but Taylor felt so confident of success that he ignored their protestations and went ahead. Finally, on Thursday morning, he bade Bliss issue a fateful order: "The army will march today at 3 o'clock, in the direction of Matamoras. It is known the enemy has recently occupied the route in force. If still in possession, the general will give him battle. The commanding general has every confidence in his officers and men. If his orders and instructions are carried out, he has no doubt of the result, let the enemy meet him in what numbers they may. He wishes to enjoin upon the battalions of Infantry that their main dependence must be in the bayonet."[36] Augmented by the addition of two hundred reinforcements at Point Isabel, the United States troops totaled two thousand, two hundred and twenty-eight when the command to advance was given.

Taylor's rank and file were weak numerically, but a more serious liability lay in his lack of top-ranking subordinate officers. Cross, the experienced quartermaster, was dead. Hitchcock had returned to New Orleans on sick leave. Worth, of whom much was expected, had obtained a furlough and departed for Washington in a huff as soon as it became known that President Polk had decided the Worth-Twiggs controversy in favor of Twiggs.[37] Of colonels of the line, Taylor and Twiggs alone were left. "One regiment," wrote William S. Henry, "had all its field officers absent; its colonel for years laid upon the shelf; its lieutenant-colonel . . . cut down by disease; its major, a gallant soldier, but broken in constitution; this regiment was commanded by a captain! Another had its colonel absent, its lieutenant-colonel enjoying à brigadier's command, its major bed-ridden for years! This regiment was commanded by a brevet major. Another regiment, its colonel and lieutenant-colonel absent, its major enjoying a brigadier's command; this regiment was commanded by a captain, and only one captain led his company. A battalion from four regiments was commanded by a captain—by brevet a lieutenant-colonel—not a field officer belonging to either was present." No wonder Henry exclaimed: "A retired list has become . . . necessary for the well-being and efficiency of the service."[38]

But now was no time to complain. It was a critical juncture, and there were compensations. Thanks to the drill and discipline undergone by the privates and non-commissioned officers, Taylor's command could be considered one of the most efficient military units placed in the field by the United States since the founding of the Republic. Nearly all his troops were regulars. Many of his captains and lieutenants were the beneficiaries of West Point training. And Taylor felt certain that his guns and equipment would prove superior to those of the enemy.

Although he would never have admitted it for a moment, his own presence at the head of the army was the greatest psychological factor in the American's favor. Already the picturesque old soldier, on whose broad shoulders fell the burden of leadership, had become less a man and more a myth in the eyes of his followers. Soon the verse-writers would be transforming him into a national hero of the homespun Jackson type:

> Though our General at best was indifferently dressed,
> In a dingy green frock coat and in pants of cottonade,
> And a broken old straw hat, still we did not care for that.[39]

Captains might look askance at his attempt to master problems of strategy. Majors might nod knowingly when they saw his plans, or lack of plans. Lieutenant colonels might pity his abysmal ignorance. But the rank and file never questioned, never wavered in their faith. They loved leaders who could be both natural and brave, and they had learned to adore Old Rough and Ready—the name by which they knew him when they did not say Old Zack.

There he was, in a "blue checked gingham coat, blue trousers without any braid, a linen waistcoat and a broad-brimmed straw hat. Neither his horse nor his saddle had any military ornament."[40] Simplicity! This well-born son of Virginia gentlefolk personified simplicity. And every time the privates saw him, plain and unpretending, mounted on Old Whitey with one leg swung over the pommel of his saddle, they felt that impelling urge to obey his orders and to march or race or ride wherever he might lead.

The first test on Texas soil was soon to come. In front of the Americans, blockading the road from Point Isabel to Fort Texas, was a Mexican army which outnumbered Zachary Taylor's force by more than two to one—led by Mariano Arista, a vital Potosían

now in the full vigor of middle life whose fiery red hair and side-
burns contrasted sharply with the Latin sleekness of the members
of his staff. Owing his present appointment primarily to political
considerations, Arista could not be classified as a typical political
appointee. His patriotism was unquestioned and, if he had but
dabbled in military science, he was certainly better qualified for
the task at hand than either Mejía, the comedian of the Arroyo
Colorado, or the imperious Ampudia, whom no one trusted.[41]
Against such a man and against an array of Mexico's best soldiers,
Taylor set out on the morning of Thursday, May 7.

# CHAPTER XIII

## Palo Alto and Resaca de la Palma

### 1

THAT night the troops bivouacked after a march of seven miles.[1] As the sun rose on Friday May 8, they continued inland. And eleven miles beyond, at the pond of Palo Alto, the masses of the enemy could be seen less than a mile distant across "an open prairie without a bush of any kind," occupying a front of nearly a mile and a half.[2] "The general immediately had his command formed in column of attack, and with the greatest deliberation ordered arms, and permitted the men, half at a time, to go and get water to fill their canteens."[3]

Several officers now advised against taking the offensive, but Taylor unhesitatingly over-ruled them. McIntosh commanded the Fifth Infantry on the extreme right. Next came Ringgold's battery, and nearer the road marched the Third and Fourth Infantry under Lieutenant Colonel John Garland. Yoke oxen plodded along the road in the center of the line, pulling Lieutenant William H. Churchill's two eighteen-pounders and flanked on the left by Brevet Lieutenant Colonel William G. Belknap's First Brigade composed of the Eighth Infantry, Duncan's battery and Brevet Lieutenant Colonel Thomas Childs's artillerymen. Because the Mexicans appeared weak on their left, Taylor placed a disproportionate number of troops upon his own right. There Twiggs's dragoons were also stationed, and behind them rode May's squadron, while the remainder of the cavalry under Captain Croghan Ker were assigned to guard the baggage wagons at the rear.[4]

Arista likewise was prepared for battle. Forming his line, he stationed General Anastasio Torrejón's thousand mounted lancers on the left slightly in advance of the other Mexican soldiers with a

pair of small cannon protecting their right flank. To their right
was Ampudia with the Fourth Infantry under Colonel José López
Uraga, the Tenth under General José María García, and the Sixth
and First commanded by De la Vega, together with a company
of sappers, two eight-pound guns and five four-pounders. On the
Mexican right appeared the Tampico Veterans, the Second Light
Infantry, a detail of sappers and a single four-pounder, with one
hundred and fifty cavalrymen under General Luis Noriega at the
extreme right.[5]

A majority of the Mexican rank and file were ignorant Indian
conscripts half-trained, half-starved, badly clothed, and underpaid.
But some were well-equipped considering the time and place, and
these were competently officered. Many of Arista's men had shown
on previous occasions that they could stand firm under fire, and
the lengthy preparations at Matamoros had resulted in improved
discipline.[6] Statistics are not available as to the exact size of the
Mexican army at Palo Alto, but it is known that it outnumbered
Zachary Taylor's force by more than two to one.

2

As Taylor advanced to meet the waiting enemy, he abandoned
an earlier decision to place his chief reliance in the bayonet. His
artillery was by all odds his strongest arm, and, following the advice of Bliss, Ringgold and Duncan, he determined to capitalize on
the advantage.[7] The muskets of Taylor's infantrymen were not
much better than Mexican muskets. The pistols of the American
dragoons were scarcely more effective than the lances and carbines
carried by Arista's cavalry, and the dragoons themselves were outnumbered ten to one. Taylor's subordinate officers felt certain that
the beautifully-wrought but unwieldy eighty-year-old Mexican
cannon could match neither the range nor the mobility of what
the United States gun crews fondly referred to as their "Flying
Artillery."[8] As soon, therefore, as the Mexicans commenced cannonading half a mile away, Taylor commanded his troops to halt.
Then, deploying, the American infantry stood at attention while

Duncan and Ringgold returned the fire of the hostiles' ineffective guns.[9]

The trend of battle could be gauged almost at the outset. Slicing and chopping through the Mexican lines, the American shot opened great gaps in Arista's ranks, unnerving the Indian conscripts and paralyzing the dumfounded Mexican officers, who had never witnessed such uncanny accuracy. General Arista had originally intended to charge the Americans regardless of the cost. Now he was on needles, a victim of vacillation. Impatiently his men awaited the signal to move forward and attack, but Arista was so distraught by the turn events were taking that the command never came.

There was little or nothing to compensate the Mexicans for their growing casualty lists which increased out of all proportion to the American losses. The Mexicans' copper cannon balls rarely reached Taylor's blue-uniformed troops except on the rebound,[10] and it was almost as easy for the trim foot soldiers of Belknap, Garland, and McIntosh to jump and sidestep the round shot as to keep high-collared jackets in place or bell-crowned forage caps securely on their heads.[11] "In the early part of the action our left suffered most," wrote Assistant Surgeon Madison Mills. "The 8th Inf[antr]y and artillery battalions stood up, the former in square, the latter in column of companies and received several rounds of cannon shot before their commanders brought them into line and gave the order to 'lie down,' and had several men wounded, while . . . [the soldiers on the right] who immediately formed line and laid down, had none wounded till we had been under fire nearly two hours."[12]

After the first hour of this unequal struggle, with each minute taking its toll in Mexican lives and each second ticking off another lapse in Mexican morale, Arista screwed up his courage so far as to order Anastasio Torrejón to harass the American right and rear. Under Torrejón's command were two guns and the full force of his cavalry. The seizure of the sheltered American wagons was the ultimate object of the attack.

General Taylor was fully aware that the lancers were coming. When his scouts apprized him of their approach, he cautioned

Twiggs to "keep a bright lookout for them." And Twiggs was waiting with the Fifth Infantry drawn up in a square when Torrejón appeared.[13] Advancing in column formation instead of in line as prudence would have dictated, the Mexicans twice exchanged volleys with the Fifth, twice were worsted, and twice recoiled. Then, when Ringgold's battery rushed to Twiggs's support, Torrejón's disheartened horsemen plunged pell-mell back through the chaparral whence they had come and conveyed the bad news to their already pessimistic general.[14]

### 3

Concurrently the prairie grass caught fire. Fanned by breezes from the coast, the flames speedily formed a smoke screen which blanketed the whole of the area intervening between the opposing armies. American could not see Mexican, nor Mexican American, and cannonading ceased. While Mexican morale crumbled further in the presence of delay, Zachary Taylor advanced a short distance on the enemy's left, swinging his own right wing forward and attaining a thirty-five-degree angle from his previous position. Arista responded with a similar movement when the smoke cleared, with the result that the two armies were soon again blasting away at each other from parallel formations.[15]

As before, the Americans did the greater damage—Duncan's battery being especially effective. "Duncan ... poured into them a few rounds of grape and cannister and mowed them down in great numbers," wrote Mills.[16] "His shells and shrapnell shot told with murderous effect," William S. Henry recorded.[17] And Philip N. Barbour wrote: "After the change of front, Duncan moved rapidly to a position not over 300 yards from the enemy's right flank which he gained unperceived under cover of a dense volume of smoke that rolled up from the burning prairie and opened so unexpected and destructive a fire upon it that their ranks were broken and hundreds of them mowed down and the whole right wing of their army thrown into the utmost confusion."[18] Together with the eighteen-pounders, the Eighth Infantry and May's dragoons,

Duncan drove Noriega's horse toward the Mexican light infantry who in turn prevented the Tampico troops from maintaining their position and pushed them blundering forward with their flank exposed to the American guns.[19] The American right meanwhile had met with similar success, and conditions would have been ripe for sallying forth on the offensive all along the line had it not been for the gathering darkness.

More than four hours had elapsed since the hostilities commenced. It was now seven o'clock. With appreciable relief the two armies obeyed commands to bivouac on the battlefield not far from their original positions, part of Taylor's force occupying the point held by the Mexican lancers at the commencement of the action, and the entire Mexican Army retiring a short distance in the direction of Matamoros and the Rio Grande before making ready for the night.[20]

The affair of Palo Alto was history, relegated by the burning present to the confine of the past, and General Taylor paused to study the results of the first pitched battle of the Mexican War. His troops had advanced since mid-afternoon, and Arista's troops had fallen back,[21] but the significance was to be found in the psychological effect rather than in the geographical. Five Americans lay dead, including the gallant Ringgold. Forty-three were numbered among the wounded, one of these being Captain John Page of the Fourth Infantry whose jaw was shot away and who already was marked for certain death.[22] Beside the Mexican casualties, however, this list seemed small indeed. For officially two hundred and fifty-two Mexican soldiers were accounted "dispersed, wounded and killed," while actually the killed and wounded alone were in all probability at least seven times the number of the American losses.[23]

Of all this Taylor had a clear idea. What he could not know was that, during the hours following the termination of the Battle of Palo Alto, Mariano Arista was being accused by his subordinates of everything from cowardice to treachery. The gravest accusation laid at Arista's door was lodged in the charge of failure to carry out the planned frontal attack at the beginning of the encounter.[24]

Taylor's cannon had given an indication of what might be expected of them in the days to come, but the full effect of their efficiency upon Mexican morale only the morrow would tell.

4

The American dead had been buried and medical care had been provided for the injured when, with the coming of dawn on Saturday, May 9, Zachary Taylor peered hopefully through the lifting haze to the spot where the enemy had spent the night. It was at this time that he began to formulate his plans for the immediate future. His soldiers were now finishing their breakfasts. Like their commander, they had been heartened by the events of the previous afternoon and were definitely in a mood for further fighting. Taylor's and their own eagerness to capitalize on the advantages gained at Palo Alto reached new heights when at length the Mexicans could be seen moving slowly away from their encampment along the road to Fort Texas, which Brown's men were still stoutly defending against that part of Arista's army which had remained in and near Matamoros.[25] By no means all the American officers, however, were inclined toward a policy of pursuit at this time.

"General Taylor called a council of war upon the presentation of Col. Twiggs that the commanders of corps . . . were in favor of intrenching our camp where it was and awaiting reinforcements. It leaked out after the council broke up that 7 out of 10 were in favor of this suggestion of inaction. Col. McIntosh, Capt. Morris and Duncan . . . were in favor of fighting again. The General sided with them. His mind was doubtless made up beforehand."[26]

Original documents fail to tell whether the attitude of Twiggs and the other conservatives seriously conditioned Taylor's own ideas but it is known that he hesitated before ordering the main body of his force to advance. A two-hour reconnaissance satisfied him that Arista's activities were more than a ruse, and that he was retreating far into the woods, but still Taylor played safe. He sent forward McCall and C. F. Smith with two hundred and twenty picked troops to follow the Mexicans and harass their rear guard, and devoted the late morning and early afternoon to throwing up a temporary breastwork for his wagon train while he awaited a report on Arista's later movements.[27]

Shortly after midday McCall sent word that the Mexicans had halted in a curving Rio Grande delta distributary known as the Resaca de la Guerra, approximately five miles from Palo Alto and immediately north of the Resaca de la Palma. This distributary had for protection such natural defenses as embankments, underbrush and chaparral, offsetting the effectiveness of the superior American cannon and necessitating reliance on infantry and cavalry in which branches the Mexicans had the advantage of numbers if not of organization and morale. When, therefore, Taylor's little army of approximately seventeen hundred troops set out at two o'clock on Saturday afternoon, both they and their commander were prepared to meet force with force, in hand-to-hand combat.

While the main body of Americans tramped onward slowly in a single column, General Taylor dispatched Lieutenant Stephen Decatur Dobbins' small detachment of infantrymen several hundred yards ahead in an attempt to draw the Mexicans' fire and thus ascertain the location of their batteries. The experiment succeeded. As Dobbins rounded a turn in the road, he "was saluted with a shower of grapeshot which wounded him and two sergeants of the 3d Infantry and killed an artillery private."[28] Enemy cannon could be seen commanding the approach from every angle, and when the report was brought to him the General correctly surmised that Arista's foot soldiers were also in the immediate vicinity.

Taking charge of the center himself, Taylor sent Lieutenant Randolph Ridgely's battery directly forward along the road. The Eighth and Fifth Infantry deployed as skirmishers on the left. The Third and Fourth received a similar assignment on the right.[29] And the fight was on.

## 5

Almost at once it was apparent to Ridgely that he could never capture the enemy cannon unless he received substantial support.

Nevertheless he wheeled his own guns forward, pouring such a murderous fire into the Mexicans' midst that their artillery, which had been assigned to guard the road, was forced to fall back a few yards. This was the best Ridgely could do unsupported.[30] Beset by hostile lancers, he sent back to Taylor for aid.

Old Rough and Ready did not hesitate. At once he ordered Captain May to charge the Mexican batteries with which Ridgely was contending. When May had ridden ahead a short distance, however, he found that General De la Vega's cannoneers now occupied a new position. And, instead of obeying without reasoning why, he returned to ask Taylor if the instructions still held good.

"Charge, Captain, *nolens volens!*" is the reply attributed to the American general.[31]

And away dashed the dragoons in the direction of the focal point of the fighting.

May and his men thundered up to Ridgely.

The Lieutenant seized the opportunity.

"Hold on, Charley, till I draw their fire," he shouted to May.[32]

May paused. The Mexican guns spoke. Then, as De la Vega futilely attempted to prepare another volley, the dragoons galloped toward the enemy gunners, lunged at them, plunged past them, turned and charged back again, capturing several of the enemy including De la Vega himself and then returning to where Taylor waited.[33]

In the spectacular raid many men had fallen on both sides, but the Mexican cannon were not dislodged from the enemy's hands until Taylor sent Belknap's Eighth Infantry and part of the Fifth Regiment along the route where May had gone before.

"Take those guns, and by God keep them!" the General commanded.[34]

And this they did.

## 6

Meanwhile, on both the right and left of the road it was a case of every man for himself as the infantry pressed on. "Chance was the lord of all."[35] By the very nature of the terrain tactical maneuvering was prevented. Regiments and even companies lost their integrity, the well-nigh impassable chaparral splitting even the smallest military units into segments and then splitting them again.

As their soldiers toiled, the conduct of the two commanders contrasted strangely. Mariano Arista, seemingly in a trance, remained in his tent and, it is said, in his underwear, long after the action became hot; he devoted his time to composing an official report of his alleged "victory" at Palo Alto instead of assuming leadership in the field. Zachary Taylor, on the other hand, sat astride Old Whitey "in the thickest of the fight, with his sword drawn, while the balls were rattling around him. Colonel C[umming], the amiable sutler of the 4th Infantry, formerly mayor of Augusta, Ga., and well known for his courage and kindness of disposition, remarked to him that he was exposing his person very much, and proposed to him to retire a short distance. . . ."

"Let us ride a little nearer, the balls will fall behind us," was the General's reply.[36]

Little headway could be made against the strong Mexican right, where Arista had stationed a disproportionate number of his troops, including two of his most impressive regiments, the Second Light Infantry and Uraga's Fourth Infantry. The left side of the Mexican line was not nearly so powerful, however, and before the insistent hammering of American infantrymen it eventually gave way.

After wandering through the underbrush in the hottest of the fire, Captain Barbour of the Third Regiment stumbled out onto the road with twelve of his command and found General Taylor and his staff, including Brevet Captain Bliss, occupying an exposed position "where the balls were falling like hailstones."

"Where will I find the enemy?" Barbour called out to Bliss.

"Straight ahead, and bear to the right," Taylor's assistant adjutant general directed.[37]

Pressing forward on the double-quick, Barbour passed "under the enemy's fire . . . 50 yards along the road, crossed the ravine on which they were entrenched and gaining the rising ground on the

other side untouched, was just in time to render important service
to a detachment of the 4th"[38] which he found being beaten back
by a large body of lancers. Twice the lancers charged, and twice
they were repulsed. This was the event on which the battle hinged.
Turning the Mexicans' flank, Barbour's small advance party led the
way against the Tampico Veterans, a handful of sappers and a single
company of Uraga's men who had crossed the road in a vain attempt to stem the tide.[39]

## 7

By this time Ridgely, manning the captured cannon with his
own artillerists, was blasting away at the enemy's center.[40] The
Mexican right, strong as it had been, now crumbled under the
American assault. The Second Light Infantry, a regiment which
Arista considered one of his crack units, became panic-stricken.
Arista, roused from his writing desk, tried to rally his forces to no
avail. And soon, ignoring the groans and wailing of their wounded
comrades, every able-bodied Mexican was in full flight.[41] "Bayonet
to bayonet, & sword to sword, we completely routed them," wrote
Taylor.[42]

Pursued to the Rio Grande, where many of their number
drowned, infantry and cavalry vied with each other in attempting
to gain the farther shore. Arista admitted that he left behind one
hundred and sixty dead, two hundred and twenty-eight wounded,
and one hundred and fifty-nine missing. His casualty list was probably much larger. Thirty-three Americans had been killed, eighty-
nine were being treated for wounds, and there could not be the
slightest trace of doubt even in Mexican minds that Taylor had
gained a sweeping victory.[43]

Not to be denied was the superiority of American man power,
equipment, training, and morale. The rout was complete. As
surgeons gave attention to the demands of the injured, confidence
of the most sanguine nature reigned in Zachary Taylor's camp not
far from the battlefield of the Resaca de la Guerra in the Resaca de
la Palma.

# CHAPTER XIV

## From Matamoros to Monterey

### 1

It does not seem to have occurred to Taylor to cross the Rio Grande at once. Had he followed this course directly after the Mexican rout, at the probable cost of a few more lives and regardless of the risks involved, Arista's entire army might have surrendered on the spot and an even prouder laurel might have been added to Taylor's brow. Not only had American morale been heightened by the success of American arms at Palo Alto and Resaca de la Palma, but the gallant defenders of Fort Texas had also won a signal victory. For nearly a week they had steadfastly resisted their assailants with little loss and, albeit fatigued, they were in good enough condition to continue fighting.[1]

If Taylor did give serious consideration to pursuing the enemy across the river, lack of siege material and inadequate transportation probably dissuaded him from attempting an offensive at the time. If the fault was partially his, it did not rest on him alone. Repeatedly he had begged the quartermaster department to supply a pontoon bridge. Repeatedly he had sought the proper mortars and ammunition for them. These requests ignored, and makeshift facilities lacking, the onus of his failure to follow up two triumphs by forcing the Mexicans to capitulate must be attributed in a great measure to inadequate support from Washington.[2] Thus justified, at least in his own eyes, the General departed from the Resaca de la Palma on Monday, May 11,[3] to confer at his depot on the coast with Commodore David Conner, the commander of the naval squadron.

This conference is memorable because of the humorous sidelight it throws on Zachary Taylor's character rather than for the routine decisions which the leaders made, for it was soon after his arrival

191

at Point Isabel that the famous "incident of the uniform" occurred. On only two occasions during the entire Mexican War did so competent an observer as Lieutenant U. S. Grant hear of the General's donning full military dress, and this was one of them.[4] Aware of Conner's propensity for the outward and visible signs of naval and military rank, Taylor sought to make a favorable impression. He rescued a wrinkled uniform from his chest, arrayed himself in the official regalia of a brigadier replete with sword and epaulets and sash and held himself in readiness for the Commodore's visit. Meanwhile Conner, knowing Taylor's love of ease and informality, decided to wear his oldest clothing in order to conform with Taylor's taste. Not unnaturally when the two men met, their amazement was scarcely greater than the amusement of their aides. Somehow they managed to make plans for the minor naval assistance that was designed to aid the army in the contemplated ascent of the Rio Grande and assault on Matamoros. But when the consultation ended and Conner departed, General Taylor relegated the crushed and creased uniform to the limbo of forgotten things with the comment that he would never again resort to formalities.[5]

## 2

Returning from Point Isabel, Taylor rejoined his army on Wednesday evening, May 13. A fever forced him to "keep my tent" the following day,[6] but by Friday he felt well again. Friday and Saturday witnessed the arrival of additional supplies of ordnance and ammunition. A few Mexican boats were secured from the opposite shore, and every energy was bent in the hope of crossing the river on Sunday. But this last was not to be. Believing that a *ruse de guerre* might gain him a safe conduct out of Matamoros, Mariano Arista sent a deputation to Taylor with a proposal that the two armies enter into an armistice until both generals could learn the outcome of the negotiations in Mexico City. This suggestion, however, did not mislead the American commander. And to it he returned a firm refusal.[7]

Arista's representative tried to persuade Taylor not to occupy

## THE BATTLE OF PALO ALTO

By Carl Nebel. First reproduced in George Wilkins Kendall's *History of the War between the United States and Mexico*. Taylor is pictured in the right foreground, astride Old Whitey. On the extreme right, Twiggs is repulsing Torrejón's attack. The two American eighteen-pound cannon are seen in the center. On the left, back, the prairie has caught fire.

Matamoros provided that all the public property, including ammunition, would be surrendered forthwith.

Taylor's refusal was straightforward. "I must have Matamoros," was the substance of his statement, "even if I am forced to batter down the town. I am fully prepared to do that very thing. These are my terms: The city must capitulate; all property must be surrendered; then and only then may the Mexican army march out and retire."[8]

Arista did not take his adversary at his word. What really interested him was delay, and this he obtained. While Old Rough and Ready awaited Arista's reply, which was to have been delivered at three o'clock on Sunday afternoon, the entire Mexican army was fleeing southward with virtually none of their injured men and only part of their munitions and supplies. "The scare," wrote Captain Henry, "was still working."[9]

On the morrow—Monday, May 18—General Taylor received confirmation of the report that Arista actually had fled, leaving civil officials in charge of Matamoros and civil laws in operation. At eight o'clock in the morning a delegation of civilian authorities appeared on the southern bank to be ferried across the Rio Grande for an interview. "Their object was . . . to ask terms for the surrender of the city. The General told them he should not molest any persons or property of a private nature nor should his troops commit any outrages upon their women."[10] Satisfied, they withdrew from Taylor's tent in time to witness the raising of the American flag high above Fort Paredes, while American soldiers on the ground below joined lustily in singing the stirring chorus of "Yankee Doodle."[11]

## 3

If the more romantic Americans expected to find in Matamoros something of the rarefied atmosphere of Castilla or Andalucía, they were doomed to disappointment. Structurally, Matamoros was not a whit different from half a hundred other Mexican towns containing populations in the neighborhood of eight thousand.

Facing the plaza were the usual two-story dwellings built of brick
or stone, with barred windows and massive walls. There was also
the Roman Catholic cathedral, an unfinished pile of masonry,
which was flanked by the prison, the market-house, and stores.[12]
"I visited the different hospitals," Henry wrote. "They are filled
with the wounded and dying. The stench that arose from the
want of police was disgusting. . . . On the whole, it is one of the
most indifferent and filthy cities I have ever seen. . . . In about one
house in three of the more humble cast, one of the family was
diligently *searching the heads* of the others. It is said they are *some*
for *lice*."[13]

Instead of establishing headquarters in the heart of Matamoros,
as some of his subordinates expected him to do, General Taylor
pitched his tent half a mile from the city, and there his staff joined
him. To Colonel Twiggs he delegated the difficult duties of military governorship, and that officer removed from the General's
shoulders many of those routine details which otherwise would
have scattered his energies and all but monopolized his attention.
More and more volunteers were now arriving from New Orleans.
These unruly troops frequently disobeyed orders and occasionally
were responsible for outrages committed upon the inhabitants. Together with the regulars, they occupied a series of camps which
stretched from Matamoros to the Gulf and bordered on both banks
of the Rio Grande—one of the camps being at Burrita, a small
Mexican settlement that had been occupied by Lieutenant Colonel
Henry Wilson on May 17 with the assistance of Commodore
Conner.[14]

Taylor's soldiers, now nearly eight thousand strong, enjoyed a
somewhat varied existence on the border. Sleeping, eating, drilling,
shooting at targets, they spent their spare time training donkeys,
listening to sermons, gambling, and attending plays. Monte and
fandangos were the order of the hour, and not a few of the officers
and men who visited Mexican families in the town or worshiped in
the cathedral were impressed by the foreign atmosphere obtaining
there. The plays were given in the Spanish Theater by a company
of American actors, one of whom was young Joseph Jefferson, who

described the audience as "the most motley that ever filled a theater...." "Victory had crowned our arms," Jefferson wrote, "so the soldiers, settlers, gamblers, rag-tag and bob-tail crowd that always follow in the train of an army ... were ready for amusement."[15]

4

Taylor himself wasted no time on fandangos or theatricals. There was work to be done. On May 11 President Polk, having received the ringing report of the Thornton affair, sent to the Senate and to the House of Representatives a dramatic message. "Mexico ...," he stated in authoritative terms, "has invaded our territory and shed American blood upon the American soil.... War exists, and, notwithstanding all our efforts to avoid it, exists by the act of Mexico herself."[16]

On May 13, 1846, Congress passed a bill officially declaring war, appropriating ten million dollars for its prosecution, and providing for the mobilization of fifty thousand additional soldiers. Taylor's problems multiplied. Already he had more volunteers than he could use,[17] and his equipment was ridiculously insufficient.[18] Though he lacked definite instructions from Washington with regard to his future operations,[19] he did not permit this lack to handicap his activities. While he was waiting for specific orders from Secretary of War Marcy as well as boats, wagons, tents, horseshoes, and medicine from Quartermaster General Jesup, he formulated a plan of campaign which would lead him as rapidly as possible toward the city of Monterey, capital of the state of Nuevo Leon and the key to further progress in northern Mexico.

Meanwhile, by no means all of Taylor's troops stood idle. As early as Tuesday, May 19, the day following the occupation of Matamoros, the General placed Lieutenant Colonel Garland in charge of all his available dragoons and sent them in pursuit of Arista's men who were fleeing to the south. Possessing neither strength enough to join battle with Arista nor provisions enough to warrant an attempt to overtake him, Garland returned on May

22 with twenty-two prisoners after engaging the Mexicans' rear guard, capturing a wagon, and killing two of the enemy.[20] Soon thereafter the law-abiding citizens of the river town of Reynosa appealed for American protection against some of their own countrymen who had turned brigands. Taylor complied with their request by detaching four companies of the First Infantry and a detail of Texas Rangers and ordering them to Reynosa where they were to act as police and garrison.[21] Finally, on June 12, the colorful Major Ben McCulloch and forty picked rangers were sent southwestward to analyze the relative advantages of marching directly to Monterey by way of Linares or proceeding as far as Camargo by the Rio Grande and the San Juan and thence continuing overland. General Taylor leaned toward the Camargo route even before McCulloch departed, and his decision was fixed when the latter returned to Matamoros with the information that neither water nor forage could satisfy the needs of a large invading army along the Linares road.[22]

## 5

As the General completed preparations for advancing upstream to hot Camargo, his personal popularity in the United States was assuming phenomenal proportions. Relayed by boat to New Orleans and thence by telegraph and special messenger to Washington and New York, reports of the victories of Palo Alto and Resaca de la Palma were greeted with excitement that was fairly electrical. Church bells rang. Bonfires blazed. There was dancing in the streets of the cities, and oratory in the public squares. "We are all agog with the news," Philip Hone confided to his diary.[23] And even the dour Polk joined in paying tribute to the hero of the hour.[24]

In the camps near Matamoros, not a few American officers frowned on Taylor's unconventional behavior in and out of battle or were jealous of his new-found fame, and these men failed to add their laurels to the tribute of the nation. "Utterly, absurdly incompetent to wield a large army," was the opinion of one captain.[25]

And even Lieutenant Meade, who admired him in most respects, criticized his "perfect inability to make use of the information" furnished by the topographical engineers.[26] But Lieutenant Grant commented on Taylor's superior ability. "No soldier could face either danger or responsibility more calmly than he," Grant wrote. "These are qualities more rarely found than genius or physical courage."[27] And other officers, equally keen, joined in comparable estimates.

Stay-at-home Americans were of but one opinion. Not stopping to pass judgment on technical details, they knew that Taylor had won two smashing victories. This was enough for them, and their enthusiasm knew no bounds. More than anything else they liked the homespun qualities of the General—his simplicity, humility and rare common sense—and their impressionistic picture of a latter-day Cincinnatus was made vivid by anecdotes which admirers sent homeward from the front.

When two delegations of Louisiana dignitaries arrived at Matamoros to announce the forthcoming presentation of a golden sword, to give him the military sash which General Edward Braddock had bequeathed to George Washington, and to convey the Louisiana Legislature's vote of thanks, Taylor refused to accept the heirloom until "the campaign, so far as I am concerned, is finished."[28] In Taylor's eyes, the Louisianians were "a high set of gentlemen," for the two baskets of champagne and the cold collation spread out for their refreshment before Taylor's tent were not enough to satisfy their thirst and hunger, and "some of them have been on a frolic pretty much ever since they have been here."[29]

And how could the newspaper-reading public fail to find a hero in the "hearty-looking old gentleman" who could win battles and yet might be found "sitting on a box, cushioned with an Arkansas blanket, dressed in Attakapas pantaloons and a linen roundabout, and remarkable for a bright flashing eye, a high forehead, a farmer look and 'rough and ready' appearance"?[30]

But apparently there was not champagne for every occasion, and Taylor himself drank none of it. One correspondent for an American paper wrote: "There was no pomp about his tent. A couple of blue chests served for his table, upon which was strewn, in masterly confusion, a variety of official documents: a quiet-looking, citizen-dressed personage made his appearance upon hearing the significant call of 'Ben,' bearing, on a tin salver, a couple of black bottles and shining tumblers, arranged around an earthen pitcher of Rio Grande water. These refreshments were deposited upon a stool, and we 'helped ourselves' by invitation. We bore to the general a complimentary gift from some of his fellow-citizens of New Orleans, which he declined receiving for the present; giving at the same time a short but 'hard sense' lecture on the impropriety of naming children and places after men before they were dead...."[31]

## 6

Taylor must have known that many a male infant was being named in his honor, and even the appellation of "Rough and Ready" was inflicted on one innocent babe. Taylor's military genius was compared to that of Washington and Jackson, and he was promoted to the brevet grade of major general on the recommendation of President Polk in recognition of his "gallant conduct and distinguished services in the successive victories over superior Mexican forces at Palo Alto and Resaca de la Palma." On June 29 he became a major general of the line. On July 18 he was tendered the thanks of Congress "for the fortitude, skill, enterprise and courage which have distinguished the recent operations on the Rio Grande...."[32]

Medals and swords were on their way. Other honors were showered on the soldier who had served thirty-seven years with little recognition. Poets penned sonnets and odes commemorating Taylor's battles, and one of the odes was written in Latin which the General could not read. Biographers gathered the reminiscences of frontiersmen and retired officers and distant relatives who "knew the great man when." Editors sent reporters scurrying to the Rio Grande for interviews, and artists arrived in Matamoros to sketch the General or to paint his portrait. And less than three weeks after Resaca de la Palma an event had occurred which lifted Taylor out of political obscurity when Thurlow Weed, editor of the Albany

UNCLE SAM'S TAYLORIFICS

A cartoon of the period, drawn by Edward Williams Clay.

*Journal* and prominent Whig leader, predicted his election to the presidency.[33]

But Warwick reckoned without his king, for on the surface Zachary Taylor did not seem to take kindly to Weed's suggestion. And soon Lieutenant Colonel Joseph P. Taylor, who had conferred with Weed, would receive this succinct statement from his celebrated brother: "Memoranda of the conversation you had with an Albany editor, and to which you request a reply, seems to me too visionary to require a serious answer. Such an idea never entered my head, nor is it likely to enter the head of any sane person. I shall be well satisfied to get creditably through this campaign. For your friend's confidence in me, however, you will make my acknowledgments."[34]

As early as June 21, referring to Polk and General Scott in connection with the next national election, the victor of Palo Alto assured his son-in-law that he cherished no political ambitions of any kind. "They need have no apprehensions," he wrote to Doctor Wood relative to the presidency, "of being interfered with by me for that high office, which I would decline if proffered & I could reach it without opposition."[35] This position would be reaffirmed in letters to other intimates for many months to come.

## 7

As the president-makers eyed him with increasing interest, the General pressed on toward Camargo from which place he proposed to march to Monterey. On July 6 and 7 the Seventh Infantry left Matamoros. By August 4, when Taylor and his staff departed aboard the *Hatchee Eagle* to reach Camargo on August 8, nearly all the regulars and many of the volunteers had gone before.[36] "The Rio Grande is a noble river at the present stage of water," wrote Captain Barbour, who preceded the commander. "There is not a snag in it. The country along its banks is decidedly pleasing, many spots being so elevated as to have escaped entirely the recent overflow. . . . The Mexicans appear to be exceedingly friendly along the river."[37]

Lieutenant Meade, writing to his wife in Philadelphia, corroborated this account: "It was quite an agreeable sight in passing up, to see the banks, which are generally high and firm, covered with fields, extending for miles, with the finest corn I have ever seen, now and then a ranch, or village, in front of which all the inhabitants were collected, staring in stupid wonder at our little boat as she puffed her way up; and when we took off our hats and kissed our hands to the girls, they would all shout and laugh and make themselves most merry."[38] Because of a lack of transportation, the land route was followed by some of the troops who found the going both difficult and disagreeable. "The heat was intense, and the men suffered very much," Captain William S. Henry recorded. "I am free to confess, had not my pride come to my rescue, I should have given out. The greatest cause of suffering was want of water. ... The men actually dropped down from thirst; the ground was so hot that it burned your feet, and the dense chaparral prevented our feeling the influence of the sea-breeze."[39]

At Camargo the blistering heat continued, reaching a peak of one hundred and twelve degrees. A shabby town of three thousand inhabitants with its dilapidated cathedral and its plaza and its typically Mexican assortment of donkeys, dogs, and fighting-cocks,[40] Camargo was a logical location for a supply depot from the geographical standpoint. However, it was a far from satisfactory rendezvous for so many unacclimated volunteers, hundreds of whom fell victims to dysentery and diarrhea.[41] "I never saw so sad a looking place," one officer recorded. "The recent overflow of the Rio Grande and San Juan did great injury to it. Scarcely a respectable looking house is left standing. There are no stores, and but one house, a druggist shop in the town, to indicate that business of any sort is carried on."[42] "What a horror I have for Camargo," a general agreed. "It is a Yawning Grave Yard. . . ."[43]

Taylor, never partial to citizen-soldiers, found his troubles doubled and redoubled as each new boat unloaded its quota of volunteers. Not only did they sicken and die, but they knew no discipline. Meade, his patience taxed, had written at Point Isabel: "So irregular and undisciplined is the force sent here that I shall be surprised if I ever find myself at Monterey. A regiment cannot move its camp eight or ten miles, without incurring the risk of starving. . . . They will overload their wagons with baggage and sutler's goods, and leave their provisions, thinking this a clever scheme by which they will force the Government officers to send on their provisions by extra transportation. The consequence is they arrive at their new position, and the next day they have nothing to eat, and then complain. . . ."[44] "Volunteers are playing the devil and disgracing the country . . . ," was Barbour's observation.[45] Taylor himself characterized the Texas Rangers as "licentious."[46] And Meade, keenly resentful, wrote: "Already are our guardhouses filled daily with drunken officers and men, who go to the town, get drunk and commit outrages on the citizens. . . . Notwithstanding the positive order of General Taylor . . . that no firing is to be allowed in camp, they come down in crowds to the bank of the river opposite to us and discharge their pieces right across, and the bullets come whizzing by us as thick as in an action, and I really consider spending a day in my tent, uninjured, equivalent to passing through a well-contested action."[47]

Such intolerable conditions continued to obtain at Camargo, where approximately eleven thousand volunteers were concentrated by the last week in August. Some of these troops were competently led by West Pointers like Colonel Jefferson Davis of the First Regiment of Mississippi Rifles, on whom his father-in-law bestowed a welcome the heartiness of which could not be mistaken.[48] Other volunteers, less fortunate, were to serve under mere politicians who were unfamiliar with even the rudiments of warfare. Taylor had decided to leave the majority on the Rio Grande during the Monterey campaign. Heading the division assigned to accompany the regulars into the interior of Mexico was Major General William O. Butler, a striking six-foot Kentuckian whom Taylor long had known.

A lawyer by profession and a politician by inclination, Butler was not unqualified for military leadership. Unlike too many of the political appointees, he had participated in the War of 1812 and had tasted defeat at the River Raisin in 1813 and victory at New

Orleans two years later.[49] One of the new brigadiers was Thomas L. Hamer, a congressman from Ohio who owed his grade to prominence in the Democratic party but whom Ulysses S. Grant considered "one of the ablest men Ohio ever produced."[50] Another was John A. Quitman, a native New Yorker who had moved to Mississippi and whom General Taylor described as a "gentleman of intelligence, of large fortune [and] long a Genl Officer of militia."[51] In charge of the regulars under Taylor were Worth, who had returned from Washington somewhat chastened in spirit and whose motto now was "a grade or a grave,"[52] and Twiggs, who had ably seconded Old Rough and Ready at Palo Alto and Resaca de la Palma and had won promotion to a brigadier generalship.

## 8

William J. Worth and the First Brigade were the first to march toward Monterey. Crossing the San Juan on August 19,[53] officers and men were thankful to escape the sickness and the mud of Camargo, the swarms of frogs and insects that plagued the soldiers with almost biblical intensity, the clammy dews and withering noonday heat, the lack of sanitation and the muffled drums of death. Persifor F. Smith, who had served creditably with Taylor in the Florida War and was now a colonel, followed shortly thereafter with the rest of Worth's Second Division. Soon the First Division, under Twiggs, was under way. Butler's volunteers, more than twenty-seven hundred strong, followed. McCulloch's and Gillespie's Texas Rangers went with Worth. Five hundred Texas cavalrymen, led by Colonel John C. Hays, accompanied Twiggs. Finally on September 5, Zachary Taylor with his personal staff and a rear guard departed. And the entire expedition, six thousand six hundred and forty strong, was under way.[54]

Throughout the summer, the army had been handicapped by lack of transportation. Two days prior to leaving Camargo, Taylor wrote to Wood: "If I depended on the Qr Masters dept to complete the necessary arrangements . . . , not only the time of the . . . [vol-

MAJOR GENERAL ZACHARY TAYLOR

This portrait of General Taylor is from an original daguerreotype in the collection of
William M. Sweeny of Astoria, New York.

unteers] would expire before they were completed, but the regulars likewise. . . . We are very much in want here of medicines and supplies. . . . As they were very particularly needed the Qr Master shipped them on the slowest boat on the river, whether by design or accident I am unable to say. . . ."[55] Exasperated by this want of foresight, the General purchased enough pack mules to take the place of the needed wagons. Horseshoes were lacking. Tents, of muslin manufacture, leaked. Most distressing of all was the absence of siege trains. Only one ten-inch mortar went forward from Camargo. "Should I ever get away from here . . . ," Taylor wrote, "I shall be very deficient in transportation to what it should have been; but I must attempt something; we have been idle too long and we must move on Monterey be the consequences what they may. . . ."[56]

Marching westward up the Rio Grande Valley the troops turned south at Mier, where "a lofty range of blue mountains burst upon us, their jagged peaks cut into fantastic shapes against the blue sky."[57] Noon of August 25 found Worth in Cerralvo.[58] Soon Twiggs, too, was there. And by September 9 Taylor, who moved more swiftly, completed the sixty-mile advance to that picturesque town[59] "through which courses a bold running stream, winding its noisy way. . . . The houses are low. . . . The fig, peach, and pomegranate are in the greatest abundance. . . . The banks of the stream are lined with them, and the lemon, orange, and peccan. . . ."[60]

Tuesday, September 15, found Taylor's entire army once more moving forward, led by McCulloch's rangers and by the pioneers. "Whether the enemy will fight for Monterey is quite uncertain," the General wrote to Doctor Wood. "It can only be ascertained by going there; my impressions are we shall meet with no resistance out of the city. . . ."[61] This prediction was substantially correct. Ineffective Mexican opposition at Ramos and at Marín served only to heighten the Americans' enthusiasm.

But, at last, on Saturday morning, September 19, advancing slowly through luxuriant fields of corn and sugar cane, General Taylor and his Texas scouts approached the city of Monterey.

"The mists still clung around the turrets of its churches, and enveloped its commanding heights; but the ... sun ... dissipated the veil, until palace and hill, barricade and fort, with long lines of tents and pendent flags presented themselves. .... All was silent; not a breath of air stirred. .... Suddenly a hot sulphurous smoke rose quickly from one of the bastions. ...."[62] "The first shot passed within 10 feet of the General and subsequently two balls passed through both the Texas regiments without touching a hair of man or horse. The army retired half a mile to a beautiful grove of pecan and walnut trees of very large size, and encamped."[63]

# CHAPTER XV

## "We Were Not Many"

### 1

THE grove to which the American army withdrew came to be known as Walnut Springs. From it on the afternoon of his arrival Taylor dispatched an engineering expedition under Major Mansfield, accompanied by Gillespie's Texas Rangers, to reconnoiter the approaches to Monterey. Situated on the north bank of the Rio Santa Catarina, the city was strongly protected both by natural defenses on the south and west and by man-made fortifications on every side.[1] At the northeast angle, nearest Walnut Springs, stood the guns of Fort Tenería. They were in front of a stone tannery building "the flat roof of which, protected with sandbags in addition to the parapet, was held by a competent garrison."[2] A single redoubt commanded the Marín road. Four hundred yards in the rear was the earthwork of El Diablo. Behind this were two demi-bastions together with a bridgehead—La Presa—which guarded the Purísima bridge over the Ojo de Agua Canal. And the entire eastern approach to the principal plaza was further fortified by barricaded streets and stone houses bristling with rifles.[3]

In the very heart of Monterey, the cathedral—where not long before devout Catholics had passed under the carved façade to worship their Maker—was transformed into a storehouse of munitions. To the north, outside the city with which it was connected by Calle El Roble, loomed a formidable mass of masonry known as the Citadel (Ciudadela) where four hundred veterans under Uraga stood ready to man the eighteen-pounders and other cannon.[4] West of Monterey, at its very edge, the Bishop's Palace on Independence Hill was defended by a sandbag redoubt facing the Sierra Madre Mountains and by the fort of La Libertad the guns of

205

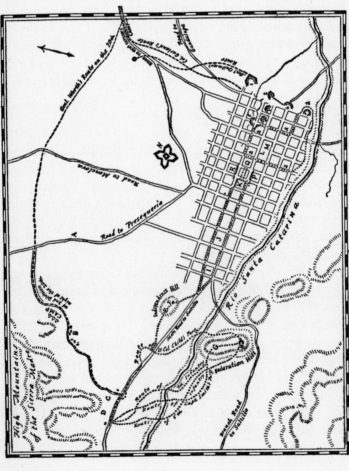

## LEGEND

A. Mexican ambuscade, afternoon of 20th of Sept.
B. Yard into which Mexicans fired at night-fall on 20th.
C. Charge of Mexican Lancers on morning of 21st.
D. Position of 2nd Division on 22nd.
E. Height stormed by Col. Childs on 22nd.
F. Bishop's Palace carried on 22nd.
G. Height stormed by Capt. Smith's party and 7th Infantry on 21st.
H. Redoubt stormed by Col. Smith on 21st.
I. Arista's house and garden.
J. Church and cemetery, with loopholes for musketry.
K. Plazuela de Carne.
L. Small Plaza.
M. Grand Plaza.
N. Citadel.
O. Mortar.
P. } Position occupied by our troops on the
Q. } morning of the 24th.
R. }
1. Redoubt of 4 guns assaulted and carried on the morning of the 21st by 1st, 83rd Division.
2. Redoubt of 3 guns.
3-8-4. Breastworks.
5. Tete de Pont.
6. Redoubt of 4 guns.
7. Redoubt of 3 guns.
aaa. Line of barricades.
—— Routes of troops.

MONTEREY AND ITS APPROACHES

A drawing showing Gen. Taylor's operations at Monterey, Mexico, in 1846, based on a drawing by Lieut. Calvin Benjamin, U. S. Army. Records of the Chief of Engineers, War Department, Washington. In custody of the National Archives, Washington.

which pointed toward the city proper. Across the river, on the south, was Federation Ridge, its eastern edge commanded by El Soldado where two nine-pounders would later be placed, its western approach less adequately protected by a small redan.[5] A total force of seven thousand three hundred and three regular and irregular troops constituted the Mexican garrison, and in charge of them was Major General Pedro de Ampudia.

When Mansfield returned to Walnut Springs at ten o'clock Saturday night,[6] Taylor pored over the reports and determined on a plan. Two thousand soldiers under Worth would skirt the Citadel. Cutting off Ampudia's source of supplies by commanding the Saltillo highway, they would blast their way into the town by storming Independence Hill, while Taylor himself was to divert attention at the eastern gates. After Worth's initial attack, regardless of its outcome, Taylor would then strike in earnest with the bulk of his force in a whirlwind invasion to the heart of Monterey.[7]

2

Two o'clock on Sunday afternoon, September 20, 1846, found Worth leaving the Walnut Springs camp. In four hours' time, his men marched to the farther side of the city beyond the range of batteries on Independence Hill but within striking distance of the highway. It was a wind-lashed night. Rain drenched the unprotected troops, who slept on their arms. Worth was nervous as he contemplated the impending assault.

By dawn on Monday the entire field force of General Worth was advancing toward the road, led by four hundred mounted Texans under Hays and Ben McCulloch. Captain Charles F. Smith followed with his skirmishing artillerymen. Then came Duncan's battery. No sooner was the column in motion than the enemy was roused to resist the attack. Sweeping toward the Americans galloped a squadron of lancers, more than two hundred strong, who fell ferociously upon McCulloch and lunged savagely at his command. For some grim minutes neither adversary gave an inch. Lances were shivered. Swords slashed without restraint. With

Smith and Hays pouring a murderous fire into the mêlée from behind a barricade, the engagement was hurrying to a crisis when Duncan and Mackall unlimbered their heavy artillery. Mexican cavalry and supporting infantry, valiant though they were, took to their heels at this fresh sally. And Worth was quick to gain his first objective—undisputed possession of the Saltillo road.[8]

"The town is ours," his scribbled note told Taylor. But he spoke too soon.[9]

### 3

Meanwhile Taylor was not idle. He made a show of strength on Sunday in order to distract Ampudia, and continued this strategy early Monday morning while his engineers were busily reconnoitering. Then, when Worth's message reached him, to Lieutenant Colonel Garland he gave the order to advance.

"Colonel," Taylor commanded, "lead the head of your column off to the left, keeping well out of reach of the enemy's Shot, and if you think . . . you can take any of them little Forts down there with the bay'net you better do it—but consult with Major Mansfield, you'll find him down there."[10]

Panting through the chaparral and cornfields adjacent to the city, Garland's eight hundred troops—regular infantry of the First and Third Regiments and the Washington-Baltimore volunteers—followed blindly where their leaders flashed a brave challenge to their derring-do. There was dynamite enough awaiting them. Brushing through the Marín road redoubt, recently abandoned, they were shortly within range of the Tenería guns. This was a direct invitation to an enemy bombardment, and the Mexicans obliged with a saturnalia of slaughter. Dazed at first, decimated and worse by the stiff barrage of musketry and grape, virtually all of Garland's men were as innocents against a firing squad. And they were forced to retreat.[11]

Taylor's plan had proved far simpler than its execution. He had taken the first step in the most ill-advised assault of his career. The second step would be equally tragic.

Americans pressed on. Part of the Fourth Infantry stormed Fort Tenería. Thirty per cent fell, killed or wounded. William S. Henry, who was in the thick of it, wrote: The Mexicans' initial shot "struck immediately in front of our line and ricoche[tte]d over it. An enfilading fire was opened upon us from the citadel. . . . For five hundred yards we advanced across a plain under fire of the two batteries. We rushed into the streets. Unfortunately, we did not turn soon enough to the left, and had advanced but a short distance when we came suddenly upon an unknown battery, which opened its deadly fire upon us. From all embrasures, from every house, from every yard, showers of ball were hurled upon us. . . . On every side we were cut down. Major Barbour . . . fell, cheering his men."[12]

Returning now into an adjoining street, Ulysses S. Grant and his comrades of the Fourth Infantry sought shelter in the shadow of Monterey's stone houses as they tried vainly to close the gaps in their riddled ranks.[13]

Here the dead were everywhere. The wounded bit their lips in pain. The dying groaned. But Mansfield, dragging his splintered leg, still stumbled on cheering his men and pointing out places of attack. And the gallant Lieutenant Colonel William H. Watson, scorning suggestions to retreat, cried: "Never, boys! never will I yield an inch! I have too much Irish blood in me to give up!"[14] Soon afterward he was a corpse.

With many men of the Fourth Regiment already killed and Garland's survivors wandering aimlessly through the maze of streets, Captain Electus Backus of the First Regiment scrambled up to the roof of a shed which overlooked Fort Tenería. From this vantage post he searched that redoubt with musketry and became the first American to penetrate its pregnable defense.[15] Then came reinforcements with General Quitman as brigadier: Tennesseans under Colonel William Bowen Campbell, Mississippi Rifles with Jefferson Davis in command.

By an echelon movement these volunteers formed a line of battle in front of Fort Tenería to the left of where the regulars had previously attacked. Five or six rounds were fired, and the enemy recip-

rocated. Quitman's horse was killed under him.[16] Then as the
Mexicans paused Davis, Campbell, and Lieutenant Colonel Alexander K. McClung seized their moment of hesitation to direct a
charge against the battery. "The combat," wrote a Mexican defender, "began to be terrible. The Americans kneeling, concealing
themselves in every sort of posture; in possession of the ground
close to the fort, within pistol shot, and even on the counter-
scarp . . . maintained a lively fire upon our parapets."[17] Here the
morale of the Mexicans broke. They fled pell-mell from Fort
Tenería just as McClung clambered over the rampart, and also
speedily abandoned the near-by tannery and sought shelter in El
Diablo or beyond.[18]

Still the struggle continued. Quitman's forces, pressing forward,
struck at El Diablo from the front[19] while the First Ohio Regiment—officered by Hamer, Butler and Taylor himself—stoutly
attempted to storm it from the rear. They only met with failure,
fighting as they did with a ferocity unsurpassed in the entire war.
Old Rough and Ready, exercising neither skill nor caution, oblivious to danger or disdainful of it, set his men a splendid example of
physical bravery by participating personally in the carnage, battling
on foot in their very midst.[20]

But even this was not enough. And the American assailants
lacked adequate artillery, though Bragg and Ridgely did their best.
With Colonel Davis at their head, the Mississippians waded the
stream that flowed below the Purísima Bridge, losing men at every
step and charging at a venture. In the face of overwhelming odds
courage was commendable, but the accumulated courage of a far
stronger force could not have captured El Diablo on that fatal day.
As the guns behind the earthwork spat defiance at the troops, an
even larger number fell before the bridgehead.[21]

"All was confusion," wrote an observant surgeon. And those
behind cried "Forward!" And those before cried "Back!" Finally,
at five o'clock, as the shadows of the Sierra Madres lengthened over
Monterey, Taylor abandoned the offensive. Only to Tenería was
a garrison assigned by the American commander.[22] And all the
other troops retired to Walnut Springs.

4

Throughout this bloody struggle General Worth was meeting better luck. Shortly after noon on Monday, now in possession of the Saltillo highway, he focused his attention on Federation Ridge with the westernmost redoubt as his first objective. After fording the Rio Santa Catarina while bullets sizzled, Texans and artillery-men under Captain Smith led the way to the ridge's top. The Seventh Infantry came next, followed by the Louisianians and also by the Fifth, with Colonel Smith assigned to direct them all. Steadily and surely Captain Smith advanced against the rear of the redoubt, while the Colonel was veering left to smother El Soldado. Almost simultaneously both bands of Mexicans were routed, and a smaller fort was also captured near the eastern edge.[23]

Independence Hill was next. But how to reach the Bishop's Palace? To attack La Libertad would be certain slaughter. So Worth reasoned. And he was correct. Detailing four hundred and fifty men to ascend the oval mesa from the west in the small hours of Tuesday morning, Worth ordered their leaders to creep up upon the sandbag redoubt as silently as possible, trusting that their stealth might take the enemy by surprise and send him sprawl-ing eastward toward the city. "At three o'clock two columns ad-vanced . . . , their progress timed so that they would converge at the summit near daylight." Brevet Colonel Childs, "accompanied by Hay's Rangers, led the right; Captain [John R.] Vinton and Walker's Rangers took the left."[24] Concurrently another detach-ment, pulsing toward the Palace under Taylor's orders, succeeded in diverting the attention of its garrison from the more important movement high above.[25]

Captain Henry, who was lying on his back in the mud of Fort Tenería, described the scene: "Just at the gray dawn of day . . . I witnessed the storming of the height which commanded the Bishop's Palace. The first intimation we had of it was the discharge of musketry near the top of the hill. Each flash looked like an electric spark. The flashes and the white smoke ascended the hill-side steadily, as if worked by machinery. The dark space between the apex of the height and the curling smoke of the musketry became less and less, until the whole became enveloped in smoke, and we knew it was gallantly carried. It was a glorious sight, and quite warmed up our cold and chilled bodies."[26]

Now at the top after braving wind and rain, Childs considered his infantry inadequate to the capture of the mammoth structure which lay below. Accordingly, in the words of George Gordon Meade, who took an important part in the proceedings, "a piece of artillery was taken to pieces and carried up by hand ... which ... threw shrapnel shells ... right into the palace and the open work in front. This made the place so untenable that the enemy undertook to drive us from the summit, and made a charge of cavalry and infantry up the hill. In this they were defeated, and, on retiring, were so vigorously pursued by our people, that they continued beyond the Bishop's Palace, leaving this work, with four pieces of artillery, in our hands, and they retired into the town."[27]

## 5

Pursuing the Mexicans no farther on that September afternoon, General Worth gave his tired troops a respite. At the other end of Monterey, Taylor also eased the strain of battle. There was no fighting on that side through the entire day. When Wednesday dawned, the offensive was resumed. Quitman, picking his way from Tenería on to El Diablo, sent back the exultant word that the latter fort had been abandoned in the night.[28] With hopes that the enemy was weakening, the Americans saw other signs of evacuation in every suburb of the town. Soon it was apparent to both Worth and Taylor that—with the single exception of the Citadel—Ampudia now occupied only the cathedral and territory two squares deep, in each direction, from the central plaza.[29]

To conclude that victory already was within the invaders' grasp, however, was an unsound assumption which Taylor did not entertain. Too much remained to be accomplished for an easy triumph to be foreseen. With what appeared to be a do-or-die spirit the Mexicans "had erected across the streets solid masonry walls, with embrasures for guns to fire grape, sweeping the street[s]; then all the houses in the neighborhood were occupied by their infantry, loopholes being made to enable them to fire in any direction."[30]

Having learned to count the cost of charging batteries head on, General Taylor directed his artillery to advance as circuitously as possible while the infantrymen with pick and crowbar cut their way through wall after wall from house to house into the very heart of Monterey.[31] Despite precautionary measures there was gallantry enough. Guns on both sides exacted their toll. Americans and Mexicans fought and fell.

When ammunition failed, Lieutenant Grant played a hero's part: "I volunteered to go back to the point we had started from, report our position to General Twiggs, and ask for ammunition to be forwarded. We were at this time occupying ground off from the street, in rear of the houses. My ride back was an exposed one. Before starting I adjusted myself on the side of my horse furthest from the enemy, and with only one foot holding to the cantle of the saddle, and an arm over the neck of the horse exposed, I started at full run. It was only at street crossings that my horse was under fire, but these I crossed at such a flying rate that generally I was past and under cover of the next block of houses before the enemy fired. I got out safely without a scratch."[32]

Taylor himself, disregarding danger and a constant source of concern to members of his staff, strolled calmly in the heat of battle where majors and colonels were more discreet. By every chance he should have been shot, one observer commented. When a watchful captain rushed to warn him, the General's years of experience of fighting where the balls were thickest served only to heat his combative spirit.

"Take that ax and knock in that door," he instructed the subordinate.[33]

And this was done.

## 6

William J. Worth's tactics were substantially the same. He tunneled a path through obstruction after obstruction eastward from

the west, passing the Plaza de la Capilla and the Plaza de Carne
while Taylor penetrated from the east. With half his force advancing by the Calle de Iturbide and the other half proceeding
along the Calle de Monterey, "sharpshooters mounted the roofs
and worked their guns from the housetops as the artillery swept the
streets. Axes crashed against doors, timbers fell, rifles cracked, and
men shouted in anger, triumph, or in pain."[34] When Zachary
Taylor, then only one square distant from the principal plaza,
made the mistake of withdrawing his troops to prepare for a general assault, the entire contest shifted to where Worth fought val-
iantly and continued to fight until darkness fell.[35] "The dead lay
in almost every possible position. Some of the wounded were
screaming in agony, as they were hauled off in wagons; others lay
on the ground, begging for water and assistance; some hobbled
along assisted by comrades; and a few . . . turned a mute but im-
ploring glance, as if they desired help, and knew it would not be
given."[36]

All night long, Worth's and Taylor's cannoneers bombarded the
cathedral which had been transformed from a place of worship into
a powder house. On Federation Ridge, in Cemetery Place and outside the city at its eastern gates, marksmanship was much too keen
for the quivering Ampudia's peace of mind.[37] This was the last
straw. Thursday found the Mexican general eager to capitulate.

Taylor wrote a letter to Doctor Wood in which he described the
preliminary negotiations: "I recd by the hands of a staff officer . . .
from Genl Ampudia . . . proposals for surrendering the city provided he was permitted to leave it with his army, arms & baggage
of every description; this I declined when he requested a personal
interview which ended after a protracted conversation in fixing on
three individuals to settle the terms. . . ."[38]

General Worth, Colonel Davis and Major General J. Pickney
Henderson of the Texas Volunteers were selected to represent the
United States. These officers met with Generals Tomás Requena
and José María Ortega of the Mexican Army and Governor Manuel M. Llano of the state of Nuevo Leon, and agreed upon nine
articles of which the following four were the most important:

ARTICLE 1. As the legitimate result of the operations before this place, and the present position of the contending armies, it is agreed that the city, the fortifications, cannon, the munitions of war, and all other public property, with the undermentioned exceptions, be surrendered to the commanding general of the United States forces now at Monterey.

ARTICLE 2. That the Mexican forces be allowed to retain the following arms, to-wit: The commissioned officers, their side arms; the infantry, their arms and accouterments; the cavalry, their arms and accouterments; the artillery, one field battery, not to exceed six pieces, with twenty-one rounds of ammunition.

ARTICLE 3. That the Mexican armed forces retire within seven days from this date beyond the line formed by the pass of the Rinconada, the city of Linares, and San Fernando de Pusos....

ARTICLE 6. That the forces of the United States will not advance beyond the line specified in the third article before the expiration of eight weeks, or until the orders of the respective governments can be received....[39]

## 7

In accordance with these terms, Friday, September 25, found the Mexicans marching out of Monterey and the Americans marching in to the tune of "Yankee Doodle" as the Stars and Stripes were hoisted overhead. Twenty-eight guns boomed forth from the Bishop's Palace.[40] And the dramatic moment bespoke the triumph of General Taylor, who at the not inconsequential cost of approximately eight hundred officers and men killed or wounded, had successfully stormed "impregnable" Monterey in three short days.

Despite the achievement of American arms, the future was not altogether rosy from Zachary Taylor's point of view. Trouble lay ahead, and on the home front. Taylor's liberality to Ampudia, a liberality compared by latter-day historians to the terms dictated by Grant to Lee at Appomattox at the insistence of Abraham Lincoln, constituted the cause of dissension between Taylor and some of his subordinates and later between Taylor and President Polk. For Old Rough and Ready had neither captured the Citadel nor

taken possession of the Mexican munitions nor won the unconditional surrender of the entire Mexican army or Ampudia himself.
And this was the formula called for by many Americans, in Mexico
and out.

Taylor himself was satisfied. "These terms were liberal," he
wrote to Wood, "but not considered too much so by all reflecting
men belonging to the army here especially considering our situation; besides it was thought it would be judicious to act with mag-
nanimity towards a prostrate foe, particularly as the president of
the United States had offered to settle all differences between the
two countries by negotiation, and the Mexican commander stating
that said propositions he had no doubt would be favorably met by
his go[vernmen]t as their was a gen[era]l wish for peace on the
part of the nation. . . ."[41]

Successful in the larger sense, or unsuccessful, the battle of Monterey gave to the American people an acute sense of American military courage such as they had not experienced since Andrew Jackson's victory at New Orleans. Physical bravery, ability to overcome
great odds, personal and group resourcefulness in the hour of
trial—all these qualities were emphasized, told, retold, and elaborated over American breakfast tables. Monterey was immortalized
in song and story. "We were not many," the poet wrote.

> We were not many—we who stood
>     Before the iron sleet that day—
> Yet many a gallant spirit would
> Give half his years, if but he could
>     Have been with us at Monterey.
>
> And on—still on our column kept
>     Through walls of flame its withering way;
> Where fell the dead, the living stept,
> Still charging on the guns which swept
>     The slippery streets of Monterey.

# CHAPTER XVI

## Polk and Santa Anna

### 1

In the United States, Zachary Taylor's victory at Monterey caused nation-wide rejoicing. The bonfires of Palo Alto blazed anew. Commemorative medals were struck off. Stay-at-home heroes held forth at public gatherings, and the name of Taylor was cheered from Maine to Texas. Just as after Resaca de la Palma "the news from the seat of war ... is the absorbing topic. 'General Taylor and the Army' is the toast which swells the ordinary allowance of wine in the glass to the generous overflow of the bumper. The squeaking voices of newspaper boys are modulated to the monotonous tune of 'Great news from Mexico,' and you cannot pass the *pave* in front of the Exchange unprepared with an answer to the only question asked, 'What news from Mexico?'"[1]

Day by day, as beautiful September gave way to the Indian summer weather of the Mexican winter, reports of his compatriots' jubilation reached Old Rough and Ready in his camp at Walnut Springs. The news which pleased him most of all was the conviction on the part of an overwhelming majority of the American people that he had acted wisely in the Mexican interior. Medals, promotions, votes of thanks, handsome swords, gifts of claret and champagne were but the superficial trappings of deeper, inner sentiment. This simple realization that his program was approved gave Taylor contentment and peace of mind, valued far above the laurels. "I am fully sensible," he wrote, "as well as duly grateful that the people or a majority of them have & are ready to award me an ample share of credid for my sacrifices in this war...."

Gratified by the reaction of the rank and file, the General encountered complaints and condemnation in certain quarters. Three groups of critics in Washington and elsewhere aimed darts of cal-

217

umny in his direction. More than once he felt the sting of "open & covert attacks & insinuations of numerous letterwriters & other[s], envious & sycophantic who envy acts they cannot emulate or are not inclined to accomplish." And one suspects the accuracy of his further statement that "so far as I am concerned their insinuations or attacks give me no concern."[2]

Taylor was correct in the assumption that much of the vitriol was poured upon him by the usual chronic troublemakers, standing ready at all times and in all ages to hurl abuse at gallant leaders who dare to be successful. A second and smaller but more important group of critics was composed of professional soldiers. And these men, either on account of some real or imagined slight or because they sincerely questioned the capacity of the commander, turned a deaf ear to the huzzaing in the forum and the market place and insisted that Taylor's tactics had not been intelligently conceived or properly executed.

A third group of fault-finders, more powerful and more proscriptive than either of the others, included members of the Democratic high command at the national capital and was led by no less a personage than the President himself. From the hour of its inception these party leaders had been prone to regard the Mexican War as a primarily private affair. In this spirit they had pursued without deviation their chosen program of Manifest Destiny and had loaded letter after letter to the front with aggressive language, recommending more extreme measures than Taylor had seen fit to carry out. James K. Polk had been ready to call openly for war even before the account of Thornton's skirmish reached him, and only the restraining voice of Secretary of the Navy George Bancroft had held him back.[3] Finally, when the report from the Rio Grande dramatized the issue, it was Polk who attempted to saddle Mexico with the entire burden of the blame by formally declaring that war "exists . . . notwithstanding all our efforts to avoid it."

2

Nowhere was the guile of the gaunt Tennessean more apparent

than in his attitude toward his generals. At the outbreak of hostilities Polk's logical first choice for the leadership of the invading
army was Winfield Scott, the ranking officer in his branch of the
service and one whose technical knowledge of military problems
supplemented qualities of unparalleled experience and almost legendary fortitude. Scott's name, nevertheless, had been crossed off
the President's list—avowedly on account of his supposed inability
to work in harness with the Administration, but actually because
Polk recognized his strength as a Whig presidential possibility.
Proud and petulant, learned and on occasion surprisingly petty,
Scott had come to be called Old Fuss and Feathers by those who
hated him. His loose use of the pen singled him out as a target for
ridicule and malice in nearly as great a measure as his genius for
generalship brought him a lion's share of laurels.[4] But even considering his peculiar talent for abusing and embarrassing the White
House and the Secretary of War, Scott's irrevocable Whigism was
the President's chief reason for passing him over. In a day of
intense partisan rivalry it would never do for an outstanding Whig
to win battle after battle in a Democratic war! So reasoned the
President of the United States.[5] And, thumbing the Army roster
for another man after Palo Alto and Resaca de la Palma, Polk had
picked the general who was on the spot and who already had twice
been victorious—Zachary Taylor.

At the start of the Monterey campaign Taylor possessed Polk's
confidence. But by the time that city capitulated Polk decided that
Old Rough and Ready was a Whig after all and, much to the President's dismay, a potential candidate for the White House in the
bargain. Polk's gradual change in attitude may readily be traced
in the day-by-day notations of his voluminous diary. In contrast
to glowing reminders of "gallant victories"[6] won by the unknown
Taylor early in 1846, jottings inscribed late in the same year testify
to altered feelings and stand in sharp relief.

The first blush of criticism, based solely on Taylor's alleged
errors in strategy and tactics, is far from unfair and tempered by
perspective. But, following an interview with Quartermaster General Jesup on September 5, Polk waxed adversely critical in the

extreme. Taylor, Polk feared, was "not the man for the command of the army. He is brave but does not seem to have resources or grasp of mind enough to conduct such a campaign. . . . He seems ready enough to obey orders, but appears to be unwilling to express any opinion or take any responsibility on himself. . . . He is, I have no doubt, a good subordinate officer, but . . . unfit for the chief command. Though this is so, I know of no one whom I can substitute in his place. After the late battles, which were well fought, the public opinion seems to point to him as entitled to the command."[7]

Up to this point one of Polk's principal objections was premised on the commander's failure to assume responsibility frequently enough. The events transpiring at Monterey lent a new aspect to the President's attitude, for now the man in the White House accused Taylor of shouldering too much responsibility: "In agreeing to this armistice Genl Taylor violated his express orders & I regret that I cannot approve his course."[8] So wrote Polk on October 11, and as the autumn wore on his disapprobation increased. By November 21 he was quite beside himself with anger at the soldier whom certain groups "controlled . . . for political purposes."[9] And he declared: "I am now satisfied that he is a narrow-minded, bigoted partisan, without resources and wholly unqualified for the command he holds."[10]

### 3

Such a characterization reflects little credit on the sincerity of the President, who was partisan enough himself and certainly— up to this time at least—more partisan than Taylor. Although Polk often assured both his friends and his enemies that his conduct of the Mexican War was non-political, the written record tells another story. Indeed, with few exceptions, every volunteer general who owed his commission to the federal government was a member of the Democratic party. Pitifully few Whigs received appointments. From Robert Patterson and William O. Butler through the brigadiers (one of whom was Polk's Nashville law partner, Gideon

J. Pillow) and down to the colonels and lieutenant colonels, "deserving Democrats" obtained nearly all the high commands.

President Polk, moreover, long toyed with the proposal that Senator Thomas Hart Benton—who was an able statesman but knew next to nothing about soldiering—should be given the rank of lieutenant general, thus automatically superseding both Scott and Taylor, and then should be sent to Mexico to take charge of the entire army in the field.[11] When even the partisan Democratic congressional leaders sidetracked this suggestion as utterly out of the question, Polk considered entrusting the chief command to General Patterson, who also lacked experience. Anyone but a Whig! But Patterson's birth had occurred in Ireland. Hence he could not run for the presidency as a military hero in 1848.[12] And Polk dismissed him from his mind. "I am now satisfied that anybody would do better than Taylor," wrote the baffled Tennessean.[13] Whereupon he performed the most contradictory about face of a varied career, and nominated Scott.

As recently as May, the President had confided to his diary "my determination to order Genl Scott to remain at Washington instead of taking command of the army on the Del Norte."[14] But, by November, Polk intimated to the Chief of Staff that "if I was satisfied that he had the proper confidence in the administration . . . I was disposed to assign him to the command. . . ."[15] "Nothing but stern necessity and a sense of public duty could induce me to place him at the head of so important [an] expedition," but Polk could not see "how it can be avoided."[16]

Scott in the meantime was playing every available card in an effort to gain the coveted assignment, even departing from his original position to support Polk's theory that Taylor was woefully incompetent.

The President, appreciating this new and radical approach, ordered Scott to head an expedition against the seaport city of Vera Cruz whence he was to advance over the mountains to Mexico City. Four-fifths of all the available troops were to accompany him, while Zachary Taylor was to stay in the vicinity of Monterey with enough men only to act on the defensive.[17] Although every civil and military leader of consequence—including Taylor—had approved just such an expedition, the latter had not unnaturally concluded that he would at least be given a subordinate command in the main column. The purpose of isolating Taylor seemed perfectly clear to anti-Administration editors, who analyzed it thus: Scott would reap a major portion of this campaign's rewards, splitting the plaudits of the populace with Taylor; Taylor had been selected for the Monterey expedition with a view to cutting short Scott's presidential chances; now the hero of Lundy's Lane would sail for Vera Cruz, where he ought to have ventured before, while Democrats hoped his successes might offset Taylor's mounting prestige; and yet Polk maintained that he was acting in the interest of the nation rather than in the interest of a party! So wrote the Whigs.[18]

### 4

Meanwhile the man in the White House, meddling in internal Mexican politics, was permitting himself to be duped into one of the most disastrous moves ever made by an American president. The notorious Antonio López de Santa Anna, now in exile at Havana, assured Polk through an intermediary that a mutually satisfactory treaty between the two belligerents could be concluded if Santa Anna were returned to power. "In adjusting a boundary...," the suasive Mexican argued, "the Del Norte should be the Western Texas line, and the Colorado of the West down through the Bay of San Francisco to the Sea should be the Mexican line on the north...." Mexico would cede "all East and North of these natural boundaries to the United States for a pecuniary consideration...." Thirty million dollars was mentioned as a proper sum.[19]

James K. Polk was suspicious and at first he gave no direct reply to the incredible proposal. The intermediary, he wrote, "is [a] person to whom I would not give my confidence.... His whole manner & conversation impressed me with a belief that he was not reliable.... I therefore heard all he said but communicated nothing to him."[20] Later, however, the credulous Polk discarded caution, and July found Commander Alexander Slidell Mackenzie en route to Cuba where Santa Anna anxiously awaited word. Soon the man who called himself the Napoleon of the West was receiving the welcome news that under Polk's orders Secretary of the Navy Bancroft had written to Commodore Conner: "If Santa Anna endeavours to enter the Mexican ports you will allow him to pass freely."[21] On August 12, 1846, the exile reached the Mexican coast and passed through the blockade. "He was much gratified that permission was given him to pass, and said his wife was more so."[22] Thus, with his child bride at his side, his favorite gamecocks included in the baggage, and his character unchanged, the firebrand came home to the country he had ruled so long and exploited so ruthlessly. The fireworks would soon begin.

5

What manner of man was this master spirit of Mexican unrest whom Polk's safe-conduct had spared the trouble of running the blockade? Born a decade after Taylor, Santa Anna was the son of a Jalapa mortgage broker and had attained the presidency of Mexico in 1833 after twenty tempestuous years of participation in every war or revolution that came his way. Graduated from a Vera Cruz military school before the days of the republic, he had served king and country for the first time at the age of seventeen. Between that initial resort to arms and the date of his ascension to the highest office in the land, he had fought twice against the Spanish, once against the French, and almost constantly in civil strife.

As an erstwhile confidant of Augustín de Iturbide, Santa Anna had aided that leader's rise to power and later aided as energetically in deposing him. As governor general of Yucatán and as dictator of Vera Cruz, he proclaimed benevolence and robbed the public coffers, and he found an outlet for his excess energy in a thwarted attempt to annex the island of Cuba.[23] Reveling in luxurious surroundings, gorging himself at lavish feasts, delighting in his gamecocks and his opium, he acquired a costly collection of Napoleonana and "five acknowledged bastards."[24] Possessor of a magnetic personality, he was a master organizer, brilliant in the defense of beleaguered cities and a captivating commander in the field so long as fate favored him. But if on occasion he exhibited courage in the hour of trial, more frequently he was the first to flee when the tide turned, reappearing to issue the inevitable *pronunciamento* and to claim a victory.

In the realm of politics, the story was similar. Adept at intrigue, aggressive when place and power seemed within his grasp, the Napoleon of the West failed to face crises squarely and too often he left trusted henchmen to reap the whirlwind while he retired to his hacienda as the storm passed by.[25] Such was the already eight-time President of Mexico and self-styled liberator of the Mexican people who admitted in an honest moment that "I threw up my cap for liberty ... but very soon found the utter folly of it."[26]

This was the person with whom the President of the United States chose to do business in concluding a treaty and ending a war.

6

Not long after Santa Anna's return to his native land, he showed his true colors. Disavowing the Polk-Mackenzie-Santa Anna bargain and refusing to exert his influence in favor of a treaty, he shouted: "Every day that passes without fighting at the north is a century of disgrace for Mexico."[27] The tangled state of affairs throughout the land led influential merchants, priests, and military leaders to echo this pronouncement, and it was to the one-legged Napoleon of the West that all factions turned for direction. On October 8, the ex-exile was ushered into San Luis Potosí "with as many *vivas* ... as his vanity desired."[28] And soon he was president for the ninth time.

Studying the map of Mexico, President Santa Anna saw an American military network spread over a full third of what had been the Mexican domain at the outbreak of the war. In distant California the colorful Lieutenant Colonel John Charles Frémont

ANTONIO LÓPEZ DE SANTA ANNA          PEDRO DE AMPUDIA

WILLIAM J. WORTH                    JOHN E. WOOL

MEXICAN AND AMERICAN GENERALS IN THE MEXICAN WAR

The photographs of General. Worth and General Wool are by Brady and are reproduced
through the courtesy of the United States Army Signal Corps.

had captured Sonoma in June, declaring the state independent and planting the famous Bear flag on California soil. More recently Commodore J. D. Sloat had raised aloft the Stars and Stripes on the California coast at Monterey before handing over land command to the more aggressive Robert F. Stockton. Farther to the east, Brigadier General Stephen W. Kearny had won over New Mexico to United States allegiance. Following a remarkable march from Missouri out to Santa Fé, Kearny had effected the bloodless occupation of that city and even now was joining forces with Stockton to guarantee American control of California against a Mexican adventurer named José María Flores.

As Santa Anna recruited his strength at San Luis Potosí, more and equally bad news came his way. Brigadier General John E. Wool was headed for Chihuahua, and it was rumored that part of Kearny's men were destined for the same place under Colonel Alexander W. Doniphan. On the Gulf Coast, Conner had taken Tampico, Patterson's troops had been sent to occupy it, and Brigadier General James Shields even now was on his way to join Patterson.[29] Taylor's line of defense across the states of Coahuila, Nuevo Leon, and Tamaulipas stretched from Saltillo and Monterey to Tampico and the sea. The Mexican army appeared hopelessly inadequate to cope with Old Rough and Ready's fourteen thousand men,[30] and Santa Anna was aware that only a most unusual combination of circumstances could justify his sallying forth in that direction. A break was needed.

The break came when Santa Anna intercepted a letter written by Scott and addressed to Taylor.[31] The purpose of this letter was to inform Taylor of the Vera Cruz undertaking, and it ordered him to send his entire command to join Scott's column with the exception of six thousand men. Most of the six thousand were untrained. Nearly all were volunteers. This was news to the Napoleon of the West, and he made the most of it. Although the ill-equipped Mexican army was hardly fit for fighting, many of its members still suffering from the effects of the Monterey catastrophe, Santa Anna saw that the intercepted message signaled for a Mexican offensive and he would not be denied. Santa Anna dreamed that, while the main American column was involved at Vera Cruz, he could sweep down upon Taylor, annihilate him, and return strengthened by the victory to face the larger and stronger force of Winfield Scott. It was an ingenious plan, and all but practical. And on February 2, 1847, clad in the fine apparel of the Mexican military, seated in a chariot drawn by eight mules, followed by a bevy of wanton women and many fighting cocks, the erratic liberator was sung out of the city of San Luis Potosí. Ahead stretched the sands of the Mexican desert with the "triple threat of starvation, illness and desertion" staring the rag-clad rank and file full in the face.[32] But beyond were the mountains. And somewhere in that beyond was General Taylor, stripped of his soldiers and shorn of support. It was the opportunity of a lifetime for Santa Anna.

### 7

If the full import of the Scott-Polk plan gave sanguine pleasure to Santa Anna, its effect on Taylor was almost apoplectic. Convinced since August that the Administration was trying to "break me down," he had managed heretofore to curb his criticism.[33] But now the dam broke. Anger and dismay flooded his correspondence. "I had been stripped of nearly the whole of the regular force & more than one half of the volunteers, & ordered here to act on the defensive," he grimly wrote from Monterey on January 26. "I cannot know what force will be left behind, until Genl S[cott] completes his command. . . . It seems to me the great object so far as I am concerned . . . is to keep me as much in the dark . . . as it was possible to do; particularly as far as the authorities at Washington are concerned."[34]

February 9 found Taylor's bitterness unassuaged: "One of the expectations of those who perpetrated the outrage against me was, that I would at once leave the country . . . in disgust & return to the U States which if I had done so, would have been used by them to my disadvantage. . . . But in this I shall disappoint them, as I have determined to remain & do my duty no matter under what circumstances until I am withdrawn. . . . I recd an answer from

Genl Scott to a communication I wrote him from Victoria, in which I did not disguise my feelings; he is somewhat tart in his reply. . . . He & myself now understand each other perfectly, & there can for the future be none other than official intercourse between us."[35]

It must of course be clearly understood that the interim between the Monterey armistice and Santa Anna's departure from San Luis Potosí was four months long. Characterized by marches and countermarches, by orders made and countermanded, it was a period of confusion and humiliation as far as Taylor was concerned. Polk and Marcy went over Taylor's head when they ordered General Patterson to occupy Victoria and the other towns in Tamaulipas, and Patterson did not consult Taylor as to the wisdom of the stroke. Then, when Old Rough and Ready got wind of the movement, his peremptory demand that Patterson cancel preparations for leaving the banks of the Rio Grande only served to strain the already unsympathetic relations between Taylor and the civilian authorities.[36]

A second bone of contention between them was the armistice to which Taylor and Ampudia had agreed at Monterey. Marcy was indignant at Taylor for having exceeded his authority, and he ordered the armistice to be terminated at once. On receipt of Marcy's instructions to this effect, the American general notified Santa Anna of their contents in accordance with the usages of war and at the same time prepared to occupy Saltillo, which the terms of the armistice had prevented him from entering hitherto. Containing between fifteen and twenty thousand inhabitants and situated less than seventy miles southwest of Monterey, Saltillo was the capital of the state of Coahuila and a key to the passes through the Sierra Madre Mountains.

This contemplated expedition was the third source of conflict between General Taylor and his civilian superiors. On November 8, 1846, Taylor had commanded Worth to make preparations for a march upon Saltillo. Four days later, Major Robert M. McLane arrived with dispatches from the Secretary of War advising Taylor that any advance beyond Monterey would be unsafe and that he should remain where he was.[37] Considering this information as an expression of opinion rather than a specific command, Taylor disregarded it in its entirety.[38] On November 13, he followed Worth's force of approximately one thousand men to Saltillo which they entered unopposed. Leaving Worth to garrison the place, Taylor retraced his steps and November 24—his sixty-second birthday—found him again at Walnut Springs outside the gates of Monterey.[39]

## 8

Prior to January 14, 1847, when a copy of Scott's intercepted order finally reached him, Zachary Taylor was busy cementing his line of defense from Saltillo to the Gulf. Late in December, he hastened to complete his inspection of the neighborhood by visiting Victoria. And then he hastened back to take charge of Monterey and Saltillo in the belief that the rumors that Santa Anna might soon attack would materialize.[40]

Although the Victoria expedition has been interpreted by Scott's historical adherents as a shabby excuse to avoid meeting Old Fuss and Feathers in a conference at Camargo, there was ample cause for bolstering American morale all along the line. Zachary Taylor was at his best in instilling the rank and file with confidence, and there was a special need for this at Victoria where the strutting and preening of Pillow and Patterson were expected to exert an adverse effect on the soldiers serving there. On January 4, Taylor rode into Victoria. Dressed for comfort and mounted on a mule, he spoke a few cheering words to the men in his simplest style. "General Taylor is the one, after all!" exclaimed a private from Tennessee in typical volunteer enthusiasm.[41] Soldiers met their commander several times before they knew him, so plain he was, so unpretending. "He is a full shaped man, not over large, but thick set, inclining to corpulency;—has a full, double chin, a very pleasant countenance, full of good humor, and has none of the pomp and show of power and dignity about him, of which many of his inferior officers possess so much. . . . He rode about Victoria, sometimes on a small Mexican horse, and sometimes on a very pretty mule, of a yellowish color, and with an easy gait."[42]

There followed a period when Taylor's command was depleted in compliance with the instructions of Winfield Scott. Well-trained regulars and volunteers were sent to the Brazos, to Tampico, and beyond. Robert E. Lee, Ulysses S. Grant, Meade, Mackall, Duncan, Charles F. Smith, and a host of equally promising young officers received the assignment to join Scott. Worth, who had shone at Monterey, left Taylor. Twiggs, whose services at Palo Alto and Resaca de la Palma had proved invaluable, departed. Quitman and Shields, Patterson and Pillow went their way, and not a single general officer of importance who had been under fire remained with Zachary Taylor. With the carrying out of Scott's instructions less than eight hundred regular troops stayed behind in northern Mexico. Taylor's volunteer soldiers totaled less than seven thousand and lacked experience in battle,[43] and of these only seventy per cent were in the Monterey-Saltillo vicinity. Faced with the problem of holding a vast area with such a slender force, Taylor departed from Victoria on January 16 and arrived at Monterey on January 24.

It was high time for Taylor to put in an appearance. His arrival was anything but premature. Fear and uncertainty were unnerving his command. Not only had it been learned that Santa Anna was preparing to march on Monterey, but equally disheartening was a series of disastrous scouting expeditions which resulted in the capture of nearly a hundred Americans by Mexican cavalrymen. Brigadier General Wool had cut short his contemplated Chihuahua expedition in response to Taylor's urgent order, reached Saltillo late in December, and was doing his best to allay anxiety. General William O. Butler was also exerting his influence.[44] Still the men lacked confidence, and Taylor was the only leader who seemed capable of instilling it in them.

His popularity at this time cannot be exaggerated. Though Polk and Marcy swore at him, the soldiers swore by him. They trusted him implicitly. It was his free and easy manner, his hatred of military pomp, and his undisguised concern for the welfare of his army that won and retained the affection of his men. In Victoria "Gen. Taylor visited the Illinois Volunteers . . . and the way the boys crowded around him threatened immediate suffocation."[45] Another Illinoisan who saw him at Saltillo described him vividly enough: "Taylor is short and very heavy with pronounced face lines and gray hair, wears an old oil cap, a dusty green coat, a frightful pair of trousers and on horseback looks like a toad."[46]

Such a commanding officer, a hero in homespun, was just the sort of leader his men could comprehend. His dress "is that of a plain country farmer," a Virginia admirer wrote. "He never wears a uniform; the neck-kerchief he has had on every time I have seen him has been of checked or striped cotton, and I believe un-hemmed."[47] "He looks more like an old farmer going to market with eggs to sell than anything I can . . . think of; jovial and good natured," commented Captain T. B. Kinder of Indiana.[48] Epaulets and plumes, sashes and glittering uniforms, and the inconsiderate harshness of a martinet were all foreign to Taylor's nature. This was well. For soon the "plain country farmer" from Baton Rouge and the Mississippi River bottoms would lead a motley array of untried troops into one of the most critical battles in the history of American arms.

# CHAPTER XVII

## The Battle of Buena Vista

### 1

Two days after Zachary Taylor rode into Monterey, Winfield Scott wrote to him: "I must ask you to abandon Saltillo, and to make no detachments, except for reconnaisances and immediate defence, much beyond Monterey. I know this to be the wish of the government, founded on reasons in which I concur."[1] Regarding this request as mere advice rather than as an order, Taylor brusquely replied to his superior: "I would do no such thing without orders to that effect from proper authority. . . ." On February 8 he wrote to Colonel Joseph P. Taylor: "I found most of the troops in & about Saltillo, & at once established a camp . . . on the San Luis road at a strong mountain pass where I shall in a day or two have near 5000 men, & altho, the greater portion of them will be volunteers yet I have no fears. . . ."[2]

Strictly speaking, the General's position when he wrote this letter was not at the Pass of La Angostura to which he referred. His camp was at the hacienda of Agua Nueva, ten and a half miles nearer the enemy and seventeen miles from Saltillo. To this relatively unprotected position in the shadow of the mountains, approximately four thousand six hundred and fifty troops had come by Sunday, February 14, 1847. And it was from there that, after considerable delay, Taylor sent out two parties of scouts six days later to discover whether the enemy was approaching and how far north Santa Anna had dared to penetrate.[3]

On February 21 word came almost simultaneously from Brevet Lieutenant Colonel May, who had ridden due east to La Hedionda, and from Major Ben McCulloch, who had led his Texas Rangers southward to La Encarnación, that the huge army of the Napoleon

231

of the West had reached the latter place and that General Vicente Miñon's cavalry was heading toward La Hedionda in an effort to block the road between Agua Nueva and Saltillo.[4] There was but a single course to take, and Taylor took it. Leaving behind Colonel Archibald Yell and his four hundred and seventy-nine Arkansas horsemen as a rear guard, the army retreated along the Saltillo road past La Encantada and the Angostura defile where Colonel William R. McKee's Second Kentucky Infantry and Colonel John J. Hardin's First Illinois Infantry respectively were stationed. Continuing on to the hacienda of Buena Vista, the main body of troops halted and General Wool assumed command, while Taylor rode into Saltillo to provide for the defense of that city in the event of an attack by Miñon.[5]

2

Taylor rejoined his command on Monday morning, February 22, to find it strongly established in the immediate vicinity of La Angostura, a mile and a half south of the Buena Vista ranch. Guarding the pass proper were the five field guns of Major John M. Washington, a distant relative of the first President, flanked by two companies of the First Illinois under Lieutenant Colonel William Weatherford. These soldiers commanded the parapet between the roadway and a labyrinth of deeply eroded gullies, which in themselves all but forbade assault in that quarter.[6] To the left of Washington's battery, Wool had stationed the remaining six companies of Hardin's men on the first of a series of spurs extending from the base of the sierra to the road. And to the north and east of this position the entire American army, four thousand seven hundred and fifty-nine strong, stood waiting expectantly.[7]

The Americans did not have long to wait. Charging down the valley from Agua Nueva, which Yell had hastily evacuated at midnight, came Antonio López de Santa Anna himself. With him were a strong advance force of twenty-five hundred cavalrymen and a small infantry detachment. The Mexican general might have directed a charge against Washington's guns with odds in favor of Mexican success, but this he did not do. Instead, he halted, surveyed the American position, bided his time until the rest of his force began to come up, and then dispatched Surgeon General Pedro Vanderlinden with a haughty summons addressed to Taylor.

It was typical of the arrogance of the man:

"You are surrounded by twenty thousand men, and can not in any human probability avoid suffering a rout, and being cut to pieces with your troops; but as you deserve consideration and particular esteem, I wish to save you from a catastrophe, and for that purpose give you this notice, in order that you may surrender at discretion, under the assurance that you will be treated with the consideration belonging to the Mexican character; to which end you will be granted an hour's time to make up your mind, to commence from the moment when my flag of truce arrives in your camp.

"With this view I assure you of my particular consideration. God and liberty!

"ANTONIO LÓPEZ DE SANTA ANNA"[8]

Tradition has it that Taylor's unofficial reply was "forcible" and required toning down.[9] But Brevet Major Bliss saw to it that the emissary took back a formal refusal, and Old Rough and Ready signed this brief and pithy note to General Santa Anna:

"Sir: In reply to your note of this date summoning me to surrender my forces at discretion, I beg leave to say that I decline acceding to your request.

"With high respect, I am, sir,
   "Your obedient servant,
                                    "Z. TAYLOR,
            *"Major-General U. S. Army, Commanding"*[10]

Notwithstanding the testiness of Taylor and the pomposity of Santa Anna, there was no fighting on Monday except on the extreme left of the American line. Here Colonel Humphrey Marshall and the Kentucky and Arkansas Cavalry, supported by a section of the Indiana Infantry, vied with General Ampudia's foot soldiers in an attempt to capture a commanding position immediately beneath the near-by mountain. In this minor test of strength the Americans lost, the Mexicans gained a slight advantage, and Marshall was eventually forced to retire whence he had come.[11]

Meanwhile, on left and right, there was considerable jockeying for position. Captain John Paul Jones O'Brien took charge of the Second Indiana Regiment and three supporting guns which backed up the Americans on the right, and the Second Kentucky and two additional cannons went to the succor of Washington and Hardin after the enemy made a show of strength along the roadway near the narrows.[12] Still nothing of consequence happened, and darkness enveloped the battlefield, but before the daylight faded Taylor again left the main body of his troops in Wool's charge and rode off to inspect the defenses of Saltillo.

### 3

All this was but prelude to the action of Tuesday, February 23, which actually took place at La Angostura but has come to be known in history as the Battle of Buena Vista. This was the battle on which the fate of the entire American army depended more than on any other in the course of the Mexican War. Zachary Taylor's military reputation, now second to that of no other living man in the estimate of the American people, stood to be lost or enhanced by its outcome. Outnumbered by more than four to one, made up almost entirely of volunteer troops and green volunteers at that, and containing only between four hundred and fifty and five hundred regulars, the force which faced the legions of Santa Anna was scarcely impressive from any point of view.[13] Still these handicaps were partially offset by the advantage of position which clearly lay with Taylor, Wool, and their courageous men.

The American right was secure. As Brigadier General Santiago Blanco discovered at eight o'clock on Tuesday morning, no headway could be made there. Supported by artillery, Blanco attempted to advance along the road. His men were slaughtered by Major Washington's guns, and first blood was drawn. On the American left, however, Wool's position was not nearly so impressive and he could not count on topography to counterbalance the numerical

## LEGEND

A. La Angostura, held by Washington's battery.
B. 1st Illinois, under Hardin.
C. 3rd Indiana, under James H. Lane.
D. 2nd Kentucky, under McKee, supported by Sherman's battery. (Actually 2nd Kentucky did not occupy this position until a later hour, moving from W.)
E. 2nd Illinois, under Bissell, and one section of Bragg's battery.
F. 2nd Indiana, under Joseph Lane and Bowles, and three pieces of Washington's battery.
G. Kentucky horse and one squadron of the 2nd Dragoons.
H. Arkansas horse and one squadron of the 1st Dragoons.
I. Mounted Texans, under McCulloch.
K. Humphrey Marshall with rifle companies of Arkansas and Kentucky cavalry dismounted, and Indiana and Illinois detachments.
M. Mississippi Regiment.
O. Mexican infantry and cavalry, under Blanco.
P. Mexican divisions, under Lombardini and Pacheco.
Q. Mexican battery of eight pieces.
R. Mexican light troops, under Ampudia.
S. Mexican reserves.
T. Mexican columns turning the American left.
V. Position of Mexican battery after gaining the left of the American line.
W. Bragg's battery and the 2nd Kentucky, under McKee. (Soon to move to D.)
X. Mexican cavalry, from head of column T, penetrated to this point.
Y. Springs, near hacienda of Buena Vista.
Z. Position of Gen. Wool, and later of Gen. Taylor.

## PLAN OF THE BATTLE OF BUENA VISTA

A drawing showing Gen. Taylor's operations at La Angostura, near Saltillo, Mexico, in 1847, the troops being represented in order of battle on the morning of Feb. 23. With the exception of the 2nd Kentucky Regiment, changes of position are omitted to avoid confusion. Based on a map drawn by Capt. Thomas B. Linnard from surveys by Capt. Linnard and Lieuts. John Pope and William B. Franklin, *Senate Executive Document 1, Thirtieth Congress, First Session*. And on a drawing by Brevet Capt. Lorenzo Sitgreaves, engraved for Capt. James H. Carleton's *The Battle of Buena Vista*.

superiority of the enemy. Part of the Second Illinois re-enforced Marshall as soon as it was seen that Santa Anna had increased the troops on the mountainside in the course of the night, but the Americans were still decidedly weaker than their antagonists.

The main body of the Mexicans now swung into action, Generals Francisco Pacheco and Manuel María Lombardini leading their infantry and cavalry through the ravines and against the plateau. Here Pacheco grappled with the Second Indiana under Brigadier General Joseph Lane. A full half-hour of fighting followed, and the Hoosiers stood their ground supported by Captain O'Brien and three of Washington's guns. Then Lane, sensing that the time was ripe, determined to repulse the Mexicans and ordered his command to charge. Exactly what happened next was soon lost in a welter of contradiction, to such an extent that the brave Indiana volunteers were falsely accused of cowardice. What actually happened was that an incompetent colonel, William A. Bowles, countermanded Lane's order immediately after his general issued it. Lacking every qualification for leadership in the field, Bowles became confused and told his men to fall back without designating a rallying point. The retreat became a rout. The Arkansas riflemen followed Bowles's troops. And O'Brien's gunners were left unprotected.[14]

O'Brien, therefore, also retreated. And Colonel William H. Bissell's Second Illinois Regiment, outflanked now, had no alternative but to follow suit. Now Marshall's men were isolated and these were obliged to give way before Ampudia, whose cavalrymen came pouring down upon them from the plateau.[15] In this drastic emergency, the regulars and McKee's Kentuckians stemmed the Mexican tide. Four of Colonel Hardin's companies also came. Joining in a desperate defense, Captain Thomas W. Sherman and Bragg, McKee and the First Dragoons kept the enemy at bay, and Hardin battled with the best.[16] Still it was by no means certain whether sufficient American reserves could be found to withstand the onrushing Mexicans throughout the afternoon. Many a brave man quailed as he wrestled with the enemy on that February day. A new incentive was needed—fresh energy and vigor directing a valiant offensive instead of being satisfied with holding the line. There was no time to be wasted, what with thousands upon thousands of Santa Anna's troops charging forward. There was no stopping them. Or so it seemed.

4

It was at this critical moment that General Taylor arrived on the scene. Absent from La Angostura since the previous evening, he had been engaged in strengthening Saltillo—a work of dubious value compared to the direction of operations on the battlefield. With courage typical of the man who had taken part in hand-to-hand fighting in the streets of Monterey, Taylor did not hesitate to expose himself as a target to enemy cannoneers. Joining his troops at approximately nine o'clock, he at once appeared astride Old Whitey high on the plateau within sight of all. The effect of his presence on the struggling American soldiers was almost magical.[17] For here was Old Rough and Ready in fact as well as in name, sitting calm and collected in the heat of battle. Instantaneously the combat stiffened, and Taylor seized the moment of regained confidence to take Santa Anna unawares—dispatching Colonel Jefferson Davis, his Mississippi Rifles, the Second Dragoons and some of the Indiana men to pit their strength against Ampudia's.

Davis did not hesitate. It was his chance for glory, and he grasped it. Throwing caution to one side, the anchorite of Brierfield charged Ampudia with a reckless fury that defied defeat. There was method in the madness of the man. Mexicans, both horse and foot, stunned by the shock of body impact at a time when victory seemed certain, recoiled from the north field and retreated toward the mountain. Lombardini and Pacheco encountered an equally impenetrable wall as McKee, Hardin, and Bissell poured shot into their midst.[18] American batteries, albeit few, were everywhere. Not excepting the Mississippians led by Davis, the Fourth Artillery under two captains of unquestioned ability— Bragg and Sherman—contributed more than any other unit to saving the day.

But when Sherman and Bragg retired with part of their forces from the broad ravine to guard the rear, it was the Mississippi men who again sprang into the breach. Here Colonel Davis summoned all the ingenuity at his command. Stationing his soldiers in a V formation with "both flanks resting on the ravine," he allowed the Mexican cavalry to come within easy rifle range when—each American singling out his object—"the whole head of the column fell.... A more deadly [cross] fire was never delivered,"[19] and only a remnant of the gaily bedecked lancers who a moment before had galloped so handsomely toward the Mississippi Regiment turned and retreated with Davis, Sherman, and the Indianians in pursuit.

It was now past noon. The battle had been in progress more than four hours. At the psychological instant, as the enemy was fleeing pell-mell from the plateau, thunder spoke and pelting rain deluged the contesting masses in the north field. The Mexican army fell back farther to a little cove on the side of the mountain near which it had emerged so triumphantly earlier in the day. As Bragg and Sherman turned the full power of their artillery upon them, "our shot went crashing through them, and our shells likewise, opening for themselves a bloody circle wherever they exploded." No quarter was asked, and none was given. At this stage of events Zachary Taylor should have been wary of Santa Anna's reliance upon the trickery of misrepresentation, especially in view of the letters exchanged on the previous morning. But when a Mexican officer under a flag of truce told Taylor that Santa Anna wished to "know what he wanted," many an American gun was silenced while Wool rode forward bearing the American general's reply to this singular request.[20] There was no lull on the Mexican side, however, and the American advantage—so dearly bought—was lost when many of the Mexican troops extracted themselves from their exposed position and withdrew out of canister range.

5

Now it was Santa Anna's turn to resume the offensive. Taylor, more courageous than prudent, resolved to match him blow for blow. General Francisco Perez had assumed command of all the Mexicans in the south field and on the plateau, and a battery was advancing on his right to an elevated position. Caution would have dictated the Americans' remaining strictly on the defensive, but Taylor ordered the First Illinois Infantry under Hardin to charge. Hardin was joined by McKee's Kentuckians and by the Second Illinois. Perez met them head on, and they more than met their match. No longer could it be said that "the bullets went over our heads . . . [and] sounded like a swarm of bees,"[21] for the firing of Perez' corps was true and "the lancers were fully six to one, and their long weapons were already reeking with blood."[22] It was too fierce an onslaught to withstand. Higgledy-piggledy, the volunteers fled. There was no other course. Hardin died gallantly, as did Lieutenant Colonel Henry Clay, son and namesake of the statesman. McKee, wounded more variously than tongue could tell, joined the Great Majority. All seemed lost. Only the artillerymen of Major John M. Washington, rushing to the rescue, prevented wholesale annihilation.[23]

General Taylor was in the hottest of the fight, calmly giving his orders. "His presence restored confidence," wrote one of the junior officers.[24] But now as the enemy's right wing threatened him, there was more than a moment when even Taylor's legendary immunity to Mexican bullets seemed soon to end. One ball passed through his "left sleeve above the elbow in the part between the arm and the body, making a large hole where it went in and came out. . . . It cut through both of his shirts . . . and grazed the skin of his arm. Another entered the breast of his coat, cut through the lining for several inches, and came out at the button hole, tearing it away."[25]

O'Brien, making an heroic effort, fired away at the troops of General Perez, checking them momentarily, but still they pressed on.

Again the tide turned. Captain Bragg, now a major by brevet as a result of his activities at Monterey, arrived from the north field in the nick of time and participated in an incident which tradition may have colored but which doubtless had its basis in truth.

"What are you using, Captain, grape or canister?" Old Rough and Ready is credited with asking Bragg.

"Canister, General."

"Single or double?"

"Single."

"Well, double-shot your guns and give 'em hell."[26]

As Braxton Bragg strove to carry out Taylor's order, Sherman came up and did the same. Supporting brave men from Mississippi and equally brave men from Indiana, the gun crews blasted the Mexican lines and kept them from advancing farther. Perspiring and powder-stained, gasping for air as they rammed the charges home, they showed as much grit and grimness as were ever shown on any battlefield in all the tide of time.

It was a terrific fight. Toward five o'clock on that Tuesday afternoon, superior American morale asserted itself and a gap opened in the Mexicans' ranks. Another instant, and those ranks collapsed—bent and broken. Here and there a last grim remnant of Santa Anna's thousands stood firm as the most courageous of the Mexicans drizzled a last shower of shot upon the vanguard of Americans.[27] It was ineffectual. The weary soldiers could fight no longer. Buena Vista was history, and the battle would be memorialized in verse by Theodore O'Hara, the Kentucky poet who was the son of Taylor's old Kentucky schoolmaster:

> The muffled drum's sad roll has beat
>   The soldier's last tattoo;
> No more on Life's parade shall meet
>   That brave and fallen few.
> On Fame's eternal camping-ground
>   Their silent tents are spread,
> And Glory guards, with solemn round,
>   The bivouac of the dead.
>
> Long had the doubtful conflict raged
>   O'er all that stricken plain,
> For never fiercer fight had waged
>   The vengeful blood of Spain;

THE BATTLE OF BUENA VISTA

By Carl Nebel. First reproduced in Kendall's *History of the War between the United States and Mexico*. By odds the best pictorial interpretation of the battle, it is not entirely satisfactory in that the terrain appears far more level and passable than it actually was. Taylor and his staff are seen in the center foreground. Bragg's battery is advancing from the right, and Davis' Mississippians from the left. The dark hill in the left background is the one which Marshall's men attempted to command on the evening of February 22.

And still the storm of battle blew,
 Still swelled the gory tide;
Not long, our stout old chieftain knew,
 Such odds his strength could bide.

'Twas in that hour his stern command
 Called to a martyr's grave
The flower of his beloved land,
 The nation's flag to save.
By rivers of their father's gore
 His first-born laurels grew,
And well he deemed the sons would pour
 Their lives for glory too. . . .[28]

## 6

Buena Vista was over, yet who had won the battle? Through the whole of one day and part of another, two evenly matched armies had fought to a standstill. Santa Anna, the aggressor, had gained no ground. Nor had Taylor, who for the most part remained on the defensive. At least eighteen hundred Mexicans had been killed or wounded compared to the American casualty list of six hundred and seventy-three, and the Mexicans who fled the field never to return could not be counted. At the close of hostilities on February 23, however, Santa Anna's army still was larger and fresher than Taylor's. And who could forecast the morrow, when another Mexican attack might be as fraught with fury as that of Tuesday morning?[29]

John Ellis Wool and others advised a general retreat, but Old Rough and Ready would not consider withdrawing. Determined to stand his ground throughout the night, he was constantly alert for the trouble that did not come. Santa Anna's worries were greater than his own, and of a different kind. Fear played its part. Canister and leveled bayonets and gun-swept causeways had taken a heavy Mexican toll not alone in lives but also in morale. Thus it was that in the dead of night, while the teeth of Taylor's subordinate generals still chattered with terror, the man who chose to call himself the Napoleon of the West led his disheartened legions in disorganized retreat.

It was a macabre procession—like an army of the dead. So gay those Mexicans had been, so confident, so heartless—and that only forty hours before. Now the Mexican army was a confused mass, withdrawing painfully to San Luis. "The sight of the dead bodies, the death rattle of the dying, the moaning of the wounded, and the cursing of all, added new griefs to the spirits already sad with so many sufferings. The spectacle presented to view infused the most painful misery: the walking over the dead, and the trampling upon those who had not yet breathed their last. Here a woman was sobbing over the body, now lifeless, of her husband, and there, another ministering to hers, tortured with his wounds. Some washed dirty clothes in the water full of mire and blood. Some hushed their little children, who cried without knowing wherefore. The wagons and trains blocked up the road, the pack animals stumbled at every step. The saddle horses and draught mules, fatigued, and without anything to eat, could scarcely move. All was confusion, all wretched, and all enduring privations. At least, on the field of battle, the night, with its protecting shades, covered half the disasters; but in Aguanueva the picture of horrors of the retreat was revealed in all its deformity."[30]

When the sun crowned the sierras at La Angostura on Wednesday morning, February 24, Taylor and his troops anticipated battle. To their delight and infinite relief, the hosts of the enemy were seen retreating.[31]

Buena Vista was no defeat.

It was an American victory. And what a victory! And what far-reaching ramifications it contained!

# CHAPTER XVIII

## A Military Apotheosis

### 1

GENERAL TAYLOR had been criticized in certain quarters for his failure to seize the army of Mariano Arista at Matamoros immediately after the Battle of Resaca de la Palma. He had been castigated by no less a personage than the President of the United States because he did not demand and obtain the unconditional surrender of Pedro de Ampudia following the attack on Monterey. It was typical of the man to let well enough alone, and never was this attitude more justifiable than on February 24, 1847, when the paralyzed condition of his men and horses led Taylor to reconnoiter and recuperate his strength instead of trailing the Mexicans immediately.

As the hours passed, the General enjoyed a steadily increasing appreciation of the significance of Buena Vista. What he had recognized at first as an important but perhaps temporary triumph of the American arms was shown to be both permanent and vital. On February 25 the indefatigable Bliss was sent to the enemy's camp at Agua Nueva to discuss an exchange of prisoners and care of the wounded, and at that time Santa Anna still cherished a scheme to renew the struggle, or so he said. Subsequent events proved that Santa Anna either was then seeking to discourage Taylor from pursuing or had deluded himself into magnifying his own diminished power, for he never again faced American troops at La Angostura or Taylor anywhere.

When the Americans advanced to La Encarnación on Tuesday, March 2, the main body of Mexicans was already out of sight and the rear guard of lancers could be seen on the horizon. The Mexican dead and wounded had been left behind, equipment had been discarded, and reports from the south included the ungallant picture of General Santa Anna fleeing with the foremost and letting the hindmost take care of themselves. Tattered legions of disgruntled Latins and confused and weary Indian conscripts, their throats parched and stomachs empty, were trudging across the interminable wasteland.[1] And the sight was enough to convince even a Doubting Thomas of the full import of Buena Vista.

## 2

Zachary Taylor's letters reflect little jubilation. "The great loss on both sides . . . ," he confided to his brother Joseph, "has deprived me of everything like pleasure. . . ."[2] He was convinced, moreover, that heavy American casualties might have been avoided, and the possibility afforded him little peace of mind: "If Scott had left me five hundred or one thousand regular Inf[antr]y the Mexican army would have been completely broken down, & the whole of their artillery & baggage taken or destroyed. . . ."[3] Granting the need of a strong column at Vera Cruz, there was no reason for stripping Taylor of his command unless the "powers that be" intended "breaking me down." These "powers" had hoped for one of three results—the resignation, retreat, or defeat of Zachary Taylor, any one of which would have caused him to lose caste in the eyes of the American people. Such, at least, was the General's theory.[4] Previously provoked at the Administration, he was now quite beside himself with anger. He was satisfied that selfish motives of political partisans had caused the needless slaughter of his troops, and he had only contempt for "Scott, Marcy & Co."[5]

To both officers and men, the General distributed laurels with a lavish hand in his report to the War Department. To Wool's instructions prior to the battle and to "his gallantry and activity on the field, a large share of our success may . . . be attributed." The Mississippi Rifles "sustained throughout the engagement the reputation of veteran troops. . . . Colonel Davis, though severely wounded, remained in the saddle until the close of the action. . . ." The artillery batteries "were nearly all detached at different times, and in every situation exhibited conspicuous skill and gallantry."

Only the Indiana Volunteers had "fallen back in disorder" and "could not be rallied"—statements which the Indiana men were to deny vehemently in after years—and they alone received a reprimand. As for the soldiers as a whole, "exposed for successive nights, without fires, to the severity of the weather, they were ever prompt and cheerful in the discharge of every duty; and finally displayed conspicuous gallantry in repulsing, at great odds, a disciplined foe."[6]

In paying tribute to the dead, Taylor's sentiments betrayed his emotions. Among the fallen were some of the noblest and the best—Yell of Arkansas, the handsome auburn-haired ex-Governor who had left his seat in Congress to die at the head of his regiment; George Lincoln of Massachusetts, the promising young officer who had been brevetted captain for gallant conduct earlier in the war and who was a son of the distinguished Levi Lincoln and a distant relative of Congressman-elect Abraham Lincoln; Captains T. B. Kinder of Indiana, William S. Willis of Kentucky, and Andrew R. Porter of Arkansas; also John J. Hardin of Illinois, daring and ingenuous, the favorite of the Whigs in the Prairie State and one of whom Abraham Lincoln could say without exaggeration, "We lost our best Whig man."[7]

These gallant patriots were typical of others who perished at Buena Vista. Referring to Clay, McKee, and Hardin, General Taylor said: "The cool and steadfast courage with which they maintained their positions during the day, fully realized my hopes. . . ." To the sorrowing Henry Clay, senior, the master of Ashland, Taylor penned the most gracious note of all: "A grateful people will do justice to the memory of those who fell. . . . To your son I felt bound by the strongest ties of private regard; and when I miss his familiar face, and those of McKee and Hardin, I can say with truth that I feel no exultation in our success."[8] Other private letters expressed similar sympathy and sadness.

3

After Buena Vista the General was certain that the Administration would not give him an opportunity to fight again in Mexico. Already Scott had captured Vera Cruz. Now he was marching up to Mexico City, but Taylor knew too much to hope for even a minor role in that campaign. The chance that hostilities might be renewed in the north was equally slim. "It seems to me," he wrote Doctor Wood, "if we have another serious fight in this direction, or with this column, it will not be this side [of] San Luis Potosi...."[9]

Reconciling himself to spending the spring and summer of 1847 in the camp at Walnut Springs, Taylor did not squander his newly acquired leisure. He wrote lengthy letters to friends and relatives about plantation and family affairs. He gradually developed a political correspondence and even a political interest. He trained volunteers for service under General Scott and he directed operations against bandit rancheros. Portrait painters consumed a portion of the General's time. Concerning Jesse Atwood's work, he wrote: "Without being decided fine, I imagine the likenesses painted of me by Mr. Atwood are tolerable; the one which has just been finished by a Mr. Brown from Richmond is said by those who understand or are judges of such matters to be a much better painting; Mr. B. has nearly completed a group of officers, myself & staff in addition to several others, which I imagine will be considered a good painting by connoisseurs; he is now engaged in making a painting describing the battle ground of Buena Vista...."[10]

If most of the dainty daubers failed to catch his spirit, written pictures were on the whole more creditable. Taylor's unaffected simplicity did nearly as much as his four victories to enhance his popularity, and the newspapermen at Monterey vied with one another in portraying this quality. Taylor made his home in a "common wall tent" which contrasted favorably with the pomp surrounding Scott, and shielded from the sun by pecan branches he maintained his voluminous correspondence from his seat on a camp stool, using a trunk for a table. Equally simple was the outdoor kitchen, over which an orderly presided and which a journalist described: "Here are barrels, tubs made out of barrels, tin dishes,

GENERAL TAYLOR AND HIS STAFF

At Taylor's Walnut Springs headquarters, near Monterey, some weeks after the Battle of Buena Vista. Bareheaded, Zachary Taylor stands near the center of the picture. The other officers are: (seated) Brevet Brigadier General Henry Whiting, Brevet Lieutenant Colonel Joseph H. Eaton, Brevet Major Robert S. Garnett; (standing) Brevet Lieutenant Colonel William W. S. Bliss, Brevet Colonel Joseph K. F. Mansfield, Brevet Lieutenant Colonel Braxton Bragg, Brevet Major George D. Ramsay, Brevet Colonel John Munroe, Brevet Major Amos B. Eaton, Surgeon Presley H. Craig. At the far left an orderly holds Old Whitey. From a lithograph formerly in Tappahannock Court House, Essex County, Virginia.

and the good old coffee-pot, arranged before you, with not a few stumps of old trees. . . . It is all out of doors, for there is nothing but a rude roof, made of slabs, with a few large rocks piled up beneath it on one side, against which the fire is made, to keep it from being utterly blown away. Don't forget the harness of General Taylor's travelling wagon, upon one of the corners of the . . . [mess-tent], part of which you see on the right, with the interpreter's tent between it and the General's."[11]

"I regard him as one of the noblest specimens of human nature I ever saw," declared a Virginia officer. He is "perfectly unaffected by his brilliant successes, plain and unassuming in his kind manners, mild and affable in his disposition, and kind and courteous in his demeanour. You feel at once comfortable and easy in his society. He paid me a visit the other day; I was sitting on a trunk writing at the time; I arose and offered him the seat, remarking that I had but a poor seat to offer him; oh, never mind, said he, all I am afraid of is that I will spoil the trunk, and he sat down and conversed in the most sociable and familiar manner for some time."[12] Tales like this were related in letters written by homesick youths to anxious mothers and were exaggerated and elaborated for political purposes. They produced a profound impression in the United States. The Taylor Tradition became embedded in current American folklore, and the General's personality grew almost legendary while he yet lived.

Even more important than the human interest element was the effect of time and distance in adding to Taylor's popularity. Many hundred miles separated the Mexican battlefields from the heart of America. Communications were primitive. Accounts of the struggles in which the General participated were frequently garbled or twisted when they were read by the people in their homes. Curiously enough, the first tidings of all four of Taylor's battles brought word of defeat. And each time the initial report was subsequently denied and, the truth being known, joy was uncontained. The significance of this psychological factor can hardly be overemphasized, for the commander who had previously been cursed or lamented because of a "defeat" inevitably emerged with the new day as a glorious hero, and each triumph was instrumental in adding to his heroic stature.

4

While Taylor remained at Monterey looking forward to his homeward journey, Winfield Scott was winning victory after victory in a campaign that carried him from Vera Cruz into central Mexico. On April 18, at Cerro Gordo, Scott's column scored its first victory over Santa Anna's men who were still suffering from the shock they had received at Taylor's hands at Buena Vista. Smashing successes followed at Contreras, Churubusco, Molino del Rey, and Chapultepec, and on September 14 Mexico City itself was occupied by the American army. Two days later Santa Anna resigned the Mexican presidency, to be succeeded by the moderate Manuel de la Peña y Peña.[13] Negotiations for a permanent treaty were about to be reopened between Peña y Peña's government and Nicholas P. Trist, whom Polk had assigned to represent the United States. General Taylor felt certain that peace was soon to come, and on October 27 he wrote from Walnut Springs: "I have fixed on the 8th of Novr for leaving here for Matamoras, & expect to reach there by the 18th where I intend to await the action of the dept on my application for permission to leave the country, & if ... favorable I will sail on the first good vessel that leaves the Brazos for N. Orleans. . . ."[14]

Accompanied by General Wool and by the staffs of both generals, Taylor at last bade farewell to Monterey on the morning of Monday, November 8. He encamped that night at Ramos, reached Marín twenty-four hours later and on Friday afternoon arrived at Mier where the officers of the Third Dragoons provided a light collation in his honor. He left Mier on Saturday aboard the steamer *Major Brown* and was saluted by salvos of artillery on his arrival at Camargo, where on Sunday he reviewed a grand parade of the Tenth Infantry. Monday morning found Wool returning to Walnut Springs, while Taylor took the *Colonel Cross* on the last leg of the journey to Matamoros.[15]

At Matamoros the General received the long-anticipated leave of absence and, journeying the remainder of the way down the Rio Grande to Brazos Island on the steamer *McKee,* he boarded the *Monmouth* on Friday, November 26, and sailed for New Orleans.[16] "There were several sick and wounded volunteers on the boat. . . . General Taylor . . . ordered these men to be placed in his state-rooms, and proper attention paid them. It was a cold, rainy day when this occurred. The deck hands . . . did not know General Taylor. The wind blew high, and the firemen had raised a sail in front of the boilers to protect themselves from the rain, and under this sail there were some old mattrasses; here General Taylor laid down and went to sleep. At supper time great inquiries were made for the General, and servants sent off to look him up. But he could not be found! At last some one going below, inquired of a fireman if he had seen any thing of such and such a man—the fireman said no, but added, 'there is a clever old fellow asleep there under the sail, in front of the fire!' It was General Taylor."[17]

This was one of the last of the Taylor anecdotes connected with his services in the United States Army on active duty. Like the many others of the bygone years, it would be spread far and wide in 1848. Now it was still 1847. On Tuesday evening, November 30, after a four-day voyage aboard the *Monmouth,* the General was transferred to another vessel, the *Mary Kingsland,* at the South-west Pass below New Orleans. The *Daily Picayune* described the scene: "We have an account from an eye witness of the reception of the General from the moment the Monmouth came into sight, and by discharges of cannon and display of her flags announced that she was bearing home to Louisiana her distinguished citizen. He was received with cheers on the Mary Kingsland, and every steamboat and every ship from the bar to the pilot station mustered its hands and cheered a welcome. . . ."[18]

On his way up the river, Taylor stopped off for an hour and a half at the plantation of Colonel Maunsel White, his agent and cotton broker, before proceeding to the Jackson Military Barracks where Mrs. Taylor, Betty Taylor and the Woods were waiting. Wednesday and Thursday he spent at the Barracks in the bosom of his family, surrounded by intimate friends and visited by acquaintances of long standing. "He appears to be in excellent health," the *Daily Picayune* noted. "In person he is thinner than when he left the United States." The reporter could not forego commenting on the General's "diffidence which increases with increasing fame."[19] Weary from handshaking but otherwise rested, Taylor was apprised of the elaborate ceremonies which had been arranged for Friday, December 3, when he was to be the recipient of the most lavish tribute in New Orleans' history since the days of Andrew Jackson and Pakenham's defeat.

5

When Friday dawned, all New Orleans was in readiness. At break of day the ships in the port hoisted their colors. Balconies, windows, housetops were festooned. Before ten o'clock, while the cannon thundered, the committee on arrangements was sailing downstream on the *Mary Kingsland* to the Barracks, where Taylor and his staff prepared to join them. Promptly at eleven, the General went aboard.[20] As the *Mary Kingsland* again got under way, more than one observer apotheosized him: "With his stalwart form distinguished from all others, his firm, erect, and military position, his head uncovered, and his grey hairs streaming in the wind, he looked . . . like a conquering hero of the olden time."[21] Walt Whitman has left a more realistic impression of a "jovial, old, rather stout, plain man, with a wrinkled and dark yellow face."[22] But such a description was not exalted enough for the enthusiast who wrote: "The cheers that greeted him could have been heard in the distant forest, while the waving handkerchiefs and glancing smiles of . . . [the ladies] testified the sincerity with which they joined in the admiration that heroism and bravery have ever won from those whose smiles the soldier deems his best reward."[23] It was an age when gallantry still survived, and Zachary Taylor was the object of greater attention and applause than had been his portion during all of the first sixty-three years of his life.

With the packet *America* towering highest in the fleet of four-

teen boats, the *Mary Kingsland* led the way upstream past shores
lined with vessels which were crowded from deck to masthead
with the cheering multitudes. Reaching the municipality of Lafay-
ette, the regatta turned and sailed back as far as the historic Place
d'Armes where the ships rounded to. Here forty thousand persons
had gathered. Taylor, alighting on the wharf, strode into the jam-
packed square between two lines of soldiers. A grand salute of a
hundred guns from each municipality proclaimed his landing. A
triumphal arch had been erected in the center of the Place d'Armes,
and the name of the hero and the hero's victories were displayed
upon it, the entire frame being covered with evergreens.[24] In such
a setting, with the crowd's huzzas echoing above the thunder of
the guns, Mayor Abdiel D. Crossman delivered the official greet-
ing:

"General: In behalf of the city of New Orleans . . . it is my
pleasing office to welcome your happy return to your country and
your home; and in behalf of the Municipal Councils, I tender to
you the hospitality of this city, whilst it is your pleasure to remain
among us. . . .

"Wherever you direct your steps, upon any spot where the star-
spangled banner triumphantly expands its folds to the breeze, you
will find a nation's love to greet you—you will bear a whole people's spontaneous applause to extol the splendour of your deeds,
which your modesty would in vain endeavour to weaken in your
own eyes.

"Again, General, I bid you a hearty welcome, in the name of all
the citizens of New Orleans."[25]

Taylor appeared to be deeply affected by the Mayor's address.
His response was typical of the speeches which he would be called
on to deliver many times in the weeks and months to come. He
made it haltingly and not without emotion:

"Mr. Mayor: The welcome which I meet this day . . . over-
whelms me with feelings which no words can express. You have

been pleased to qualify, with terms of the highest approbation, the services of the army which I have had the honour to command in Mexico. Could those brave officers and soldiers, whose gallantry achieved the successes to which you refer, be present on this occasion ..., the measure of my satisfaction would be complete. For them and myself, I thank, from my heart, the people of New Orleans, and accept, Mr. Mayor, the offer of their hospitality."[26]

Following General Taylor's speech, he repaired with his staff and the officials of the day to the Cathedral of Saint Louis—Catholic center of a predominantly Catholic city—where the *Te Deum* was sung and Taylor's moderation and humanity in battle were lauded by Bishop Antoine Blanc.

Soon the company was leaving the cathedral, and the enthusiasm of the crowd soared to a new height when—instead of taking his seat in a carriage as had been originally planned—Zachary Taylor mounted the weather-beaten white horse that had shared the trials of Buena Vista with its master. During the war Old Whitey had become a symbol of Taylor's prowess on the field of arms; now hairs were pulled from his tail by those among the onlookers who sought a souvenir. From the cathedral the seemingly endless procession with the General and his staff on horseback at its head, wound its way through the Vieux Carré and across Canal Street to the palatial St. Charles Hotel. Here Taylor dismounted and took his stand between the pillars of the colonnade while the parade passed before him.

"The whole of the colonnade, the pavement below, the street in front, the windows of the St. Charles, the doors of all the buildings near, the large galleries of the verandah, and the neighboring streets, presented one mass of human beings; so dense was the crowd ... that the procession was frequently brought to a complete pause by the pressure and inability to proceed. The cheering was loud and incessant, and there seemed no bounds to the delight and enthusiasm of the congregated multitude. At length the procession had passed, and as the general turned to enter the hotel, the long, loud, and continued cheer, made the very welkin ring."[27]

6

But the adulation of the throng was not appeased, and the General's fellow citizens pressed about him. He retired to a private parlor in the St. Charles and there he was lionized, and at seven o'clock in the evening he received the Governor of Louisiana, Isaac Johnson, an old Feliciana friend, who conducted him to the grand banqueting hall of the hotel. Here he was toasted by two hundred and fifty of the city's most distinguished residents, and the orchestra saluted him with "Hail to the Chief!" Taylor rose and raised his glass. "The citizens of New Orleans!" he exclaimed. "Unsurpassed for their hospitality, intelligence and enterprise."[28] Tremendous enthusiasm throughout the hall. More music. And more toasts.

The toasts continued interminably, and the festivities went on far into the night, but at a relatively early hour General Taylor and Mayor Crossman left their fellow diners at their brandy and liqueurs and departed to visit the principal theaters. Their first stop was the St. Charles Theater where a musical "extravaganza," *The Fair One with the Golden Locks,* was being performed. At the American they saw George Jamieson, one of the most talented actors of his day, in Bulwer's *Richelieu.* At the Orleans the General's entrance was heralded by "Taylor's March," and he and his party witnessed a more varied program—the first act of *La Dame Blanche* and vaudeville.[29]

The hotel was still illuminated when the General returned from his dramatic debauch. "Between the pillars of the colonnade . . . were suspended . . . variegated lanterns under chaplets of live oak. In front of the ladies' parlor was a transparency of the General, in the old brown coat, with the motto—'A little more grape, Captain Bragg!' In front of the gentlemen's parlor was another transparency of the General, with the words—'I have no reinforcements to give you, but Major Bliss and I will sustain you!' "[30]

Thus the essence of reality expanded into the realm of mythological exaggeration, and Zachary Taylor's acts of bravery, simplicity, or kindness were magnified by the adoring multitudes and by clever party managers. On Saturday the festivities continued,[31] and it was not until nine o'clock Sunday morning, December 5, 1847, that the hero and his suite fled the plaudits of the Crescent City aboard the steamboat *Missouri* bound for Baton Rouge.

There was glory enough higher up the Mississippi. Shortly after leaving New Orleans, the *Missouri* overtook the *Majestic* and *Pride of the West*—and the passengers cheered Taylor wildly. On either bank clusters of men and women, surrounded by their children, waved and cried out to him and called him good. The Negroes joined in the riverside acclaim, improvising a merry song in honor of "ole Massa Rough an' Ready." As the *Missouri* neared Donaldsonville, artillery flashed and thundered, and Taylor saw flags flying from every staff that could have been erected. The mayor of Donaldsonville, accompanied by Lieutenant Governor Trasimond Landry, came aboard to salute the General and to escort him through the little town to the banquet hall where, after being eloquently toasted, Zachary Taylor gallantly raised his glass to "The Ladies of Donaldsonville—Unsurpassed in beauty and grace; health and prosperity to those who have husbands, and early marriages to those who have not."[32]

When the *Missouri* reached Baton Rouge, the reception almost overwhelmed the General. Here were friends and neighbors. Here was home. Stiff was the spokesman's speech: "I feel, sir, that I cannot convey to you in adequate terms the pleasure and gratification with which those who now surround you, once more welcome you home. Of this, however, be assured that I but faintly reflect their feelings of attachment and respect ... in tendering you a thrice hearty welcome."[33]

Spontaneous was the crowd's acclaim. Tears welled in Taylor's eyes.

It was at Baton Rouge in the old "Spanish cottage" on the military reservation, just outside the city limits and a few yards from the Barracks, that Taylor was to spend the greater portion of the ensuing thirteen months.

In Zachary Taylor's life, and in the nation's, a campaign year waited in the offing—a year in which the General was to be given the command of the entire Western Division of the Army but in which he was to see no active service in the field. A long and not inglorious chapter of his life was ended. Henceforth Old Rough and Ready would forsake the military to plunge into political pursuits.

THE END

# NOTES

# CHAPTER I

[1] Zachary Taylor's autobiographical sketch, Zachary Taylor Papers, Manuscript Division, Library of Congress, Washington.

[2] James Taylor, the first, came to America about 1660. He was probably born in Carlisle, England. A landowner, lawyer and public official, he lived in Saint Stephen's Parish, New Kent County (later King and Queen County), Virginia. He died April 30, 1698. The last name of his first wife, Frances, is unknown. She died April 22, 1680, and was the great-great-grandmother of General Zachary Taylor. *Cf.* Fred G. Taylor *et al., James Taylor, Emigrant* (1933), *passim.*

[3] Fear Brewster, daughter of Elder William Brewster, married Isaac Allerton, a *Mayflower* Pilgrim, Assistant Governor of the Plymouth Colony and later a prominent New York merchant. Their son, Isaac Allerton, moved to Virginia where his daughter, Sarah Allerton, married Hancock Lee. The Hancock Lees' daughter, Elizabeth Lee, married Zachary Taylor, grandson of James Taylor, the first. Their son was Lieutenant Colonel Richard Taylor, father of General Zachary Taylor. Through Isaac Allerton, the elder, General Taylor was a fourth cousin, three degrees removed, of Franklin D. Roosevelt. Through Hancock Lee's father, he was a fourth cousin, one degree removed, of Robert E. Lee. *Cf.* Alvin Page Johnson to Editor of Louisville *Courier-Journal, Courier-Journal,* July 9, 1934.

[4] James Taylor, the second, was born in 1673 and died January 23, 1729. On December 23, 1699, he married Martha Thompson. *Cf.* Alice E. Trabue, " 'Spring Hill,' Oldham County, Ky.," *Register of the Kentucky State Historical Society,* XVIII, *passim.*

[5] James Madison and Zachary Taylor. Although Madison was thirty-three years older than Taylor, they were of the same generation in Taylor genealogy.

[6] Zachary Taylor, the General's grandfather, was born April 17, 1707, and died in 1768. For a picture of Taylor family life in Orange County at a slightly later date, see the diary of Colonel Francis Taylor. A typewritten copy of this diary is owned by Jaquelin P. Taylor of Orange and Richmond, Virginia.

[7] Zachary Taylor to Lyman C. Draper, October 30, 1848, Kentucky Papers, Draper Collection, Wisconsin State Historical Society, Madison.

[8] *Idem;* F. B. Heitman, *Historical Register of Officers of the Continental Army During the War of the Revolution* (1893), 394; Louise Phelps Kellogg (editor), *Frontier Advance on the Upper Ohio, 1778-1779* (1916), *passim.*

[9] Richard Taylor, father of the General, was the third and youngest son of Zachary Taylor and Elizabeth Lee. He was born April 3, 1744 (March 22, 1744, Old Style), and died January 19, 1829. Sarah Dabney Strother,

the General's mother, was the daughter of William Strother and Sarah Bayley Pannill. She was born December 14, 1760, and died December 13, 1822 (Taylor Family Papers, Trist Wood Collection, New Orleans).

[10] John Chaplin Strother *et al.*, "The Strother Family," *Register of the Kentucky State Historical Society*, XXV, 300.

[11] Reminiscences of Samuel Woolfolk, Louisville *Courier-Journal*, July 16, 1893.

[12] In 1784 Montebello was the home of Valentine Johnson and of his widowed mother, Mrs. Elizabeth Cave Johnson, who was a sister of Mrs. Richard Taylor's stepmother. The principal authorities for the statement that Zachary Taylor was born at Montebello are: Benjamin Valentine Johnson of Montebello, son of Valentine Johnson; Colonel Benjamin Johnson Barbour, who derived the information from his mother, a niece of Valentine Johnson; Colonel Mercer Slaughter, who was intimately associated with the Taylor and Johnson families; Colonel John Willis, who had it "direct from Mr. Charles Howard," Zachary Taylor's cousin by marriage. Mrs. Winifred Brent Russell of Gordonsville, Virginia, a direct descendant of Valentine Johnson, told the author in September, 1934, that members of her family always believed Zachary Taylor to have been born at Montebello. William Wallace Scott gave full credence to the Montebello version in his *History of Orange County, Virginia* (1907), 207-208. Trist Wood of New Orleans, whose study of Tayloriana is exhaustive, likewise leans toward Montebello. The late Philip Fall Taylor, who contemplated writing a biography of the General, compiled a sketch in which he said that Zachary Taylor was born at the Johnson place. H. J. Eckenrode, Director of the Virginia Division of History and Archaeology, believes Montebello to be the birthplace though admitting the difficulty of identifying it with any degree of finality. On the other hand, W. S. Trimmer, who owned Hare Forest prior to his death in 1929, was adamant in the conviction that Hare Forest was the birthplace. Since neither the General nor his parents stated exactly where he was born, campaign biographers assumed he was born at Hare Forest—and this conjecture early became embedded in the Taylor tradition. The author visited both "birthplaces" in 1934; listened to both sides of what has become a favorite topic of conversation in the vicinity of Orange Courthouse; and viewed the two commemorative markers, one placed at Hare Forest by the Daughters of the American Revolution, the other at Montebello by the Commonwealth of Virginia. The absence of documentary evidence, definitely establishing the place of birth, leaves the door open to doubt. The weight of traditional evidence, however, as outlined above, is decidedly in favor of Montebello.

[13] Richard Taylor was at the Falls of the Ohio on March 31, 1785 *(Calendar of Virginia State Papers*, IV, 20). There is no record of Richard Taylor's presence in Kentucky from May to August 2, a period somewhat longer than the time necessary to go from Kentucky to Virginia and return. On August 2 he personally took the oath of fidelity to the Commonwealth as Justice of the Peace for Jefferson County (Ludie J. Kinkead, editor, "Minute Book No. 1, Jefferson County, Kentucky, April 6, 1784-Decem-

ber 7, 1785," *Filson Club History Quarterly*, VI, 290). It is possible but improbable that Zachary Taylor was brought to Kentucky by an overland route. Richard Taylor was familiar with the water route, which was easier on women and children. All members of the Taylor family who went from Orange County, Virginia, to Kentucky in the years immediately following 1785 traveled overland to Redstone and then floated down the rivers to their new homes (Diary of Colonel Francis Taylor, typewritten copy, in possession of Jaquelin P. Taylor of Orange and Richmond, Virginia).

[14] Reuben T. Durrett, *The Centenary of Louisville* (1893), 47.

[15] *Ibid.*, 57-58; Lewis Collins and Richard H. Collins, *History of Kentucky* (1874), II, 359.

[16] Durrett, *op. cit.*, 61.

[17] Edward P. Humphrey and Thomas H. Cleland, *Memoirs of the Rev. Thomas Cleland . . .* (1859), 18.

[18] Kitty Anderson, "Soldiers Retreat: A Historic House and Its Famous People," *Register of the Kentucky State Historical Society*, XVII (51), 72.

[19] George Croghan's mother was Lucy Clark, sister of General George Rogers Clark, and of William Clark of Lewis and Clark fame, and of Elizabeth Clark, first wife of Richard Clough Anderson the elder. George Croghan's father, William Croghan, served with distinction in the Revolution. It is probable that Zachary Taylor often heard tales of heroism and hardship from George Rogers Clark's own lips.

[20] Elisha Ayer's last name is erroneously spelled Ayres in previous biographies of Zachary Taylor. The eldest son of Nathan Ayer and Desire Tracy, he was born in 1767 and died December 18, 1858. His home was near Preston, Connecticut, six miles east of Norwich. *Cf.* Frances Manwaring Caulkins, *History of Norwich, Connecticut* (1866), 538n.; Norwich *Chronicle*, December 22, 1858; *New England Genealogical Register*, XIII, 181.

[21] J. Reese Fry and Robert T. Conrad, *A Life of Gen. Zachary Taylor* (1848), 16. This was probably Lewis Wetsel. "Whetsel" is an incorrect spelling.

[22] Oliver Otis Howard, *General Taylor* (1892), 23.

[23] A. C. Quisenberry, "Colonel George Croghan, the Hero of Fort Stephenson," *Register of the Kentucky State Historical Society*, X (29), 23-24; *Biographical Encyclopaedia of Kentucky* (1878), 444-445; J. Stoddard Johnston, "Sketch of Theodore O'Hara," *Register of the Kentucky State Historical Society*, XI (33), 67.

[24] Zachary Taylor to Secretary of War Henry Dearborn, June 6, 1808, Organization Records Section, Old Records Division, Adjutant General's Office, War Department, Washington.

[25] These seven brothers and sisters of Zachary Taylor reached maturity. Hancock Taylor was born January 29, 1781, and died March 29, 1841; his first wife was Sophia Elizabeth Hord, his second Annah Hornsby Lewis. William Dabney Strother Taylor was born in 1782 and died *circa* June 3, 1808; he never married. George Taylor was born in 1790 and died in September, 1829; he, too, died unmarried. Elizabeth Lee Taylor was born

January 14, 1792, and died April 22, 1845; she married her cousin, John Gibson Taylor. Joseph Pannill Taylor was born May 4, 1796, and died June 29, 1864; he married Eveline McLean. Sarah Bailey Taylor was born June 11, 1799, and died September 6, 1851; she married French Strother Gray. Emily Richard Taylor was born June 30, 1801, and died November 30, 1841; she married John Stadler Allison. Zachary Taylor had a fifth brother, who died in infancy. This baby was named either Strother Taylor or, more probably, Richard Taylor, junior; tradition places his birth between Zachary's and George's. This information has been gathered from several sources, notably the Taylor Family Papers, Trist Wood Collection, New Orleans; the James Madison Papers, Manuscript Division, Library of Congress, Washington, and the Taylor Family Papers, Trabue Collection, Louisville. The author consulted many genealogical articles and books, none of which is entirely accurate. He also examined the tombstones in the Zachary Taylor National Cemetery, near Louisville.

[26] General James Taylor Autobiography, copy of the original manuscript, Philip Fall Taylor Collection, Kentucky State Historical Society, Frankfort.

[27] Alice E. Trabue, " 'Spring Hill,' Oldham County, Kentucky," *Register of the Kentucky State Historical Society*, XVIII, *passim*.

[28] R. Alexander Bate, *Commodore Richard Taylor, A Colonial Sketch* (1924), *passim*.

[29] Louisville *Courier-Journal*, July 16, 1893.

[30] William E. Railey, "Woodford County, Kentucky," *Register of the Kentucky State Historical Society*, XIX, 57-61.

[31] Louisville *Courier-Journal*, July 16, 1893.

[32] *Idem.*

[33] Kentucky land was listed in three grades. In 1800 Zachary Taylor's father owned 700 acres of "first rate" land; 8,160 acres of "second rate" land; and 2,125 acres of "third rate" land. His property was located in Jefferson, Montgomery, Barren, Warren, Christian, Henderson, and Logan counties. Fifteen of the twenty-six slaves were children. Richard Taylor disposed of more than half of his Kentucky land prior to 1806. *Cf.* Jefferson County Tax Books, 1800-1810, Kentucky State Historical Society, Frankfort.

[34] Work on the brick dwelling began about 1790. In 1940 the house was in good repair, and was one of the show places of Jefferson County.

[35] Collins and Collins, *op. cit.*, I, 354-357; A. C. Quisenberry, "The Battle of New Orleans," *Register of the Kentucky State Historical Society*, XIII (37), 23-24.

[36] Durrett, *op. cit.*, 45, 66-72, 79, 83-86, 89.

[37] Collins and Collins, *op. cit.*, II, 373.

[38] Durrett, *op. cit.*, 74-76, 103.

[39] There is a tradition that Zachary Taylor joined a Kentucky militia company in 1806, to oppose the Burr-Blennerhasset expedition. The author spent three months in an attempt to verify this tradition, and was unable to do so.

## CHAPTER II

[1] "Zachariah Taylor" was one of four men whom the Kentucky congressional delegation recommended for commissions as first lieutenants (Buckner Thruston to Secretary of War, April 16, 1808, Old Files Section, Executive Division, Adjutant General's Office, War Department, Washington). William Dabney Strother Taylor had hoped to become a midshipman in the United States Navy. He owed his second lieutenancy to the influence of Secretary of State James Madison (Richard Taylor to Madison, March 3, 1805, January 23, 1808, James Madison Papers, Manuscript Division, Library of Congress, Washington).

[2] F. B. Heitman, *Historical Register of the United States Army from . . . September 29, 1789 to September 29, 1889* (1890), 634.

[3] Taylor to Secretary of War Henry Dearborn, June 6, 1808, Organization Records Section, Old Records Division, Adjutant General's Office, War Department, Washington.

[4] Taylor to Dearborn, November 24, 1808, Organization Records Section, Old Records Division, Adjutant General's Office, War Department, Washington.

[5] Taylor to Richard Taylor, November 24, 1808, typewritten copy, Zachary Taylor Papers, R. Alexander Bate Collection, Louisville. In a postscript, the young officer asks his father to "let me know whether my horse has recovered."

[6] Taylor to Dearborn, November 24, 1808, Organization Records Section, Old Records Division, Adjutant General's Office, War Department, Washington.

[7] Lewis Collins and Richard H. Collins, *History of Kentucky* (1874), II, 556-557.

[8] Taylor to Richard Taylor, November 24, 1808, typewritten copy, Zachary Taylor Papers, R. Alexander Bate Collection, Louisville.

[9] Receipts for pay, Zachary Taylor Papers, William Henry Smith Memorial Library, Indiana Historical Society, Indianapolis. When the officers of the Seventh Infantry received their commissions, the regiment contained neither private soldiers nor non-commissioned officers. Recruiting, therefore, was the subalterns' first duty. Lieutenant Taylor recruited until March 6, 1809, and probably continued until after April 1. He left Newport before April 22 (James Taylor to the Secretary of War, February 24, March 6, April 22, 1809, Organization Records Section, Old Records Division, Adjutant General's Office, War Department, Washington). Captains and lieutenants brought their recruits from various points in Kentucky and Ohio to Newport, where they were stationed a few days before setting out for the South. James Taylor, the fourth, was quartermaster and government agent in charge of erecting barracks at Newport. The Seventh Infantry "was moved down and cantoned under Gen'l Wilkinson at some distance below New Orleans . . ." (General James Taylor Autobiography, typewritten copy, Philip Fall Taylor Collection, Kentucky State Historical Society, Frankfort).

<sup>10</sup> The exact date and circumstances of William Dabney Strother Taylor's death are difficult to determine. On October 29, 1913, the Adjutant General of the United States Army informed Trist Wood of New Orleans: "The records show that William D. S. Taylor . . . died May 30, 1808, at Fort Pickering, Tenn." However, in two official military letters, reference is made to a letter written by Lieutenant William D. S. Taylor on June 1, 1808. It is the opinion of the author that he died shortly after that date, probably on June 3 (Official transcripts of letters to Lieutenant W. D. S. Taylor, dated Inspector's Office Near Fort Adams, June 3, 16, 1808, Inspector General's Letter Book, Executive Division, Adjutant General's Office, War Department, Washington). From the above it is clear that, contrary to tradition, Zachary Taylor entered the Army before his brother's death.

<sup>11</sup> Reuben Gold Thwaites (editor), *Early Western Travels, 1748-1846*, IV, 293-295.

<sup>12</sup> *American State Papers, Military Affairs*, I, 268-296.

<sup>13</sup> Zachary Taylor Papers, Trist Wood Collection, New Orleans.

<sup>14</sup> William Russell to the Secretary of War, March 15, 1811, Organization Records Section, Old Records Division, Adjutant General's Office, War Department, Washington.

<sup>15</sup> Taylor probably spent the months of September and October, 1809, in Kentucky. On November 13 he wrote to the Adjutant General, reporting himself fit for duty. On November 29 a letter left Washington, District of Columbia, ordering Taylor to report at Washington Village, Mississippi Territory (Inspector General's Letter Book, Executive Division, Adjutant General's Office, War Department, Washington). There is a tradition that he did not reach Washington Village until March, 1810 (Memorandum by William W. S. Bliss, Taylor Family Papers, Trist Wood Collection, New Orleans). Another tradition says Taylor built a flatboat near Westport, Kentucky, loaded it with produce, and proceeded to New Orleans (Louisville *Courier-Journal*, July 16, 1893). Both traditions are plausible.

<sup>16</sup> "Lieut. Taylor of the 7th Regiment having been deranged by the above order and there being no use for his services in this territory he is directed to return to his native state and to report himself to the Honble. the secretary of the war department . . ." (Brigadier General Wade Hampton to Taylor, April 27, 1810). On May 20, at Louisville, Taylor wrote to the Secretary of War: "I hold myself in readiness at this place to execute any order I may receive" (Taylor to the Secretary of War, May 20, 1810, Organization Records Section, Old Records Division, Adjutant General's Office, War Department, Washington).

<sup>17</sup> Margaret Mackall Smith was born September 21, 1788. Her father was Major Walter Smith of Saint Leonard's, Saint Leonard's Creek, Calvert County, Maryland. Her mother was Ann Mackall (pronounced Maykle), daughter of James John Mackall and Mary Hance. Miss Smith was visiting her sister, Mrs. Mary Smith Chew, in 1809 when Lieutenant Zachary Taylor was introduced to her. The marriage license was issued June 18, 1810 (Marriage License Book Number 1, p. 67, Jefferson County, Louisville, Kentucky). They were married June 21 (Statement in Zachary Taylor's

handwriting, Taylor Family Register, Taylor Family Papers, Trist Wood Collection, New Orleans).

[18] Taylor Family Register, Taylor Family Papers, Trist Wood Collection, New Orleans.

[19] Jefferson County Tax Books, 1800-1810, Kentucky State Historical Society, Frankfort.

[20] Heitman, *op. cit.*, 634.

[21] Taylor to the Secretary of War, July 16, 1811, Organization Records Section, Old Records Division, Adjutant General's Office, War Department, Washington.

[22] William Henry Harrison to the Secretary of War, August 6, 1811, Logan Esarey (editor), *Messages and Letters of William Henry Harrison* (1922), I, 547-548.

[23] Harrison to Captain Daniel Bissell, August 9, 1811, Esarey, *op. cit.*, I, 551-552.

[24] Taylor to James Taylor, October 1, 1811, *American Autograph Shop Catalogue*, Merion Station, Pennsylvania, September, 1937.

[25] Adjutant and Inspector General to Taylor, July 27, 1811, Inspector General's Letter Book, Executive Division, Adjutant General's Office, War Department, Washington.

[26] Zachary Taylor's autobiographical sketch, Zachary Taylor Papers, Manuscript Division, Library of Congress, Washington; Taylor to James Taylor, October 1, 1811, *American Autograph Shop Catalogue*, Merion Station, Pennsylvania, September, 1937.

[27] Adjutant and Inspector General to Taylor, December 6, 1811, January 4, 13, 19, March 6, 1812, Inspector General's Letter Book, Executive Division, Adjutant General's Office, War Department, Washington.

[28] Zachary Taylor's autobiographical sketch, Zachary Taylor Papers, Manuscript Division, Library of Congress, Washington.

[29] Adjutant and Inspector General to Taylor, May 23, 1812, Inspector General's Letter Book, Executive Division, Adjutant General's Office, War Department, Washington.

[30] Henry Adams, *History of the United States of America . . .* (1891), VI, 314, 333-335; Benson J. Lossing, *The Pictorial Field-Book of the War of 1812* (1869), 270-271, 288-291, 307-311.

[31] Harrison to the Secretary of War, May 13, May 27, July 8, 1812, Esarey, *op. cit.*, II, 49, 56, 57, 69, 70.

[32] Taylor to Harrison, August 9, 1812, Esarey, *op. cit.*, II, 82-83.

[33] Harrison to the Secretary of War, August 18, 1812, Esarey, *op. cit.*, II, 88-89.

[34] J. T. Scovell *et al.* (editors), *Fort Harrison on the Banks of the Wabash*, 1812-1912 (1912), 46.

[35] Fort Harrison was erected in October, 1811, by Major Joseph Hamilton Daviess (George Pence, "General Joseph Bartholomew," *Indiana Magazine of History*, XIV, 291).

[36] Taylor to Harrison, September 10, 1812, Esarey, *op. cit.*, II, 124.

[37] This account of the defense of Fort Harrison is based almost entirely

on Captain Taylor's detailed report to General Harrison (Taylor to Harrison, September 10, 1812, Esarey, *op. cit.*, II, 124-128). Excluding the two deserters and the two young haymakers, two white men were killed and two injured. It is not known whether one or both of the injured men died of wounds. Taylor did not determine the Indian loss. He wrote: "The Indians suffered smartly, but were so numerous as to take off all that were shot."

[38] Taylor to Harrison, September 13, 1812, Esarey, *op. cit.*, II, 134. A Taylor-signed abstract of provisions destroyed by the Indians is to be found in the Zachary Taylor Papers, William Henry Smith Memorial Library, Indiana Historical Society, Indianapolis.

[39] John Gibson to William Russell, September 16, 1812, [George S. Cottman, editor], "Some Letters of John Gibson," *Indiana Magazine of History*, I, 130-131.

[40] Lossing, *op. cit.*, 334.

[41] *The War* (New York), October 10, 1812.

[42] Washington *National Intelligencer*, October 1, 1812.

[43] Gibson to Hargrove, September 12, 1812, Esarey, *op. cit.*, II, 133.

[44] Hopkins to Shelby, November 27, 1812, Esarey, *op. cit.*, II, 231-234.

[45] Washington *National Intelligencer*, October 31, 1812; Heitman, *op. cit.*, 634.

## CHAPTER III

[1] Zachary Taylor's autobiographical sketch, Zachary Taylor Papers, Manuscript Division, Library of Congress, Washington.

[2] Taylor to James Taylor, November 9, 1812, *The Collector*, XXII, 62.

[3] Benson J. Lossing, *The Pictorial Field-Book of the War of 1812* (1869), 335-336; Logan Esarey, *History of Indiana* (1918), I, 222.

[4] Esarey, *op. cit.*, I, 222-223.

[5] Taylor to James Taylor, November 9, 1812, *The Collector*, XXII, 62.

[6] Hopkins to Shelby, November 27, 1812, *Niles' National Register*, III, 264; Sarah Jane Line, "The Indians on the Mississinewa," *Indiana Magazine of History*, IX, 188-189; Lossing, *op. cit.*, 336-337.

[7] Hopkins to Shelby, November 27, 1812, *Niles' National Register*, III, 264.

[8] "I was ordered to superintend the Recruiting service in the Territories of Indiana & Illinois & likewise to muster & Inspect the Troops of those Territories . . ." (Zachary Taylor's autobiographical sketch, Zachary Taylor Papers, Manuscript Division, Library of Congress, Washington). *Cf.* Taylor to Thomas H. Cushing, April 14, 1813, Zachary Taylor Papers, Hamilton Collection, Fort Wayne, Indiana.

[9] George Pence, "Indian History of Bartholomew County,"*Indiana Magazine of History*, XXIII, 223-227.

[10] Colonel Russell's force consisted of five divisions. Brevet Major Zachary Taylor commanded the center division. His eldest brother, Hancock Taylor, served as quartermaster's sergeant. *Cf.* Russell to Governor Thomas

Posey, July 25, 1813, Logan Esarey (editor), *Messages and Letters of William Henry Harrison* (1922), II, 497-498. Also Zachary Taylor's autobiographical sketch, Zachary Taylor Papers, Manuscript Division, Library of Congress, Washington.

[11] Lossing, *op. cit.*, 530; Taylor to Thomas H. Cushing, February 2, 1813, Zachary Taylor Papers, William Henry Smith Memorial Library, Indiana Historical Society, Indianapolis.

[12] W. A. Croffut (editor), *Fifty Years in Camp and Field, the Diary of Major General Ethan Allen Hitchcock, U. S. A.* (1909), 350.

[13] Taylor to Hancock Taylor, December 22, 1813, typewritten copy, Zachary Taylor Papers, R. Alexander Bate Collection, Louisville.

[14] Monthly return for Fort Knox for March, 1814, Zachary Taylor Papers, Manuscript Division, Library of Congress, Washington.

[15] According to Taylor the total force at Howard's command amounted to one hundred and twenty regulars, ten companies of poorly organized rangers and a few militiamen. With these troops he was expected to defend the "immence frontier of Indiana, Illinois & Missouri" (Zachary Taylor's autobiographical sketch, Zachary Taylor Papers, Manuscript Division, Library of Congress, Washington).

[16] Frank E. Stevens, *The Black Hawk War* (1903), 48-50; Bruce E. Mahan, *Old Fort Crawford and the Frontier* (1926), 53-60; William E. Meese, "Credit Island, 1814-1914," *Journal of the Illinois State Historical Society*, VII, 352-354; Frank E. Stevens, "Illinois in the War of 1812-1814," *Transactions of the Illinois State Historical Society* (1904), 162-163.

[17] Zachary Taylor's autobiographical sketch, Zachary Taylor Papers, Manuscript Division, Library of Congress, Washington.

[18] Edgar Bruce Wesley, "James Callaway in the War of 1812," *Missouri Historical Society Collections*, V, 74.

[19] *Missouri Gazette* (Saint Louis), September 3, 1814.

[20] Wesley, "James Callaway in the War of 1812," *loc. cit.*, 74.

[21] Taylor to Howard, September 6, 1814, *Niles' National Register*, supplement to Volume VII, 137.

[22] Lieutenant Graham, the British commander, gives September 6 as the date of the battle of Credit Island (Meese, "Credit Island, 1814-1914," *loc. cit.*, 364). However, Taylor and Callaway agree that the battle took place on September 5.

[23] According to Callaway, two sentinels were wounded (Wesley, "James Callaway in the War of 1812," *loc. cit.*, 70).

[24] Taylor to Howard, September 6, 1814, *Niles' National Register*, supplement to Volume VII, 137-138; Wesley, "James Callaway in the War of 1812," *loc. cit.*, 70.

[25] Zachary Taylor's autobiographical sketch, Zachary Taylor Papers, Manuscript Division, Library of Congress, Washington.

[26] Captain Thomas G. Anderson to Lieutenant Colonel McDonall, August 29, 1814, *Wisconsin State Historical Society Collections*, IX, 220-221; Graham to Anderson, September 7, 1814, *Wisconsin State Historical*

*Society Collections*, IX, 226-228; Milo M. Quaife, "A Forgotten Hero of Rock Island," *Journal of the Illinois State Historical Society*, XXIII, 652-653.

[27] Estimates vary as to the number of Indians participating in this battle. One thousand is a conservative estimate. Sauk and Fox braves composed the majority, but a few Sioux also saw action. Black Hawk, whom Taylor helped defeat eighteen years later, was active at Credit Island.

[28] For Harpole's exploit see John Shaw, "Shaw's Narrative," *Wisconsin State Historical Society Collections*, II, 220-222. The reports of Taylor and Graham differ in two particulars. *Cf.* John T. Kingston, "Early Western Days," *Wisconsin State Historical Society Collections*, VII, 311.

[29] Taylor to Howard, September 6, 1814, *Niles' National Register*, supplement to Volume VII, 138. The reduction of Taylor's force from four hundred and thirty to three hundred and thirty-four was due to the fact that some soldiers were sick, others were scouting, still others had been left behind in charge of supplies.

[30] Zachary Taylor's autobiographical sketch, Zachary Taylor Papers, Manuscript Division, Library of Congress, Washington; Wesley, "James Callaway in the War of 1812," *loc. cit.*, 47; *Kentucky Gazette* (Lexington), November 7, 1814. Contrary to the popular impression, Zachary Taylor did not construct Fort Edwards near the site of Fort Johnson. Fort Edwards was built in June, 1815, by Brevet Brigadier General Thomas A. Smith. *Cf.* Henry Putney Beers, *The Western Military Frontier, 1815-1846* (1935), 33.

[31] Zachary Taylor's autobiographical sketch, Zachary Taylor Papers, Manuscript Division, Library of Congress, Washington.

[32] Taylor to Perkins, April 29, Anderson to Monroe, May 19, Anderson to the Inspector General, September 10, Anderson to Monroe, October 27, 1814, Old Files Section, Executive Division, Adjutant General's Office, War Department, Washington.

[33] Anderson to the Inspector General, September 10, 1814, Old Files Section, Executive Division, Adjutant General's Office, War Department, Washington.

[34] Wilkinson to Anderson, October 6, 1814, Old Files Section, Executive Division, Adjutant General's Office, War Department, Washington.

[35] Jennings and Johnson to Monroe, undated, Old Files Section, Executive Division, Adjutant General's Office, War Department, Washington. Johnson and Jennings were men of influence as early as 1814.

[36] Hopkins to Richard Cutts, January 8, 1815, Old Files Section, Executive Division, Adjutant General's Office, War Department, Washington.

[37] Ormsby to Monroe, October 21, 1814, Old Files Section, Executive Division, Adjutant General's Office, War Department, Washington.

[38] Stuart to Monroe, December 3, 1814, Old Files Section, Executive Division, Adjutant General's Office, War Department, Washington.

[39] Adjutant and Inspector General to Taylor, January 2, 1815, Adjutant General's Letter Book, Executive Division, Adjutant General's Office, War Department, Washington.

[40] F. B. Heitman, *Historical Register of the United States Army from ... September 29, 1789, to September 29, 1889* (1890), 634.

[41] Statement in Zachary Taylor's own handwriting, Taylor Family Register, Taylor Family Papers, Trist Wood Collection, New Orleans.

[42] Taylor to Thomas S. Jesup, April 20, 1820, photostatic copy, Zachary Taylor Papers, Manuscript Division, Library of Congress, Washington.

[43] Heitman, *op. cit.*, 634.

## CHAPTER IV

[1] Except for a few months in 1830 and 1831, and briefer interludes at other times, Zachary Taylor never lived in the heart of a city until he became president. At Baton Rouge the "Spanish cottage" stood on the border between town and country.

[2] Lewis Collins and Richard H. Collins, *History of Kentucky* (1874), II, 356.

[3] F. B. Heitman, *Historical Register of the United States Army from ... September 29, 1789, to September 29, 1889* (1890), 632-633; Colonel William Russell to Governor Thomas Posey, July 25, 1813, Logan Esarey (editor), *Messages and Letters of William Henry Harrison*, II, 497-498.

[4] Taylor to Major Taylor Berry, April 25, 1816, Presidential Papers, Missouri Historical Society, Jefferson Memorial, Saint Louis.

[5] Heitman, *op. cit.*, p. 634; Henry Putney Beers, *The Western Military Frontier, 1815-1846* (1935), 34n.

[6] J. B. S. Jacobs, senior, "List of Inhabitants at Green Bay, September 14, 1818," *Wisconsin State Historical Society Collections*, X, 136-140.

[7] William L. Evans, "The Military History of Green Bay," *Proceedings of the State Historical Society of Wisconsin, 1899* (1900), 136-138.

[8] Taylor to Major General Alexander Macomb, August 15, 1816, Old Files Section, Executive Division, Adjutant General's Office, War Department, Washington.

[9] Dickson to John Lawe, November 25, 1816, "Lawe and Grignon Papers, 1794-1821," *Wisconsin State Historical Society Collections*, X, 133-134.

[10] Deborah B. Martin, *History of Brown County, Wisconsin, Past and Present* (1913), I, 139.

[11] *Ibid.*, 137 et seq.

[12] Ella Hoes Neville *et al.*, *Historic Green Bay, 1634-1840* (1893), 165; Martin, *op. cit.*, I, 138; Louise Phelps Kellogg, "Old Fort Howard," *Wisconsin Magazine of History*, XVIII, 128.

[13] Taylor to Thomas S. Jesup, October 25, 1817, photostatic copy, Zachary Taylor Papers, Manuscript Division, Library of Congress, Washington.

[14] Octavia Pannill Taylor was born August 16, 1816. Statement in Zachary Taylor's handwriting, Taylor Family Register, Taylor Family Papers, Trist Wood Collection, New Orleans.

[15] Martin, *op. cit.*, I, 138.

16 Samuel A. Storrow, "The Northwest in 1817, a Contemporary Letter," *Wisconsin State Historical Society Collections*, VI, 169.

17 Taylor to Assistant Adjutant General, August 14, 1817, Old Files Section, Executive Division, Adjutant General's Office, War Department, Washington. Taylor's Green Bay reports were often tactless. He was obviously irritable. But it should be remembered that he was isolated, and unfamiliar with many Army regulations. Macomb's refusal to comply with reasonable routine requests meant a failure to do what was no more than common decency.

18 Taylor to Assistant Adjutant General, February 24, 1818, Old Files Section, Executive Division, Adjutant General's Office, War Department, Washington. With this letter Taylor enclosed a copy of his regimental order of February 5, 1818, prohibiting the issuing of liquor until further notice.

19 *Idem.*

20 Taylor to Assistant Adjutant General, January 17, 1818, Old Files Section, Executive Division, Adjutant General's Office, War Department, Washington.

21 Taylor to Assistant Adjutant General, August 14, 1817, Old Files Section, Executive Division, Adjutant General's Office, War Department, Washington.

22 Taylor to Macomb, July 29, 1817, Old Files Section, Executive Division, Adjutant General's Office, War Department, Washington.

23 Colonel James L. Smith to Major R. M. Kirby, June 16, Taylor to Kirby, August 31, Taylor to the Adjutant and Inspector General, October 27, 1818, Old Files Section, Executive Division, Adjutant General's Office, War Department, Washington.

24 Heitman, *op. cit.*, 634.

25 Marquis James, *Andrew Jackson, the Border Captain* (1933), 330.

26 Mrs. John Brown to Orlando Brown, July 1, 1819, Alice E. Trabue, *A Corner in Celebrities* (1922), 63.

27 Margaret Smith Taylor, fourth daughter of Zachary Taylor, was born July 27, 1819. Statement in Zachary Taylor's own handwriting, Taylor Family Register, Taylor Family Papers, Trist Wood Collection, New Orleans.

28 Heitman, *op. cit.*, 634.

29 Taylor to Jesup, April 20, 1820, photostatic copy, Zachary Taylor Papers, Manuscript Division, Library of Congress, Washington.

30 Taylor to Jesup, September 18, 1820, photostatic copy, Zachary Taylor Papers, Manuscript Division, Library of Congress, Washington.

31 W. A. Croffut (editor), *Fifty Years in Camp and Field, the Diary of Major General Ethan Allen Hitchcock, U. S. A.* (1909), 46-47.

32 Taylor to Jesup, December 15, 1820, photostatic copy, Zachary Taylor Papers, Manuscript Division, Library of Congress, Washington; Louisville *Weekly Courier*, July 1, 1848.

33 Taylor to Jesup, September 18, 1820, photostatic copy, Zachary Taylor Papers, Manuscript Division, Library of Congress, Washington.

[34] *Idem.*

[35] Taylor to Jesup, December 15, 1820, photostatic copy, Zachary Taylor Papers, Manuscript Division, Library of Congress, Washington.

[36] Taylor to Jesup, September 18, 1820, photostatic copy, Zachary Taylor Papers, Manuscript Division, Library of Congress, Washington.

[37] Statement in Zachary Taylor's own handwriting, Taylor Family Register, Taylor Family Papers, Trist Wood Collection, New Orleans; Taylor to Hancock Taylor, August 26, 1820, Zachary Taylor Papers, Ott Collection, Ocala, Florida.

[38] Taylor to Jesup, September 18, 1820, photostatic copy, Zachary Taylor Papers, Manuscript Division, Library of Congress, Washington.

[39] Statement in Zachary Taylor's own handwriting, Taylor Family Register, Taylor Family Papers, Trist Wood Collection, New Orleans.

[40] Taylor to Jesup, December 15, 1820, photostatic copy, Zachary Taylor Papers, Manuscript Division, Library of Congress, Washington; Taylor to Hancock Taylor, August 26, 1820, Zachary Taylor Papers, Ott Collection, Ocala, Florida.

[41] Taylor to Jesup, June 18, 1821, photostatic copy, Zachary Taylor Papers, Manuscript Division, Library of Congress, Washington.

[42] Taylor to Jesup, June 15, 1821, photostatic copy, Zachary Taylor Papers, Manuscript Division, Library of Congress, Washington.

[43] Taylor to Jesup, June 18, 1821, photostatic copy, Zachary Taylor Papers, Manuscript Division, Library of Congress, Washington.

## CHAPTER V

[1] F. B. Heitman, *Historical Register of the United States Army from . . . September 29, 1789, to September 29, 1889* (1890), 634.

[2] Henry Putney Beers, *The Western Military Frontier, 1815-1846* (1935), 57.

[3] *Ibid.,* 67-68; Taylor to Hancock Taylor, October 28, 1821, Zachary Taylor Papers, Ott Collection, Ocala, Florida.

[4] J. Fair Hardin, "Four Forgotten Frontier Posts of Western Louisiana," *Louisiana Historical Quarterly,* XVI, 9-10.

[5] *Ibid.,* 15-16.

[6] Edmund P. Gaines to James Gadsden, March 31, 1822, *ibid.,* 14-15.

[7] Special Order Number 19, March 28, 1822, *ibid.,* 15.

[8] Beers, *op. cit.,* 68.

[9] Heitman, *op. cit.,* 634.

[10] Cantonment Jesup Post Return, Officers' Division, Adjutant General's Office, War Department, Washington.

[11] Hardin, "Four Forgotten Frontier Posts of Western Louisiana," *loc. cit.,* 16-17; *American State Papers, Military Affairs,* II, 456.

[12] Notary Record Book B, Feliciana Parish, Saint Francisville, Louisiana, 587-588.

[13] Taylor to Jesup, January 20, 1824, photostatic copy, Zachary Taylor Papers, Manuscript Division, Library of Congress, Washington.

[14] W. A. Croffut (editor), *Fifty Years in Camp and Field, the Diary of Major General Ethan Allen Hitchcock, U. S. A.* (1909), 47.

[15] Taylor to Hancock Taylor, April 10, 1821, typewritten copy, Zachary Taylor Papers, R. Alexander Bate Collection, Louisville.

[16] Taylor to Mrs. Elizabeth Lee Taylor, August 4, 1823, typewritten copy, Zachary Taylor Papers, R. Alexander Bate Collection, Louisville.

[17] Taylor to Mrs. Elizabeth Lee Taylor, October 8, 1823, typewritten copy, Zachary Taylor Papers, R. Alexander Bate Collection, Louisville.

[18] *Idem.*

[19] Taylor to Jesup, June 18, 1820, photostatic copy, Zachary Taylor Papers, Manuscript Division, Library of Congress, Washington.

[20] *Idem.*

[21] Taylor to Jesup, January 20, 1824, photostatic copy, Zachary Taylor Papers, Manuscript Division, Library of Congress, Washington.

[22] Baton Rouge Garrison Return, February, 1824, Officers' Division, Adjutant General's Office, War Department, Washington.

[23] Taylor to Adjutant General Charles J. Nourse, April 30, 1824, Old Files Section, Executive Division, Adjutant General's Office, War Department, Washington; Taylor to Jesup, June 17, 1824, photostatic copy, Zachary Taylor Papers, Manuscript Division, Library of Congress, Washington.

[24] Taylor to Mrs. Elizabeth Lee Taylor, October 8, 1823, typewritten copy, R. Alexander Bate Collection, Louisville.

[25] Taylor Family Papers, Trist Wood Collection, New Orleans.

[26] Statement in Zachary Taylor's own handwriting, Taylor Family Register, Taylor Family Papers, Trist Wood Collection, New Orleans.

[27] *Idem.*

[28] Taylor to the Adjutant General, April 30, July 3, September 18, 1824, April 4, June 25, August 8, September 8, December 31, 1825, February 1, 1826, *et al.*, Old Files Section, Executive Division, Adjutant General's Office, War Department, Washington; Taylor to Jesup, June 17, 1824, photostatic copy, Zachary Taylor Papers, Manuscript Division, Library of Congress, Washington.

[29] Register of Officers, 1814-1833, 54, Officers' Division, Adjutant General's Office, War Department, Washington.

[30] *Idem;* Wilhelmus Bogart Bryan, *A History of the National Capital* (1916), II, 59, 59n.

[31] N. P. Willis, *American Scenery* (1840), II, 49.

[32] Washington *National Intelligencer,* October 4, 1826.

[33] *Ibid.,* October 3, 1826.

[34] *Ibid.,* October 17, 1826.

[35] *Ibid.,* October 6, 1826.

[36] *Ibid.,* October 7, 1826.

[37] *Ibid.,* October 3, 1826.

[38] Taylor to Jesup, January 29, 1827, photostatic copy, Zachary Taylor Papers, Manuscript Division, Library of Congress, Washington.

[39] New Orleans Post Return, February, 1827, Officers' Division, Adjutant General's Office, War Department, Washington.

[40] Heitman, *op. cit.*, 443; Taylor to Hancock Taylor, January 19, 1828, Zachary Taylor Papers, Hawes Collection, Yellow Springs, Ohio.

[41] New Orleans Garrison Returns, March-June, 1827, Baton Rouge Garrison Returns, July-October, 1827, Officers' Division, Adjutant General's Office, War Department, Washington.

[42] New Orleans Garrison Returns, November, 1827-May, 1828, Officers' Division, Adjutant General's Office, War Department, Washington. Major William S. Foster assumed command at New Orleans on May 1, 1828.

[43] Marcus L. Hansen, *Old Fort Snelling, 1819-1858* (1918), 75.

[44] *Ibid.*, 76.

[45] *Idem.*

[46] Beers, *op. cit.*, 73-79.

[47] Fort Snelling Post Returns, May, 1828-July, 1829, Officers' Division, Adjutant General's Office, War Department, Washington.

[48] Beers, *op. cit.*, 81-82.

[49] Taylor to William Berry Taylor, April 12, 1830, original in possession of Reuben Thornton Taylor, Bagdad, Kentucky.

[50] Taylor to John Gibson Taylor, March (May?) 2, 1829, typewritten copy, Zachary Taylor Papers, R. Alexander Bate Collection, Louisville.

[51] *Idem.*

[52] *Idem.*

[53] Taylor to William Berry Taylor, April 12, 1830, original in possession of Reuben Thornton Taylor, Bagdad, Kentucky.

[54] Taylor to Jesup, January 29, 1827, photostatic copy, Zachary Taylor Papers, Manuscript Division, Library of Congress, Washington.

[55] Beers, *op. cit.*, 77-78.

[56] Fort Crawford Post Return, July, 1829, Officers' Division, Adjutant General's Office, War Department, Washington.

[57] Taylor to Jesup, December 15, 1829, photostatic copy, Zachary Taylor Papers, Manuscript Division, Library of Congress, Washington.

[58] Bruce E. Mahan, *Old Crawford and the Frontier* (1926), 127-128.

[59] Taylor to Jesup, December 15, 1829, photostatic copy, Zachary Taylor Papers, Manuscript Division, Library of Congress, Washington.

[60] *Idem.*

[61] Mahan, *op. cit.*, 128, 312; Heitman, *op. cit.*, 117.

[62] Taylor left Fort Crawford on or about July 3, 1830 (Fort Crawford Post Return, July, 1830, Officers' Division, Adjutant General's Office, War Department, Washington).

[63] Dr. Robert C. Wood and Ann Mackall Taylor were married September 20, 1829 (Statement in Zachary Taylor's own handwriting, Taylor Family Register, Taylor Family Papers, Trist Wood Collection, New Orleans).

[64] Charles Anderson to Mrs. Varina Jefferson Davis, June 5, 1893, typewritten copy, Taylor Family Papers, Trist Wood Collection, New Orleans.

[65] Deed Book G, 114-115, Wilkinson County, Woodville, Mississippi.

[66] New Orleans Garrison Returns, August-October, 1831, Officers' Division, Adjutant General's Office, War Department, Washington.

[67] First Infantry Regimental Returns, August, 1830-February, 1832, Officers' Division, Adjutant General's Office, War Department, Washington.

[68] Taylor to Josiah Stoddard Johnston, December 24, 1831, Presidential Papers, Manuscript Division, Historical Society of Pennsylvania, Philadelphia; Taylor to George Poindexter, December 26, [1831], Zachary Taylor Papers, Manuscript Division, Library of Congress, Washington.

[69] Heitman, *op. cit.*, 40-48, 91, 95, 141-142, 147, 190, 404, 451, 477.

[70] *Ibid.*, 477.

[71] *Ibid.*, 634.

## CHAPTER VI

[1] Taylor to Thomas S. Jesup, December 4, 1832, photostatic copy, Zachary Taylor Papers, Manuscript Division, Library of Congress, Washington.

[2] Henry Putney Beers, *The Western Military Frontier, 1815-1846* (1935), 80.

[3] *Ibid.*, 81.

[4] Reuben Gold Thwaites, "The Story of the Black Hawk War," *Wisconsin State Historical Society Collections*, XII, 222, 225.

[5] Beers, *op. cit.*, 82.

[6] *Ibid.*, 82-83.

[7] Elkanah Babcock and S. T. Fiske, junior, *A War History of the Sixth U. S. Infantry . . . from 1798 to 1903* (1903), 18.

[8] Beers, *op. cit.*, 83-84.

[9] Taylor to Jesup, December 4, 1832, photostatic copy, Zachary Taylor Papers, Manuscript Division, Library of Congress, Washington.

[10] Beers, *op. cit.*, 84.

[11] Frank E. Stevens, *The Black Hawk War* (1903), 111.

[12] *Ibid.*, 112.

[13] *Ibid.*, 113.

[14] Taylor to Jesup, December 4, 1832, photostatic copy, Zachary Taylor Papers, Manuscript Division, Library of Congress, Washington.

[15] Stevens, *op. cit.*, 112-113.

[16] Allen Johnson and Dumas Malone (editors), *Dictionary of American Biography* (1928-1936), I, 410.

[17] Beers, *op. cit.*, 41-44, 50-52; Hiram Martin Chittenden, *The American Fur Trade of the Far West* (1902), 567, 608 *et seq.*

[18] F. B. Heitman, *Historical Register of the United States Army from . . . September 29, 1789, to September 29, 1889* (1890), 95.

[19] Taylor to Jesup, December 4, 1832, photostatic copy, Zachary Taylor Papers, Manuscript Division, Library of Congress, Washington.

[20] Stevens, *op. cit.*, 21.

[21] *Ibid.*, 17, 19.

[22] *Ibid.*, 17.

[23] *Ibid.*, 21, 51-52.

[24] *Ibid.*, 111; William Preston Johnston, *Life of Albert Sidney Johnston* (1879), 33; Beers, *op. cit.*, 84.

[25] Stevens, *op. cit.*, 111; Johnston, *op. cit.*, 33.

[26] Stevens, *op. cit.*, 130.

[27] *Ibid.*, 114-115, 119.

[28] Sarah Knox Taylor to Zachary Taylor, June 5, 1832, Taylor Family Papers, Trist Wood Collection, New Orleans.

[29] First Infantry Regimental Return, June, 1832, Officers' Division, Adjutant General's Office, War Department, Washington.

[30] Parke Godwin (editor), *Prose Writings of William Cullen Bryant* (1884), II, 20.

[31] Stevens, *op. cit.*, 120.

[32] *Ibid.*, 126.

[33] *Ibid.*, 127.

[34] Taylor to Jesup, December 4, 1832, photostatic copy, Zachary Taylor Papers, Manuscript Division, Library of Congress, Washington.

[35] Stevens, *op. cit.*, 126.

[36] *Ibid.*, 128.

[37] *Ibid.*, 128, 128n.

[38] *Ibid.*, 131-139.

[39] Taylor to Jesup, December 4, 1832, photostatic copy, Zachary Taylor Papers, Manuscript Division, Library of Congress, Washington.

[40] Stevens, *op. cit.*, 146.

[41] Beers, *op. cit.*, 85.

[42] Stevens, *op. cit.*, 161-162.

[43] *Ibid.*, 172.

[44] *Ibid.*, 161, 164, 172.

[45] *Ibid.*, 295, 298-299; Johnston, *op. cit.*, 36.

[46] Stevens, *op. cit.*, 180-183.

[47] Godwin, *op. cit.*, II, 20.

[48] Elijah Iles, *Sketches of Early Life and Times in Kentucky, Missouri and Illinois* (1883), 46-47.

[49] Stevens, *op. cit.*, 197.

[50] *Ibid.*, 198. John Dement's narrative.

[51] Thomas P. Reep, *Lincoln at New Salem* (1927), 41-42.

[52] John G. Nicolay and John Hay (editors), *Complete Works of Abraham Lincoln* (1894), I, 142.

[53] Albert J. Beveridge, *Abraham Lincoln, 1809-1858* (1928), I, 122.

[54] Stevens, *op. cit.*, 298-299.

[55] *Ibid.*, 291.

[56] *Ibid.*, 202-205.

[57] Beers, *op. cit.*, 86.

[58] Stevens, *op. cit.*, 205.

[59] *Ibid.*, 206, 210-211.

[60] *Ibid.*, 214-220.

[61] *Ibid.*, 307.

[62] *Ibid.*, 222-223; Beers, *op. cit.*, 86-87.

[63] Stevens, *op. cit.*, 227.

[64] *Ibid.*, 223-224; Thwaites, "The Story of the Black Hawk War," *loc. cit.*, 259-260.

[65] Atkinson to Macomb, August 25, 1832, Bruce E. Mahan, *Old Fort Crawford and the Frontier* (1926), 176.

[66] Stevens, *op. cit.*, 229-230.

[67] Fort Crawford Post Return, August, 1832, Officers' Division, Adjutant General's Office, War Department, Washington.

[68] Charles Winslow Elliott, *Winfield Scott, the Soldier and the Man* (1937), 269.

[69] *Niles' National Register*, XLIII, 78.

[70] Stevens, *op. cit.*, 306; Robert McElroy, *Jefferson Davis, the Unreal and the Real* (1937), 30.

[71] Taylor to Jesup, December 4, 1832, photostatic copy, Zachary Taylor Papers, Manuscript Division, Library of Congress, Washington.

[72] *Idem.*

[73] *Idem.*

[74] Beers, *op. cit.*, 87-91.

## CHAPTER VII

[1] Walter L. Fleming, "Jefferson Davis' First Marriage," *Mississippi Historical Society Publications*, XII, 35.

[2] Charles Anderson to Mrs. Varina Jefferson Davis, June 5, 1893, typewritten copy, Taylor Family Papers, Trist Wood Collection, New Orleans.

[3] Statement of Mrs. Anne Taylor Edwards, Fleming, "Jefferson Davis' First Marriage," *loc. cit.*, 35.

[4] According to Anderson, Sarah Knox Taylor inherited "with much of her father's self-will also a good share of his most level-headed, good common (so-called) sense."

[5] Statement of Mrs. Mary Louise Taylor Robinson, Fleming, "Jefferson Davis' First Marriage," *loc. cit.*, 32. It is exceedingly unlikely that Emily V. Mason saw Davis. She was certainly mistaken in stating that he accompanied Black Hawk to Detroit (Fleming, "Jefferson Davis' First Marriage," *loc. cit.*, 24).

[6] Walter L. Fleming, "The Early Life of Jefferson Davis," *Mississippi Valley Historical Review*, IX, Part I, 176; Milo M. Quaife, "The Northwestern Career of Jefferson Davis," *Journal of the Illinois State Historical Society*, XVI, 2, 5, 8.

[7] Quaife, "The Northwestern Career of Jefferson Davis," *loc. cit.*, 10-11; Frank E. Stevens, *The Black Hawk War* (1903), 290-308.

[8] Fleming, "Jefferson Davis' First Marriage," *loc. cit.*, 24.

[9] Statement of Mrs. Mary Elizabeth Taylor Dandridge, New York *Times*, October 20, 1906. Mrs. Dandridge was the former Betty Taylor, youngest daughter of Zachary Taylor. Her first husband was William Wallace Smith Bliss, her second Philip Pendleton Dandridge.

[10] Charles Anderson to Mrs. Varina Jefferson Davis, June 5, 1893, type-written copy, Taylor Family Papers, Trist Wood Collection, New Orleans.

[11] Varina Jefferson Davis, *Jefferson Davis, a Memoir* (1890), I, 93 *et seq.*

[12] Nehemiah Matson, *Memories of Shaubena* (1878), 76-81.

[13] New York *Times*, October 20, 1906.

[14] Fleming, "Jefferson Davis' First Marriage," *loc. cit.*, 27.

[15] New York *Times*, October 20, 1906.

[16] Quaife, "The Northwestern Career of Jefferson Davis," *loc. cit.*, 15.

[17] Fleming, "Jefferson Davis' First Marriage," *loc. cit.*, 28-29.

[18] Sarah Knox Taylor to Mrs. Zachary Taylor, June 17, 1835, Taylor Family Papers, Trist Wood Collection, New Orleans.

[19] Reminiscence of Mrs. Archibald Magill Robinson, Louisville *Herald*, July 4, 1909.

[20] Marriage License Book Number 2, 154, Jefferson County, Louisville, Kentucky. Jefferson Davis and Hancock Taylor signed the marriage bond. The priest made no return.

[21] Fleming, "Jefferson Davis' First Marriage," *loc. cit.*, 33; Louisville *Herald*, July 4, 1909.

[22] Louisville *Herald*, July 4, 1909.

[23] Fleming, "Jefferson Davis' First Marriage," *loc. cit.*, 32.

[24] Robert McElroy, *Jefferson Davis, the Unreal and the Real* (1937), I, 35.

[25] Mrs. Sarah Knox Davis to Mrs. Zachary Taylor, August 11, 1835, Taylor Family Papers, Trist Wood Collection, New Orleans.

[26] Fleming, "Jefferson Davis' First Marriage," *loc. cit.*, 34.

[27] New York *Times*, October 20, 1906; Fleming, "Jefferson Davis' First Marriage," *loc. cit.*, 34.

[28] In 1938 the author visited the grave of Mrs. Sarah Knox Davis, Zachary Taylor's daughter, in the cemetery adjoining Locust Grove Plantation, West Feliciana Parish, Louisiana.

[29] Armistead C. Gordon, *Jefferson Davis* (1918), 29-31.

## CHAPTER VIII

[1] Fort Crawford Post Returns, August, 1832-November, 1836, Officers' Division, Adjutant General's Office, War Department, Washington.

[2] Caleb Atwater, *Remarks Made on a Tour to Prairie du Chien; Thence to Washington City, in 1829* (1831), 178.

[3] Sarah Knox Taylor to Zachary Taylor, June 5, 1832, Taylor Family Papers, Trist Wood Collection, New Orleans.

[4] James H. Lockwood, "Early Times and Events in Wisconsin," *Wisconsin State Historical Society Collections*, II, 156.

[5] Mrs. Sarah Knox Davis to Mrs. Zachary Taylor, August 11, 1835, Taylor Family Papers, Trist Wood Collection, New Orleans.

[6] John H. Bliss, "Reminiscences of Fort Snelling," *Minnesota Historical Society Collections*, VI, 338.

[7] Taylor to Jesup, September 18, 1820, photostatic copy, Zachary Taylor Papers, Manuscript Division, Library of Congress, Washington.

[8] Bruce E. Mahan, *Old Fort Crawford and the Frontier* (1926), 242.

[9] *Ibid.*, 203, 209, 211, 242.

[10] *Ibid.*, 241-242.

[11] *Ibid.*, 264.

[12] Atwater, *op. cit.*, 179.

[13] W. A. Croffut (editor), *Fifty Years in Camp and Field, the Diary of Major General Ethan Allen Hitchcock, U. S. A.* (1909), 70-71.

[14] Taylor to Dr. F. S. Bronson, August 10, 1847, [Thomas B. Thorpe], *Taylor Anecdote Book* (1848), 145.

[15] Statement of Mrs. Mary Elizabeth Taylor Dandridge, New York *Times*, October 20, 1906.

[16] Mahan, *op. cit.*, 244.

[17] John E. Chapin, "Sketch of Cutting Marsh," *Wisconsin State Historical Society Collections*, XV, 31.

[18] Charles W. Moore, "Was Gen. Taylor a Mason?", *Freemasons' Monthly Magazine* (Boston), IX, 329; Rob. Morris, *History of Freemasonry in Kentucky* (1859), 491-492; Rob. Morris, "Masonic Recollections," *Masonic Review* (Cincinnati), LVII, 200.

[19] Taylor to Mary Elizabeth Taylor, December 15, 1845, *The Autograph*, I, 48.

[20] Bliss, "Reminiscences of Fort Snelling," *loc. cit.*, 338.

[21] Mahan, *op. cit.*, 197, 200, 202, 204-206.

[22] Henry Putney Beers, *The Western Military Frontier, 1815-1846* (1935), 120.

[23] Mahan, *op. cit.*, 156, 190-191.

[24] John H. Fonda, "Early Reminiscences of Wisconsin," *Wisconsin State Historical Society Collections*, V, 237.

[25] Lawrence Taliaferro, "Autobiography of Maj. Lawrence Taliaferro," *Minnesota Historical Society Collections*, VI, 211.

[26] *Idem.*

[27] E. D. Neill, "Occurrences in and around Fort Snelling, from 1819 to 1840," *Minnesota Historical Society Collections*, II, 122.

[28] [Winfield Scott], *Memoirs of Lieut.-General Scott, LL.D., Written by Himself* (1864), II, 382-383.

[29] From Charles Winslow Elliott, *Winfield Scott, the Soldier and the Man* (1937), 383. By permission of the Macmillan Company, publishers.

[30] Croffut, *op. cit.*, 71.

[31] Fonda, "Early Reminiscences of Wisconsin," *loc. cit.*, 240-241.

[32] Charles W. Upham, *Eulogy on the Life and Character of Zachary Taylor* (1850), 52-53.

[33] Statement of Robert C. Wood, junior, to Trist Wood. Robert C. Wood, junior, was Zachary Taylor's grandson and at times lived under his grandfather's roof.

[34] Croffut, *op. cit.*, 70-71.

[35] Bliss, "Reminiscences of Fort Snelling," *loc. cit.*, 337-338.

[36] Quoted in Mahan, *op. cit.*, 246.

[37] Charles Augustus Murray, *Travels in North America During the Years 1834, 1835, and 1836* (1839), II, 110.

[38] Henry Merrell, "Pioneer Life in Wisconsin," *Wisconsin State Historical Society Collections*, VII, 379.

[39] Charles Fenno Hoffman, *A Winter in the West* (1882), 61-62.

[40] Fort Crawford Post Return, Jefferson Barracks Garrison Return, November, 1836, Officers' Division, Adjutant General's Office, War Department, Washington.

[41] Order Number 12, Right Wing, Western Department, November 30, 1836, Old Files Section, Executive Division, Adjutant General's Office, War Department, Washington.

[42] Beers, *op. cit.*, 122.

[43] Taylor to Adjutant General Roger Jones, March 19, 1837, Old Files Section, Executive Division, Adjutant General's Office, War Department, Washington.

[44] Taylor to Jones, May 8, 1837, Old Files Section, Executive Division, Adjutant General's Office, War Department, Washington.

[45] Jefferson Barracks Garrison Return, May, 1837, Fort Crawford Post Returns, May, June, 1837, Officers' Division, Adjutant General's Office, War Department, Washington.

[46] Taylor to Jones, July 14, 1837, Old Files Section, Executive Division, Adjutant General's Office, War Department, Washington.

[47] Taylor to Jones, July 24, 1837, Old Files Section, Executive Division, Adjutant General's Office, War Department, Washington; *Army and Navy Chronicle*, V, 104.

[48] Not long before his Florida assignment, Colonel Taylor dictated a nineteen-page discussion of Army affairs. This discussion was entitled: "Proposed Additions and Alterations to Revised Army Regulations." It is said to have commended its author to the favorable attention of official Washington.

## CHAPTER IX

[1] December 28, 1835, was the date of the Dade Massacre. Zachary Taylor left Prairie du Chien on July 18, 1837.

[2] Frederick W. Hodge (editor), *Handbook of American Indians* (1912), II, 500.

[3] John T. Sprague, *Origin, Progress and Conclusion of the Florida War* (1848), 20-25.

[4] Grant Foreman, *Indian Removal* (1932), 319, 320, 324.

[5] *Ibid.*, 320-322.

[6] Alfred Jackson Hanna, *Fort Maitland, Its Origin and History* (1936), 47-48; Foreman, *op. cit.*, 326; Charles Winslow Elliott, *Winfield Scott, the Soldier and the Man* (1937), 289-290.

[7] *American State Papers, Military Affairs*, VI, 565; George A. McCall, *Letters from the Frontier* (1868), 299; Foreman, *op. cit.*, 326-327; Elliott, *op. cit.*, 289-290.

[8] *Army and Navy Chronicle*, II, 99.

[9] *Niles' Weekly Register*, XLIX, 366.

[10] Elliott, *op. cit.*, 294-310.

[11] Sprague, *op. cit.*, 166.

[12] *Ibid.*, 168-171, 174-180.

[13] Foreman, *op. cit.*, 349-354; Sprague, *op. cit.*, 217-219.

[14] At Fort Brooke on November 20, 1837, Taylor made what he believed might be his last will and testament. *Cf.* Agreement of settlement between the widow and heirs of Zachary Taylor, witnessed by A. Mazineau, notary public, New Orleans, December 9, 1850, Taylor Family Papers, Stauffer Collection, New Orleans.

[15] Taylor to Jesup, November 26, 1837, Old Files Section, Executive Division, Adjutant General's Office, War Department, Washington.

[16] *Idem.*

[17] Taylor to Jesup, December 4, 1837, Old Files Section, Executive Division, Adjutant General's Office, War Department, Washington.

[18] Taylor to Jones, January 4, 1838, *Niles' National Register*, LIII, 369.

[19] Taylor to Jesup, December 19, December 27, 1837, Old Files Section, Executive Division, Adjutant General's Office, War Department, Washington.

[20] Taylor to Jones, January 4, 1838, *Niles' National Register*, LIII, 370-371.

[21] *Idem.*

[22] *Army and Navy Chronicle*, IV, 234.

[23] Taylor to Jones, January 4, 1838, *Niles' National Register*, LIII, 370-371.

[24] *Idem*; Taylor to Jesup, December 27, 1837, Old Files Section, Executive Division, Adjutant General's Office, War Department, Washington.

[25] Taylor to Jones, January 4, 1838, *Niles' National Register*, LIII, 371.

[26] *Idem.*

[27] *Idem.*

[28] Sprague, *op. cit.*, 213.

[29] *Ibid.*, 210-211, 214; Taylor to Jones, January 4, 1838, *Niles' National Register*, LIII, 370-371. This account is based primarily on Zachary Taylor's reports. The denials made by some of the volunteers are fully treated in the next chapter.

[30] Taylor to Jones, January 4, 1838, *Niles' National Register*, LIII, 370-371; Sprague, *op. cit.*, 213-214.

[31] Taylor to Jones, January 4, 1838, *Niles' National Register*, LIII, 370-371.

[32] *Idem.*

[33] Taylor to William Davenport, March 20, 1838, Presidential Papers, Manuscript Division, Historical Society of Pennsylvania, Philadelphia.

[34] Jesup to Secretary of War Poinsett, July 6, 1838, Sprague, *op. cit.*, 189, 196.

[35] Jesup to Poinsett, February 11, 1838, Old Files Section, Executive Division, Adjutant General's Office, War Department, Washington.

[36] Jesup to Poinsett, June 7, 1838, Old Files Section, Executive Division, Adjutant General's Office, War Department, Washington.

[37] Sprague, *op. cit.*, 221; Taylor to Hancock Taylor, August—, 1838, typewritten copy, Zachary Taylor Papers, R. Alexander Bate Collection, Louisville. Taylor was assigned to the Florida command in April; he did not formally succeed Jesup until May 15.

[38] Taylor to Hancock Taylor, August —, 1838, typewritten copy, Zachary Taylor Papers, R. Alexander Bate Collection, Louisville.

[39] Tallahassee *Floridian*, August 25, 1838; *Niles' National Register*, LV, 19.

[40] Foreman, *op. cit.*, 368; Taylor to Jones, July 20, 1839, Sprague, *op. cit.*, 221-222.

[41] Taylor to Jones, July 20, 1839, Sprague, *op. cit.*, 223-227.

[42] Taylor to Jones, January 10, 1839, Zachary Taylor Papers, Hamilton Collection, Fort Wayne, Indiana; Taylor to Governor Richard K. Call, March 11, 1839, Edward E. Ayer Collection, Newberry Library, Chicago.

[43] Sprague, *op. cit.*, 228-229.

[44] Macomb to Poinsett, May 22, 1839, Sprague, *op. cit.*, 232.

[45] Sprague, *op. cit.*, 232-233.

[46] Taylor to Jones, July 28, 1838, Sprague, *op. cit.*, 241.

[47] Poinsett to President Martin Van Buren, November 30, 1839, *Niles' National Register*, LVII, 314.

[48] Taylor to Joseph P. Taylor, January 11, 1840, Zachary Taylor Papers, Manuscript Division, Library of Congress, Washington.

[49] *Idem.*

[50] Sprague, *op. cit.*, 247.


## CHAPTER X

[1] *Army and Navy Chronicle*, X, 360, 366.

[2] *Ibid.*, XI, 56.

[3] Taylor to Jones, September 19, 1840, *John Heise Autograph Catalogue*, Number 2468, Syracuse, New York; Charles W. Upham, *Eulogy on the Life and Character of Zachary Taylor* (1850), 21-22; Don C. Seitz, *The James Gordon Bennetts, Father and Son* (1928), 127.

[4] Taylor to Jesup, November 4, 1840, photostatic copy, Zachary Taylor Papers, Manuscript Division, Library of Congress, Washington.

[5] Baton Rouge Garrison Return, December, 1840, Officers' Division, Adjutant General's Office, War Department, Washington.

[6] Notary Record Book F, 446-447, West Feliciana Parish, Saint Francisville, Louisiana.

[7] Taylor to Edmund P. Gaines, August 6, 1841, Fort Smith Letter Book 111A, Old Files Section, Executive Division, Adjutant General's Office, War Department, Washington.

[8] Taylor to Ethan Allen Hitchcock, May 19, 1841, Zachary Taylor Papers, Manuscript Division, Library of Congress, Washington.

[9] Taylor to Jones, January 4, 1838, *Niles' National Register,* LIII, 370-371.

[10] *Missouri Argus* (Saint Louis), April 3, 1838.

[11] Quoted in William Richard Gentry, junior, *"Full Justice": The Story of Richard Gentry and His Missouri Volunteers in the Seminole War* (1937), 26-27.

[12] The author acknowledges the utter impossibility of being equally fair to every participant, regular and volunteer, either in the Battle of Okeechobee or in any other battle ever fought. At least fifty carefully-documented pages would be necessary to sift all the evidence for and against Taylor's report, or for and against the record of the Missouri Volunteers. For example, Captain Cornelius Gilliam and Adjutant H. G. Parks of the volunteers testified before the Legislative Committee that the rations given the Missouri men by Taylor were inferior to those allotted the regular soldiers. Yet Lieutenant William H. Winlock, one of Gentry's subordinates, asserted that the volunteers' rations were as good as the regulars'. Surgeon I. H. Hannah declared: "We fared about as well as they did." And Captain John Sconce testified: "We didn't have much cause to complain." One Missourian, Private Robert A. Raphael, accused a majority of the Regular Army officers of using "the Missouri Volunteers more like negroes than any thing else I can mention." Another Missourian, Captain William Henry Russell, considered the conduct and bearing of the regular officers toward the volunteers kind and even generous. Several volunteers complained because Colonel Taylor assigned them the unpleasant duty of crossing swamps ahead of the regulars during the march down the Kissimmee River. On the other hand, as Taylor pointed out, the regulars performed the drudgery of opening roads, building bridges, and erecting blockhouses. The debate seems approximately even on that particular score. It is known that ill-feeling between Gentry and Taylor developed several days before the battle; which colonel was more in the wrong it is impossible to tell. Not a single Regular Army officer had cause to testify in this connection; what testimony does exist is, of course, decidedly pro-Gentry. It seems almost certain that, immediately prior to the engagement, Taylor gave Gentry explicit instructions to fall back with his men in good order as soon as he should succeed in drawing the Indians' fire (Depositions of Captain John Sconce, Lieutenant Charles B. Rogers, Surgeon I. H. Hannah, Manuscript Journal of the Missouri Legislative Committee on the Florida Campaign, Missouri Historical Society, Jefferson Memorial, Saint Louis; statement of Thomas Benton Gentry, T. B. Gentry, *Souvenir of General Richard Gentry: A Missouri Pioneer and Soldier* [1899], 11). It may be that Taylor failed to make his instructions perfectly clear. It is equally possible that Colonel Gentry, hunting glory, rushed upon the Indians in the hope of becoming the successful hero of the conflict. In any event, Gentry told his subordinates that Taylor had commanded him to charge the hammock (Deposition of Lieutenant John Reed). On this and other points, the testimony given by Missouri volunteer officers and privates is without exception the most contradictory the author has ever encountered.

[13] Taylor to Hitchcock, July 28, 1841, Zachary Taylor Papers, Manuscript Division, Library of Congress, Washington.

[14] Taylor to Hitchcock, November 3, 1841, Zachary Taylor Papers, Manuscript Division, Library of Congress, Washington.

[15] Henry Putney Beers, *The Western Military Frontier, 1815-1846* (1935), 67-69, 122, 133.

[16] Prior to Taylor's arrival in the Second Department, General Arbuckle had planned a transfer of headquarters to Fort Smith (Taylor to Jones, July 8, 1841, Fort Smith Letter Book 111A, Old Files Section, Executive Division, Adjutant General's Office, War Department, Washington).

[17] Carolyn Thomas Foreman (editor), "Journal of a Tour in the Indian Territory," *Chronicles of Oklahoma*, X, 231.

[18] Taylor to Hitchcock, July 28, 1841, Zachary Taylor Papers, Manuscript Division, Library of Congress, Washington.

[19] Taylor to Hitchcock, November 3, 1841, Zachary Taylor Papers, Manuscript Division, Library of Congress, Washington.

[20] Taylor to Jones, July 21, 1841, Old Files Section, Executive Division, Adjutant General's Office, War Department, Washington.

[21] Taylor to William Armstrong, September 22, 1841, Fort Smith Letter Book 111A, Old Files Section, Executive Division, Adjutant General's Office, War Department, Washington.

[22] Taylor to Jones, October 14, 1841, Fort Smith Letter Book 111A, Old Files Section, Executive Division, Adjutant General's Office, War Department, Washington.

[23] Taylor to Jones, April 17, 1842, Old Files Section, Executive Division, Adjutant General's Office, War Department, Washington.

[24] Grant Foreman, *Advancing the Frontier, 1830-1860* (1933), 78-80; Ethan Allen Hitchcock to Secretary of War John C. Spencer, January 9, 1842, Hitchcock Papers, Manuscript Division, Library of Congress, Washington.

[25] Memorial to President John Tyler, July 4, 1843, Old Files Section, Executive Division, Adjutant General's Office, War Department, Washington.

[26] *Army and Navy Chronicle, and Scientific Repository*, III, 573-574.

[27] Taylor to Jones, March 28, 1843, Fort Smith Letter Book 111A, Old Files Section, Executive Division, Adjutant General's Office, War Department, Washington.

[28] Taylor to Jones, March 29, 1843, Fort Smith Letter Book 111A, Old Files Section, Executive Division, Adjutant General's Office, War Department, Washington.

[29] William Armstrong to Commissioner of Indian Affairs T. Hartley Crawford, May 24, 1842, Choctaw Agency Papers, Western Superintendency File, Office of Indian Affairs, Department of the Interior, Washington.

[30] *Arkansas Intelligencer* (Van Buren), May 27, 1842.

[31] Armstrong to Crawford, August 14, 1842, Choctaw Agency Papers,

Western Superintendency File, Office of Indian Affairs, Department of the Interior, Washington.

[32] Taylor to Jones, May 31, 1842, Fort Smith Letter Book 111A, Old Files Section, Executive Division, Adjutant General's Office, War Department, Washington.

[33] *Idem.*

[34] George W. Cullum, *Biographical Register of the Officers and Graduates of . . . West Point* (1879), 542–545; W. A. Croffut (editor), *Fifty Years in Camp and Field, the Diary of Major General Ethan Allen Hitchcock, U. S. A.* (1909), 147, 159; statement of Trist Wood, New Orleans; statement of the late Mrs. Betty Taylor Stauffer, New Orleans.

[35] From Justin H. Smith, *The War with Mexico* (1919), I, 141. By permission of the Macmillan Company, publishers.

[36] Pierce M. Butler to Crawford, June 21, 1843, Cherokee Agency Papers, Western Superintendency File, Office of Indian Affairs, Department of the Interior, Washington.

[37] Taylor to Jones, June 14, 1843, Fort Smith Letter Book 111A, Old Files Section, Executive Division, Adjutant General's Office, War Department, Washington.

[38] Taylor to Jones, August 15, 1843, Old Files Section, Executive Division, Adjutant General's Office, War Department, Washington.

[39] Taylor to Jones, October 8, 1843, Old Files Section, Executive Division, Adjutant General's Office, War Department, Washington.

[40] Taylor to Jones, February 14, 1844, Old Files Section, Executive Division, Adjutant General's Office, War Department, Washington.

[41] Fred W. Allsopp, *Folklore of Romantic Arkansas* (1931), I, 130–135.

[42] Taylor to Hitchcock, November 3, 1841, Zachary Taylor Papers, Manuscript Division, Library of Congress, Washington; Second Department Returns, January, February, 1843, January, February, 1844, Officers' Division, Adjutant General's Office, War Department, Washington.

[43] Deed Book M, 427–428, Wilkinson County, Woodville, Mississippi.

[44] Notary Record Book H, 106–109, West Feliciana Parish, Saint Francisville, Louisiana.

[45] Deed Book E, 520 *et seq.*, Jefferson County, Fayette, Mississippi.

[46] Taylor to Joseph P. Taylor, June 17, 1843, Zachary Taylor Papers, Manuscript Division, Library of Congress, Washington. One of Taylor's minor disappointments at Fort Smith was his failure to secure a West Point cadetship for his son (Taylor to Dr. Robert C. Wood, July 2, 1843, Zachary Taylor Papers, Miss Lola M. Wood Collection, Maddox, Maryland).

## CHAPTER XI

[1] Jones to Taylor, April 23, 1844, *Army and Navy Chronicle, and Scientific Repository*, III, 654.

[2] *The Rough and Ready* (Louisville), October 9, 1847.

[3] Jones to Taylor, April 27, 1844, *Army and Navy Chronicle, and Scientific Repository*, III, 655.

[4] Taylor to Jones, June 18, 1844, Old Files Section, Executive Division, Adjutant General's Office, War Department, Washington.

[5] Taylor to President Sam Houston, June 17, 1844, true copy attested by Taylor, Old Files Section, Executive Division, Adjutant General's Office, War Department, Washington.

[6] W. A. Croffut (editor), *Fifty Years in Camp and Field, the Diary of Major General Ethan Allen Hitchcock, U. S. A.* (1909), 187.

[7] [Ulysses S. Grant], *Personal Memoirs of U. S. Grant* (1885), I, 54.

[8] Harry E. Chambers, *Mississippi Valley Beginnings* (1922), 352-362; J. Fair Hardin, "Four Forgotten Frontier Posts of Western Louisiana," *Louisiana Historical Quarterly*, XVII, 144-145.

[9] Eugene Irving McCormac, *James K. Polk, a Political Biography* (1922), *passim*.

[10] Justin H. Smith, *The War with Mexico* (1919), I, 84.

[11] Joseph Schafer, *A History of the Pacific Northwest* (1905), 180-185.

[12] Secretary of War William L. Marcy to Taylor, May 2, 1845, W. S. Henry, *Campaign Sketches of the War with Mexico* (1847), 9.

[13] Croffut, *op. cit.*, 192; Taylor to Mary Elizabeth Taylor, July 3, 1845, *The Autograph*, I, 21; J. Reese Fry and Robert T. Conrad, *A Life of Gen. Zachary Taylor* (1848), 73.

[14] Henry, *op. cit.*, 10-11; Croffut, *op. cit.*, 193.

[15] Varina Jefferson Davis, *Jefferson Davis, a Memoir* (1890), I, 199.

[16] [Thomas B. Thorpe], *Taylor Anecdote Book* (1848), 101-102.

[17] Henry, *op. cit.*, 12-13.

[18] *Ibid.*, 13.

[19] *Ibid.*, 15-18; Smith, *op. cit.*, I, 142; Richard E. Cochrane, junior, to Richard E. Cochrane, senior, September 4, 1845, Florence Johnson Scott, *Old Rough and Ready on the Rio Grande* (1935), 40-41; George G. Meade to Mrs. Meade, September 18, 1845, George Meade, *The Life and Letters of George Gordon Meade* (1913), I, 27; Emma J. Blackwood (editor), *To Mexico with Scott, Letters of Captain E. Kirby Smith to His Wife* (1917), 17-18. The author visited Corpus Christi in 1940. A stretch of beach immediately north of the Breakers Hotel was pointed out as the site of Taylor's camp.

[20] Henry, *op. cit.*, 13; Croffut, *op. cit.*, 193-194; Taylor to Jones, August 15, 1845, *House Executive Document 196, Twenty-ninth Congress, First Session*, 84.

[21] Croffut, *op. cit.*, 194.

[22] Henry, *op. cit.*, 39.

[23] Smith, *op. cit.*, I, 241.

[24] [Grant], *op. cit.*, I, 123.

[25] Meade to Mrs. Meade, May 24, 1846, Meade, *op. cit.*, I, 88.

[26] From Justin H. Smith, *The War with Mexico* (1919), II, 48. By permission of the Macmillan Company, publishers.

[27] Henry, *op. cit.*, 39, 44; Walter Prescott Webb, *The Texas Rangers* (1935), 91.

[28] Croffut, *op. cit.*, 198-199; Charles Larned to Ethan Allen Hitchcock,

May 6, 1846, Hitchcock Papers, Manuscript Division, Library of Congress, Washington.

29 Meade to Mrs. Meade, November 3, 1845, Meade, *op. cit.*, I, 35.

30 Henry, *op. cit.*, 40.

31 Cochrane to Richard E. Cochrane, senior, September 4, 1845, Florence Johnson Scott, *op. cit.*, 40.

32 Love to Johnston, September—, 1845, William Preston Johnston, *The Life of Albert Sidney Johnston* (1879), 131.

33 Henry, *op. cit.*, 28, 35; Taylor to Marcy, September 6, 1845, *House Executive Document 60, Thirtieth Congress, First Session,* 105; Taylor to Jones, August 15, 1845, *House Executive Document 196, Twenty-ninth Congress, First Session,* 85.

34 Meade, *op. cit.*, I, 27-29, 36. A third expedition went along the coast (*Ibid.*, I, 46). *Cf.* Blackwood, *op. cit.*, 20; Taylor to Marcy, September 14, November 7, 1845, *House Executive Document 60, Thirtieth Congress, First Session,* 107, 111.

35 Louis C. Duncan, "A Medical History of General Zachary Taylor's Army of Occupation in Texas and Mexico, 1845-1847," *The Military Surgeon,* XLVIII, 78-79.

36 Henry, *op. cit.*, 44.

37 Croffut, *op. cit.*, 204-206, 220-221; Meade, *op. cit.*, I, 26.

38 [Grant], *op. cit.*, I, 69; Meade to Mrs. Meade, October 21, December 9, December 25, 1845, Meade, *op. cit.*, I, 32, 37, 42.

39 Meade to Mrs. Meade, December 1, 1845, Meade, *op. cit.*, I, 37.

40 Taylor to Mary Elizabeth Taylor, December 15, 1845, *The Autograph,* I, 48.

41 George Lockhart Rives, *The United States and Mexico, 1821-1848* (1913), II, 135. Justin H. Smith outlines President Polk's side of the boundary argument on pages 138 and 139 of the first volume of his *The War with Mexico,* but on page 449 Smith states that the American claim was unsound.

42 Smith, *op. cit.*, I, 70-83, 117-118, 136.

43 *Ibid.*, I, 85-87.

44 *Ibid.*, I, 91-92.

45 Marcy to Taylor, January 13, 1846, *House Executive Document 60, Thirtieth Congress, First Session,* 90.

## CHAPTER XII

1 Taylor to Jones, February 16, February 26, 1846, *House Executive Document 60, Thirtieth Congress, First Session,* 117-118.

2 Louis C. Duncan, "A Medical History of General Zachary Taylor's Army of Occupation in Texas and Mexico, 1845-1847," *Military Surgeon,* XLVIII, 80.

3 Taylor to Jones, March 8, 1846, *House Executive Document 60, Thirtieth Congress, First Session,* 118.

4 W. S. Henry, *Campaign Sketches of the War with Mexico* (1847), 50.

[5] Taylor to Jones, March 8, 1846, *House Executive Document 60, Thirtieth Congress, First Session*, 118.

[6] Henry, *op. cit.*, 52. Under Taylor's direction, two mules hauled his personal property from Corpus Christi to the Rio Grande (Taylor to Thomas W. Ringgold, May 13, 1846, James F. Drake Collection, New York City).

[7] Taylor to Jones, March 8, 1846, *House Executive Document 60, Thirtieth Congress, First Session*, 118; Diary of Surgeon Robert C. Wood, Taylor Family Papers, Trist Wood Collection, New Orleans.

[8] Henry, *op. cit.*, 53.

[9] Emma J. Blackwood (editor), *To Mexico with Scott, Letters of Captain E. Kirby Smith to His Wife* (1917), 23.

[10] Samuel G. French, *Two Wars: An Autobiography* (1901), 41.

[11] Henry, *op. cit.*, 54-57.

[12] French, *op. cit.*, 42-43.

[13] Order Number 30, March 8, 1846, J. Reese Fry and Robert T. Conrad, *A Life of Gen. Zachary Taylor* (1848), 90-91.

[14] Henry, *op. cit.*, 51.

[15] *Ibid.*, 59-60; Justin H. Smith, *The War with Mexico* (1919), I, 146; French, *op. cit.*, 44.

[16] Taylor to Jones, March 21, 1846, *House Executive Document 60, Thirtieth Congress, First Session*, 124; W. A. Croffut (editor), *Fifty Years in Camp and Field, the Diary of Major General Ethan Allen Hitchcock, U. S. A.* (1909), 211. Hitchcock's version of events transpiring at the Arroyo Colorado differs in minor details from Henry's version.

[17] Henry, *op. cit.*, 59-60; Croffut, *op. cit.*, 211; Blackwood, *op. cit.*, 30.

[18] Taylor to James Taylor, May 24, 1846, copy, Taylor Family Papers, Stauffer Collection, New Orleans; Taylor to Jones, March 25, 1846, *House Executive Document 60, Thirtieth Congress, First Session*, 129-130. Justin H. Smith errs when he says Taylor and Worth separated on March 23 (Smith, *op. cit.*, I, 148).

[19] Rhoda van Bibber Tanner Doubleday (editor), *Journals of the Late Brevet Major Philip Norbourne Barbour . . . and His Wife . . .* (1936), 17.

[20] Taylor to Jones, April 6, 1846, *House Executive Document 60, Thirtieth Congress, First Session*, 133.

[21] Ampudia to Taylor, April 12, 1846, *House Executive Document 60, Thirtieth Congress, First Session*, 140.

[22] Croffut, *op. cit.*, 220; Henry, *op. cit.*, 72; Taylor to James Taylor, May 24, 1846, copy, Taylor Family Papers, Stauffer Collection, New Orleans.

[23] On April 7 Zachary Taylor wrote to his daughter: "I have thrown up a heavy work & placed in it today some heavy guns brought up from Point Isabel" (Taylor to Mary Elizabeth Taylor, April 7, 1846, *The Autograph*, I, 74).

[24] Meade to Mrs. Meade, April 15, 1846, George Meade, *The Life and Letters of George Gordon Meade* (1913), I, 59.

[25] "Their force . . . is equal if not greater than ours, but very inferior in

quality & equipment, & should we come to blows there cannot be a doubt as to the result. We must beat them" (Taylor to Mary Elizabeth Taylor, April 7, 1846, *The Autograph*, I, 74).

[26] Meade to Mrs. Meade, April 15, 1846, Meade, *op. cit.*, I, 59.

[27] Henry, *op. cit.*, 83.

[28] *Ibid.*, 73. Meade says Colonel Cross died on April 15 (Meade, *op. cit.*, I, 62). Analysis of the statements in the two texts shows Meade to have been mistaken.

[29] Henry, *op. cit.*, 77; Blackwood, *op. cit.*, 39; Charles Larned to Ethan Allen Hitchcock, May 6, 1846, Hitchcock Papers, Manuscript Division, Library of Congress, Washington.

[30] George Lockhart Rives, *The United States and Mexico, 1821-1848* (1913), II, 143; Blackwood, *op. cit.*, 39-43; Henry, *op. cit.*, 82-85; W. H. Chatfield, *The Twin Cities of the Border* (1893), 13, 23.

[31] Taylor to Jones, April 26, 1846, *House Executive Document 60, Thirtieth Congress, First Session*, 288. The authorship of Zachary Taylor's Mexican War dispatches was frequently attributed to Bliss, who denied the allegation. It is probable that the dispatches were dictated by Taylor, revised and edited by Bliss.

[32] Taylor to Jones, May 3, 1846, *House Executive Document 60, Thirtieth Congress, First Session*, 289-290.

[33] One of many Mexican War diarists was Surgeon Madison Mills, whose observations are noteworthy because of his extreme anti-Taylor bias. On May 2, 1846, Mills wrote: "We marched till 2 o'clock this morning and halted and slept on our arms till morning without fire or supper. I did not get my blankets till after 3 o'clock AM and scarcely got asleep before . . . [we] were ordered to march on. Marched 2 miles and halted to take a little something in the way of breakfast. Our meal consisted of a little cold meal and bread (hard bread) without coffee. There is much complaint against the Genl. He is becoming very unpopular. The march yesterday afternoon and last night was the most harassing I ever saw or performed and quite unnecessarily so. Both officers and men speak boldly and say it is an outrage. Marched after a half of an hour and reached Pt. Isabel at 1 o'clock, making several short halts on the way. It is these short halts that annoy the men so much" (Mexican War Diary of Surgeon Madison Mills, typewritten copy, Kentucky Papers, Filson Club Archives, Louisville).

[34] Taylor to Jones, May 5, 1846, *House Executive Document 60, Thirtieth Congress, First Session*, 292-293; Taylor to Mary Elizabeth Taylor, May 13, 1846, *The Autograph*, I, 100-101.

[35] Doubleday, *op. cit.*, 52-53; Blackwood, *op. cit.*, 44-45.

[36] Henry, *op. cit.*, 89. According to Madison Mills, Taylor originally ordered the main body to march on May 3 at one o'clock in the afternoon, but later countermanded the order—dispatching May and Walker instead.

[37] Croffut, *op. cit.*, 220-223; Meade, *op. cit.*, I, 87-88.

[38] Henry, *op. cit.*, 129-131.

[39] Taylor to James Taylor, May 24, 1846, copy, Taylor Family Papers,

Stauffer Collection, New Orleans; Farnham Bishop, *Our First War in Mexico* (1916), 89.

40 Manuel Balbontín, *La Invasión Americana* (1883), 38.

41 Meade, *op. cit.*, I, 61; Rives, *op. cit.*, II, 150; Smith, *op. cit.*, I, 161.


## CHAPTER XIII

1 George G. Meade to Mrs. Meade, May 9, 1846, George Meade, *The Life and Letters of George Gordon Meade* (1913), I, 79; J. Reese Fry and Robert T. Conrad, *A Life of Gen. Zachary Taylor* (1848), 128; Rhoda van Bibber Tanner Doubleday (editor), *Journals of the Late Brevet Major Philip Norbourne Barbour . . . and His Wife . . .* (1936), 53; W. S. Henry, *Campaign Sketches of the War with Mexico* (1847), 90; Mexican War Diary of Surgeon Madison Mills, typewritten copy, Kentucky Papers, Filson Club Archives, Louisville. Meade, Mills, and Fry and Conrad are authorities for the statement that the May 7 march was seven miles long. Barbour says it was six miles. Henry says it was five miles.

2 Meade to Mrs. Meade, May 9, 1846, Meade, *op. cit.*, I, 79; Taylor to Mary Elizabeth Taylor, May 13, 1846, *The Autograph*, I, 101.

3 Henry, *op. cit.*, 90; Taylor to James Taylor, May 24, 1846, copy, Taylor Family Papers, Stauffer Collection, New Orleans.

4 Henry, *op. cit.*, 91; Emma J. Blackwood (editor), *To Mexico with Scott, Letters of Captain E. Kirby Smith to His Wife* (1917), 47-48; Samuel G. French, *Two Wars: An Autobiography* (1901), 49; George Lockhart Rives, *The United States and Mexico, 1821-1848* (1913), II, 150; Doubleday, *op. cit.*, 54; Fry and Conrad, *op. cit.*, 121, 128.

5 Albert C. Ramsey (editor), *The Other Side: or Notes for the History of the War Between Mexico and the United States* (1850), 45. The author is indebted to Brigadier General Blas Corral of the Mexican Army for information concerning the full names and exact commands of De la Vega, Noriega, Torrejón and Uraga.

6 Rives, *op. cit.*, II, 148-149.

7 Henry, *op. cit.*, 89; Justin H. Smith, *The War with Mexico* (1919), I, 465-466.

8 Manuel Balbontín, *La Invasión Americana* (1883), 76-77; Rives, *op. cit.*, II, 149.

9 Henry, *op. cit.*, 91; Doubleday, *op. cit.*, 54.

10 Smith, *op. cit.*, I, 166; Henry, *op. cit.*, 91; Ramsey, *op. cit.*, 48.

11 [Ulysses S. Grant], *Personal Memoirs of U. S. Grant* (1885), I, 95-96.

12 Mexican War Diary of Surgeon Madison Mills, typewritten copy, Kentucky Papers, Filson Club Archives, Louisville.

13 Meade to Mrs. Meade, May 9, 1846; Meade, *op. cit.*, I, 79; Henry, *op. cit.*, 92; Smith, *op. cit.*, I, 166-167; Doubleday, *op. cit.*, 55.

14 Henry, *op. cit.*, 91-92; French, *op. cit.*, 50; Doubleday, *op. cit.*, 55-56; Ramsey, *op. cit.*, 49.

15 Smith, *op. cit.*, I, 167; Blackwood, *op. cit.*, 49; Taylor to James Taylor,

May 24, 1846, copy, Taylor Family Papers, Stauffer Collection, New Orleans.

[16] Mexican War Diary of Surgeon Madison Mills, typewritten copy, Kentucky Papers, Filson Club Archives, Louisville.

[17] Henry, *op. cit.*, 93.

[18] Doubleday, *op. cit.*, 56.

[19] Smith, *op. cit.*, I, 168; Charles Larned to Ethan Allen Hitchcock, June 13, 1846, Hitchcock Papers, Manuscript Division, Library of Congress, Washington.

[20] Meade to Mrs. Meade, May 9, 1846, Meade, *op. cit.*, I, 79; Smith, *op. cit.*, I, 168-169; Henry, *op. cit.*, 93; Taylor to Mary Elizabeth Taylor, May 13, 1846, *The Autograph*, I, 101.

[21] "We encamped on the field of battle, having gained the point occupied by the enemy's lancers in the commencement of the action" (Mexican War Diary of Surgeon Madison Mills, typewritten copy, Kentucky Papers, Filson Club Archives, Louisville).

[22] This is a minimum figure. Other estimates place the number of men killed at nine and ten. Some, mortally wounded, were at first officially listed as wounded rather than killed.

[23] Smith, *op. cit.*, I, 169, 466.

[24] Ramsey, *op. cit.*, 50.

[25] Henry, *op. cit.*, 94-95; Meade to Mrs. Meade, May 9, 1846, Meade, *op. cit.*, I, 80; Taylor to Mary Elizabeth Taylor, May 13, 1846, *The Autograph*, I, 101; Taylor to James Taylor, May 24, 1846, copy, Taylor Family Papers, Stauffer Collection, New Orleans.

[26] Doubleday, *op. cit.*, 57; Braxton Bragg to James Henry Hammond, August 26, 1847, Hammond Papers, Manuscript Division, Library of Congress, Washington.

[27] Doubleday, *op. cit.*, 57-58; [Grant], *op. cit.*, I, 97; French, *op. cit.*, 51; Mexican War Diary of Surgeon Madison Mills, typewritten copy, Kentucky Papers, Filson Club Archives, Louisville.

[28] Doubleday, *op. cit.*, 58.

[29] *Idem;* Henry, *op. cit.*, 96; Blackwood, *op. cit.*, 50-51.

[30] Doubleday, *op. cit.*, 58; Henry, *op. cit.*, 96-97.

[31] Henry, *op. cit.*, 97.

[32] *Idem;* French, *op. cit.*, 52-53. After the battle, a dispute arose as to whether May or Ridgely was the more audacious at this stage of the fighting.

[33] "I gave them a volley, and he [May] gallantly dashed forward in column of fours at the head of his squadron. I followed as quickly as possible, at a gallop, only halting when I came upon the edge of the ravine, where I found three pieces of artillery but no *cannoniers;* however, their infantry poured into me a most galling fire at from twenty-five to fifty paces and here ensued a most desperate struggle, but our infantry coming up, they were completely routed" (*Senate Executive Document 388, Twenty-ninth Congress, First Session*, 21).

[34] Smith, *op. cit.*, I, 174-175.

35 Quoted in Smith, *op. cit.*, I, 173.

36 Henry, *op. cit.*, 100; Charles Larned to Ethan Allen Hitchcock, June 13, 1846, Hitchcock Papers, Manuscript Division, Library of Congress, Washington.

37 Doubleday, *op. cit.*, 59.

38 *Idem.*

39 Ramsey, *op. cit.*, 52-53.

40 Doubleday, *op. cit.*, 60.

41 Meade, *op. cit.*, I, 81; Ramsey, *op. cit.*, 52-53.

42 Taylor to Mary Elizabeth Taylor, May 13, 1846, *The Autograph*, I, 101.

43 Henry, *op. cit.*, 98-99; Smith, *op. cit.*, I, 176; French, *op. cit.*, 57. Taylor wrote: "We succeeded in gaining a complete victory, dispersing them in every direction[,] taking their artillery, baggage or means of transportation, a number of standards &c, with a great loss of killed, wounded & prisoners. . . . The war I have no doubt is completely brought to a close on this side the Rio Grande; the enemy who escaped having re-crossed said river" (Taylor to Dr. Robert C. Wood, May 9, 1846, William H. Samson [editor], *Letters of Zachary Taylor from the Battle-fields of the Mexican War* [1908], 1).

## CHAPTER XIV

1 Major Jacob Brown was the only American officer to die as a result of the bombardment of Fort Texas. The modern city of Brownsville stands near the site of Fort Texas, which Zachary Taylor renamed Fort Brown in honor of its deceased commander.

2 George G. Meade to Mrs. Meade, May 11, 1846, George Meade, *The Life and Letters of George Gordon Meade* (1913), I, 82; Oliver Otis Howard, *General Taylor* (1892), 130; Samuel G. French, *Two Wars: An Autobiography* (1901), 57-58; Taylor to Jones, May 18, 1846, *House Executive Document 60, Thirtieth Congress, First Session*, 297-298.

3 Rhoda van Bibber Tanner Doubleday (editor), *Journals of the Late Brevet Major Philip Norbourne Barbour . . . and His Wife . . .* (1936), 180.

4 [Ulysses S. Grant], *Personal Memoirs of U. S. Grant* (1885), I, 100-102.

5 [Thomas B. Thorpe], *Taylor Anecdote Book* (1848), 134-135; Grant, *op. cit.*, I, 102.

6 Taylor to Dr. Robert C. Wood, May 19, 1846, William H. Samson (editor) *Letters of Zachary Taylor from the Battle-fields of the Mexican War* (1908), 3. Other sources indicate that General Taylor returned from Point Isabel on May 14.

7 Doubleday, *op. cit.*, 61-64; W. S. Henry, *Campaign Sketches of the War with Mexico* (1847), 107; Albert C. Ramsey (editor), *The Other Side: or Notes for the History of the War Between Mexico and the United States* (1850), 57-58.

8 Henry, *op. cit.*, 107.

⁹ *Ibid.*, 108.

¹⁰ Doubleday, *op. cit.*, 64-65.

¹¹ *Ibid.*, 65; Henry, *op. cit.*, 108-109; Meade to Mrs. Meade, May 19, 1846, Meade, *op. cit.*, I, 85; Taylor to James Taylor, May 24, 1846, copy, Taylor Family Papers, Stauffer Collection, New Orleans.

¹² George C. Furber, *The Twelve Months Volunteer; or, Journal of a Private . . . in Mexico* (1857), 189-190; Henry, *op. cit.*, 110.

¹³ Henry, *op. cit.*, 110-111.

¹⁴ Taylor to Mary Elizabeth Taylor, June 9, 1846, *The Autograph*, I, 127; Justin H. Smith, *The War with Mexico* (1919), I, 204-206; J. Reese Fry and Robert T. Conrad, *A Life of Gen. Zachary Taylor* (1848), 167, 171; Henry, *op. cit.*, 111-115. At least two of these camps were badly situated from the standpoint of health. *Cf.* [Lew Wallace], *Lew Wallace, an Autobiography* (1906), I, 121-128.

¹⁵ [Joseph Jefferson], *Autobiography of Joseph Jefferson* (1897), 67.

¹⁶ James D. Richardson (editor), *Messages and Papers of the Presidents* (1897), VI, 2292.

¹⁷ "I much fear too many volunteers will come," Taylor wrote (Taylor to Wood, May 19, 1846, Samson, *op. cit.*, 4).

¹⁸ Doubleday, *op. cit.*, 75; Meade to Mrs. Meade, June 12, June 14, 1846, Meade, *op. cit.*, I, 103, 105; Henry, *op. cit.*, 117; Louis C. Duncan, "A Medical History of General Zachary Taylor's Army of Occupation in Texas and Mexico, 1845-1847," *The Military Surgeon*, XLVIII, 82; John R. Kenly, *Memoirs of a Maryland Volunteer* (1873), 56.

¹⁹ Meade to Mrs. Meade, June 28, 1846, Meade, *op. cit.*, I, 108; Taylor to Wood, June 12, June 30, 1846, Samson, *op. cit.*, 9, 20.

²⁰ Fry and Conrad, *op. cit.*, 173; Doubleday, *op. cit.*, 66, 68; Henry, *op. cit.*, 113; Meade to Mrs. Meade, May 24, 1846, Meade, *op. cit.*, I, 88; Mexican War Diary of Surgeon Madison Mills, typewritten copy, Kentucky Papers, Filson Club Archives, Louisville. These authorities differ slightly as to details.

²¹ Henry, *op. cit.*, 117; Thomas B. Thorpe, *Our Army at Monterey* (1848), 9-10.

²² Walter Prescott Webb, *The Texas Rangers* (1935), 95; Samuel C. Reid, junior, *The Scouting Expeditions of McCulloch's Texas Rangers* (1848), 43-52; Doubleday, *op. cit.*, 69; Taylor to Jones, July 2, 1846, *House Executive Document 60, Thirtieth Congress, First Session*, 329-332.

²³ Allan Nevins (editor), *The Diary of Philip Hone, 1828-1851* (1927), II, 764.

²⁴ Milo M. Quaife (editor), *The Diary of James K. Polk* (1910), I, 428-429; Polk to Taylor, May 30, 1846, *House Executive Document 60, Thirtieth Congress, First Session*, 283.

²⁵ Quoted in Smith, *op. cit.*, I, 179.

²⁶ Meade, *op. cit.*, I, 101. Unlike Mills (who disliked Taylor intensely) and Henry (whose admiration was outspoken), Meade rarely revealed a bias. Though occasionally inaccurate in details, Meade's letters are especially valuable because of their author's fairness. Pages 98 and 101 of

Volume I provide an example of this quality. On both pages Meade praises Taylor, and then on the latter page Meade criticizes Taylor adversely on what he considers justifiable grounds.

[27] Grant, *op. cit.*, I, 100.

[28] Fry and Conrad, *op. cit.*, 326; Meade to Mrs. Meade, June 12, July 9, 1846, Meade, *op. cit.*, I, 104, 112; *Virginia Historical Register*, IV, 218-220; *William and Mary College Quarterly*, First Series, XVIII, 12-13.

[29] Taylor to Wood, June 12, 1846, Samson, *op. cit.*, 10; Meade, *op. cit.*, I, 104; Mexican War Diary of Surgeon Madison Mills, typewritten copy, Kentucky Papers, Filson Club Archives, Louisville.

[30] Fry and Conrad, *op. cit.*, 326.

[31] *Idem.*

[32] F. B. Heitman, *Historical Register of the United States Army from . . . September 29, 1789, to September 29, 1889* (1890), 634.

[33] Harriet A. Weed (editor), *Autobiography of Thurlow Weed* (1883), 571-572.

[34] Taylor to Joseph P. Taylor, undated, Weed, *op cit.*, 573.

[35] Taylor to Wood, June 21, 1846, Samson, *op. cit.*, 14.

[36] Henry, *op. cit.*, 120, 123-125, 132; Doubleday, *op. cit.*, 98. Thorpe says Taylor boarded the *Whitesville* at Matamoros on August 5 (Thomas B. Thorpe, *Our Army at Monterey* [1848], 26).

[37] Doubleday, *op. cit.*, 91-92.

[38] Meade to Mrs. Meade, June 28, 1846, Meade, *op. cit.*, I, 106-107.

[39] Henry, *op. cit.*, 136.

[40] *Ibid.*, 152-153; Kenly, *op. cit.*, 64-65; James K. Holland, "Diary of a Texan Volunteer in the Mexican War," *Southwestern Historical Quarterly*, XXX, 18-19; William A. McClintock, "Journal of a Trip through Texas and Northern Mexico in 1846-1847," *Southwestern Historical Quarterly*, XXXIV, 240; Mexican War Diary of Surgeon Madison Mills, typewritten copy, Kentucky Papers, Filson Club Archives, Louisville.

[41] Duncan, "A Medical History of General Zachary Taylor's Army of Occupation in Texas and Mexico, 1845-1847," *loc. cit.*, 82.

[42] Doubleday, *op. cit.*, 95.

[43] Quoted in Smith, *op. cit.*, I, 212.

[44] Meade to Mrs. Meade, July 24, 1846, Meade, *op. cit.*, I, 115-116.

[45] Doubleday, *op. cit.*, 89.

[46] Taylor to George T. Wood, July 7, 1846, Governors' Letters, Texas State Capitol, Austin.

[47] Meade to Mrs. Meade, May 27, 1846, Meade, *op. cit.*, I, 91.

[48] Taylor to Davis, August 3, 1846, *Boston Public Library Monthly Bulletin*, V, 320; Taylor to Robert C. Wood, August 4, 1846, Samson, *op. cit.*, 36.

[49] Allen Johnson and Dumas Malone (editors), *Dictionary of American Biography* (1928-1936), III, 371.

[50] Grant, *op. cit.*, I, 103.

[51] Taylor to Robert C. Wood, August 19, 1846, Samson, *op. cit.*, 41.

[52] Smith, *op. cit.*, I, 241.

[53] Meade to Mrs. Meade, August 18, 1846, Meade, *op. cit.*, I, 123.

[54] Taylor to Jones, September 3, September 4, September 12, 1846, *House Executive Document 60, Thirtieth Congress, First Session*, 417-421; Thorpe, *Our Army at Monterey* (1848), 30-32.

[55] Taylor to Robert C. Wood, September 3, 1846, Samson, *op. cit.*, 50-51; Taylor to Wood, July 31, 1846, Zachary Taylor Papers, Miss Lola M. Wood Collection, Maddox, Maryland.

[56] Taylor to Robert C. Wood, August 23, 1846, Samson, *op. cit.*, 46; Mexican War Diary of Surgeon Madison Mills, typewritten copy, Kentucky Papers, Filson Club Archives, Louisville.

[57] Henry, *op. cit.*, 170.

[58] Kenly, *op. cit.*, 83.

[59] Taylor to Robert C. Wood, September 10, 1846, Samson, *op. cit.*, 54.

[60] Henry, *op. cit.*, 177.

[61] Taylor to Robert C. Wood, September 10, 1846, Samson, *op. cit.*, 54; Holland, "Diary of a Texan Volunteer in the Mexican War," *loc. cit.*, 25.

[62] Thorpe, *Our Army at Monterey* (1848), 45-46.

[63] Doubleday, *op. cit.*, 106-107.

## CHAPTER XV

[1] W. S. Henry, *Campaign Sketches of the War with Mexico* (1847), 192; George Lockhart Rives, *The United States and Mexico, 1821-1848* (1913), II, 260; Thomas B. Thorpe, *Our Army at Monterey* (1848), 49; Mexican War Diary of Surgeon Madison Mills, typewritten copy, Kentucky Papers, Filson Club, Louisville.

[2] Justin H. Smith, *The War with Mexico* (1919), I, 249; George C. Furber, *The Twelve Months Volunteer; or, Journal of a Private . . . in Mexico* (1857), 97; Samuel G. French, *Two Wars: An Autobiography* (1901), 61.

[3] Samuel C. Reid, junior, *The Scouting Expeditions of McCulloch's Texas Rangers* (1848), 149; Thorpe, *op. cit.*, 100-101; Smith, *op. cit.*, I, 232-233, 249. According to Rives, La Libertad was near El Diablo. This is incorrect. La Libertad was near the Bishop's Palace at the other end of the city. The third fort at the northeastern corner of Monterey, near El Diablo and Tenería, was known as La Casa Colorada.

[4] Rives, *op. cit.*, II, 262; Smith, *op. cit.*, I, 233; Albert C. Ramsey (editor), *The Other Side: or Notes for the History of the War Between Mexico and the United States* (1850), 76; William A. McClintock, "Journal of a Trip through Texas and Northern Mexico in 1846-1847," *Southwestern Historical Quarterly*, XXXIV, 251.

[5] Thorpe, *op. cit.*, 65, 70, 101; Reid, *op. cit.*, 150; Smith, *op. cit.*, I, 239, 241; McClintock, "Journal of a Trip through Texas and Northern Mexico in 1846-1847," *loc. cit.*, 249-251.

[6] Henry, *op. cit.*, 192.

[7] Braxton Bragg to James Henry Hammond, May 4, 1848, James Henry Hammond Papers, Manuscript Division, Library of Congress, Washington.

Bragg is one authority for the statement that Taylor planned the attack on Monterey. Other authorities credit Worth with originating it. Both possibilities deserve consideration. It is probable that Worth outlined a rudimentary plan to Taylor, and that the two generals developed it together. Always to be remembered is the fact that—although Twiggs was an efficient second-in-command at Palo Alto and Resaca de la Palma, Worth at Monterey, and Wool at Buena Vista—Zachary Taylor himself was the responsible chief.

[8] Reid, *op. cit.*, 151, 156-158; Thorpe, *op. cit.*, 63-64; Smith, *op. cit.*, I, 241-244; John R. Kenly, *Memoirs of a Maryland Volunteer* (1873), 98; Ramsey, *op. cit.*, 71.

[9] Worth to Bliss, September 21, 1846, quoted in Smith, *op. cit.*, I, 244.

[10] Quoted in Justin H. Smith, *The War with Mexico* (1919), I, 250. By permission of the Macmillan Company, publishers.

[11] Thorpe, *op. cit.*, 50, 52; Kenly, *op. cit.*, 106-112; Furber, *op. cit.*, 100, 103; Reid, *op. cit.*, 170-171; Mexican War Journal of Electus Backus, Manuscript Division, Burton Historical Collection, Detroit Public Library, Detroit.

[12] Henry, *op. cit.*, 194-195.

[13] *Ibid.*, 195; [Ulysses S. Grant], *Personal Memoirs of U. S. Grant* (1885), I, 111-112.

[14] Henry, *op. cit.*, 195; Kenly, *op. cit.*, 115.

[15] Mexican War Journal of Electus Backus, Manuscript Division, Burton Historical Collection, Detroit Public Library, Detroit; Kenly, *op. cit.*, 111; Henry, *op. cit.*, 196.

[16] J. F. H. Claiborne, *Life and Correspondence of John A. Quitman* (1860), II, 305.

[17] Manuel Balbontín, *La Invasión Americana* (1883), 30.

[18] Claiborne, *op. cit.*, II, 306-307; Ramsey, *op. cit.*, 73; Thorpe, *op cit.*, 54-55; Reid, *op. cit.*, 176.

[19] Claiborne, *op. cit.*, II, 306-307; Eleanor Damon Pace (editor), "The Diary and Letters of William P. Rogers, 1846-1862," *Southwestern Historical Quarterly*, XXXII, 266-267.

[20] Thorpe, *op. cit.*, 59-62; Smith, *op. cit.*, I, 253.

[21] French, *op. cit.*, 62; Thorpe, *op. cit.*, 57-58; Claiborne, *op. cit.*, II, 306-307; Mexican War Diary of Surgeon Madison Mills, typewritten copy, Kentucky Papers, Filson Club Archives, Louisville.

[22] Smith, *op. cit.*, I, 254-255.

[23] Thorpe, *op. cit.*, 66-69; Furber, *op. cit.*, 105; Reid, *op. cit.*, 162-164.

[24] Walter Prescott Webb, *The Texas Rangers* (1935), 107; Henry, *op. cit.*, 204; Reid, *op. cit.*, 181-183.

[25] Henry, *op. cit.*, 205; Webb, *op. cit.*, 108-109.

[26] Henry, *op. cit.*, 203-204.

[27] George G. Meade to Mrs. Meade, September 27, 1846, George Meade, *The Life and Letters of George Gordon Meade* (1913), I, 136; Thorpe, *op. cit.*, 70-73; French, *op. cit.*, 64-65; Reid, *op. cit.*, 181-182, 185.

[28] Reid, *op. cit.*, 190.

29 Meade to Mrs. Meade, September 27, 1846, Meade, *op. cit.*, I, 136; Henry, *op. cit.*, 207.

30 Meade to Mrs. Meade, September 27, 1846, Meade, *op. cit.*, I, 136.

31 Taylor to Dr. Robert C. Wood, September 28, 1846, William H. Samson (editor), *Letters of Zachary Taylor from the Battle-fields of the Mexican War* (1908), 61; Ramsey, *op. cit.*, 77; Furber, *op. cit.*, 109; James K. Holland, "Diary of a Texan Volunteer in the Mexican War," *Southwestern Historical Quarterly*, XXX, 26.

32 Grant, *op. cit.*, I, 115-116.

33 Henry, *op. cit.*, 207; French, *op. cit.*, 66; Reid, *op. cit.*, 180, 196-198.

34 Webb, *op. cit.*, 109; Reid, *op. cit.*, 190-191; French, *op. cit.*, 67. Arturo L. Gonzalez, who accompanied the author on a tour of Monterrey and who has made a careful study of the battle, believes that Worth's men advanced by either the Calle de Matamoros or the Calle de Bolivar rather than by the Calle de Monterey.

35 Webb., *op. cit.*, 109; Thorpe, *op. cit.*, 78-80.

36 Reid, *op. cit.*, 180.

37 Smith, *op. cit.*, I, 258-259.

38 Taylor to Wood, September 28, 1846, Samson, *op. cit.*, 61. Thorpe presents a detailed discussion of events leading up to the capitulation, including an intensely interesting statement by Colonel Jefferson Davis (Thorpe, *op. cit.*, 81-94).

39 *House Executive Document 60, Thirtieth Congress, First Session*, 349-350.

40 Henry, *op. cit.*, 215.

41 Taylor to Wood, September 28, 1846, Samson, *op. cit.*, 61; Claiborne, *op. cit.*, I, 253, 255, 270; Mexican War Diary of Surgeon Madison Mills, typewritten copy, Kentucky Papers, Filson Club Archives, Louisville.

## CHAPTER XVI

1 Allan Nevins (editor), *The Diary of Philip Hone, 1826-1851* (1927), II, 766.

2 Taylor to Dr. Robert C. Wood, December 10, 1846, William H. Samson (editor), *Letters of Zachary Taylor from the Battle-fields of the Mexican War* (1908), 75-76.

3 Milo M. Quaife (editor), *The Diary of James K. Polk* (1910), I, 384-385; Isaac Smith, *Reminiscences of a Campaign in Mexico* (1848), 19.

4 Charles Winslow Elliott, *Winfield Scott, the Soldier and the Man* (1937), *passim*.

5 Allan Nevins (editor), *Polk, the Diary of a President* (1929), 101n; Elliott, *op. cit.*, 420-431.

6 Quaife, *op. cit.*, I, 428-429.

7 *Ibid.*, II, 119.

8 *Ibid.*, II, 181.

9 *Ibid.*, II, 236.

10 *Ibid.*, II, 250.

[11] *Ibid.*, II, 242-243.

[12] *Ibid.*, II, 275-276; Justin H. Smith, *The War with Mexico* (1919), I, 351.

[13] Quaife, *op. cit.*, II, 250.

[14] *Ibid.*, I, 428.

[15] *Ibid.*, II, 244.

[16] *Ibid.*, II, 242.

[17] Taylor to Wood, January 26, 1847, Samson, *op. cit.*, 80.

[18] Justin H. Smith, *op. cit.*, I, 354, 356.

[19] Quaife, *op. cit.*, I, 224.

[20] *Ibid.*, I, 230.

[21] M. A. DeWolfe Howe, *Life and Letters of George Bancroft* (1908), I, 289.

[22] John M. Ellicott, *Life of John Ancrum Winslow* (1902), 37.

[23] Frank C. Hanighen, *Santa Anna, the Napoleon of the West* (1934), 1-7, 15-20, 23, 26-29, 34-36, 50-51, 53-60, 65, 69, 149-153; Wilfrid Hardy Callcott, *Santa Anna, the Story of an Enigma Who Once Was Mexico* (1936), 5, 7-11, 20, 32-45, 53-56, 66-69, 156, 158.

[24] Hanighen, *op. cit.*, 181; Callcott, *op. cit.*, 348-349.

[25] Hanighen, *op. cit.*, *passim*; Callcott, *op. cit.*, *passim*.

[26] Hanighen, *op. cit.*, 134.

[27] Justin H. Smith, *op. cit.*, I, 223.

[28] Hanighen, *op. cit.*, 315. But there are authorities who say that Santa Anna did not reach San Luis Potosí until October 14. *Cf.* Albert C. Ramsey (editor), *The Other Side: or Notes for the History of the War between Mexico and the United States* (1850), 83.

[29] Justin H. Smith, *op. cit.*, I, *passim*; George C. Furber, *The Twelve Months Volunteer; or, Journal of a Private . . . in Mexico* (1857), *passim*.

[30] New Orleans *Picayune*, December 27, 1846; Furber, *op. cit.*, 240.

[31] Taylor to Wood, January 26, 1847, Samson, *op. cit.*, 82; Walter Prescott Webb, *The Texas Rangers* (1935), 111-112; Justin H. Smith, *op. cit.*, I, 379.

[32] Hanighen, *op. cit.*, 208-209; Ramsey, *op. cit.*, 114-115.

[33] Taylor to Joseph P. Taylor, January 14, 1847, Zachary Taylor Papers, Manuscript Division, Library of Congress, Washington.

[34] Taylor to Wood, January 26, 1847, Samson, *op. cit.*, 80-82.

[35] Taylor to Wood, February 9, 1847, Samson, *op. cit.*, 85, 87.

[36] W. S. Henry, *Campaign Sketches of the War with Mexico* (1847), 240, 247-248; Justin H. Smith, *op. cit.*, I, 263, 507; Taylor to Joseph P. Taylor, December 12, 1846, Zachary Taylor Papers, Manuscript Division, Library of Congress, Washington.

[37] Marcy to Taylor, October 22, 1846, *House Executive Document 60, Thirtieth Congress, First Session*, 364; Isaac Smith, *op. cit.*, 20.

[38] Taylor to Joseph P. Taylor, February 8, March 27, 1847, Zachary Taylor Papers, Manuscript Division, Library of Congress, Washington.

[39] John R. Kenly, *Memoirs of a Maryland Volunteer* (1873), 165-169.

[40] *Ibid.*, 175, 193, 210; J. F. H. Claiborne, *Life and Correspondence of*

*John A. Quitman* (1860), I, 276 *et seq.*, 289; Taylor to Joseph P. Taylor, January 14, 1847, Zachary Taylor Papers, Manuscript Division, Library of Congress, Washington; Taylor to Mrs. Zachary Taylor, December 22, 1846, *The Autograph*, I, 128; Taylor to Mary Elizabeth Taylor, December 26, 1846, *The Autograph*, I, 181.

[41] Furber, *op. cit.*, 279, 322-323, 329; Justin H. Smith, *op. cit.*, I, 361-362; Kenly, *op. cit.*, 197.

[42] Furber, *op. cit.*, 329.

[43] Justin H. Smith, *op. cit.*, I, 544.

[44] Otto B. Engelmann (editor), "The Second Illinois in the Mexican War, Mexican War Letters of Adolph Engelmann, 1846-1847," *Journal of the Illinois State Historical Society*, XXVI, 417-421; Kenly, *op. cit.*, 167.

[45] Claiborne, *op. cit.*, I, 288; Eleanor Damon Pace (editor), "The Diary and Letters of William P. Rogers, 1846-1862," *Southwestern Historical Quarterly*, XXXII, 274.

[46] Engelmann, "The Second Illinois in the Mexican War, Mexican War Letters of Adolph Engelmann, 1846-1847," *loc. cit.*, 438.

[47] Fletcher H. Archer to Mrs. Prudence Archer, May 30, 1847, Petersburg, Virginia, newspaper clipping in possession of Severn L. Nottingham, Orange, Virginia.

[48] Oran Perry (editor), *Indiana in the Mexican War* (1908), 140.

## CHAPTER XVII

[1] Scott to Taylor, January 26, 1847, *House Executive Document 60, Thirtieth Congress, First Session*, 864.

[2] Taylor to Joseph P. Taylor, February 8, 1847, Zachary Taylor Papers, Manuscript Division, Library of Congress, Washington.

[3] James Henry Carleton, *The Battle of Buena Vista* (1848), 2-5, 12-13; Samuel G. French, *Two Wars: An Autobiography* (1901), 74.

[4] Taylor to Jones, June 8, 1847, *House Executive Document 60, Thirtieth Congress, First Session*, 1176; Carleton, *op. cit.*, 16, 19; [Luther Giddings], *Sketches of the Campaign in Northern Mexico* (1853), 287; Samuel C. Reid, junior, *The Scouting Expeditions of McCulloch's Texas Rangers* (1848), 233-236.

[5] Carleton, *op. cit.*, 20-21, 32; Justin H. Smith, *The War with Mexico* (1919), I, 383, 555; Eleanor Damon Pace (editor), "The Diary and Letters of William P. Rogers, 1846-1862," *Southwestern Historical Quarterly*, XXXII, 274.

[6] Frank C. Hanighen, *Santa Anna, the Napoleon of the West* (1934), 212-213; Oliver Otis Howard, *General Taylor* (1892), 243; Carleton, *op. cit.*, 7-8, 32-33; French, *op. cit.*, 76-77; Louisville *Weekly Courier*, November 11, 1848.

[7] [Lew Wallace], *Lew Wallace, an Autobiography* (1906), I, 165-166, 183, 188-189; Carleton, *op. cit.*, 33-34; Smith, *op. cit.*, I, 386, 555; W. S. Henry, *Campaign Sketches of the War with Mexico* (1847), 311.

[8] Carleton, *op. cit.*, 32, 36-37; Howard, *op. cit.*, 246-247.

[9] French, *op. cit.*, 77.

[10] Howard, *op. cit.*, 247; Carleton, *op. cit.*, 37.

[11] Carleton, *op. cit.*, 39-42; Smith, *op. cit.*, I, 386.

[12] Henry, *op. cit.*, 313; Carleton, *op. cit.*, 40-42.

[13] Smith, *op. cit.*, I, 386, 553, 555; Carleton, *op. cit.*, 44; Louisville *Weekly Courier*, November 11, 1848.

[14] Oran Perry (editor), *Indiana in the Mexican War* (1908), 160-161, 170-171, 187-189, 293-295, 307-311; Carleton, *op. cit.*, 53-62, 80-83; Smith, *op. cit.*, I, 389-391; Wallace, *op. cit.*, I, 170-171; French, *op. cit.*, 80; Isaac Smith, *Reminiscences of a Campaign in Mexico* (1848), 98-112.

[15] Carleton, *op. cit.*, 62-63, 65, 70-71; French, *op. cit.*, 80.

[16] Carleton, *op. cit.*, 68-69, 83-84; Justin H. Smith, *op. cit.*, I, 390-391; Wallace, *op. cit.*, I, 171-172; Braxton Bragg to James Henry Hammond, May 4, 1848, Hammond Papers, Manuscript Division, Library of Congress, Washington.

[17] Carleton, *op. cit.*, 72, 74; Louisville *Weekly Courier*, November 11, 1848.

[18] Justin H. Smith, *op. cit.*, I, 391; Carleton, *op. cit.*, 74-78; French, *op. cit.*, 81.

[19] J. F. H. Claiborne, *Life and Correspondence of John A. Quitman* (1860), I, 291; Carleton, *op. cit.*, 94-99; Wallace, *op. cit.*, I, 175; Taylor to Edmund Haynes Taylor, March 8, 1847, Louisville *Courier-Journal*, December 13, 1873.

[20] French, *op. cit.*, 83; Carleton, *op. cit.*, 105-106. The Mexican version of this incident is substantially different. *Cf.* Alexander C. Ramsey (editor), *The Other Side: or Notes for the History of the War between Mexico and the United States* (1850), 126-127.

[21] Otto B. Engelmann (editor), "The Second Illinois in the Mexican War, Mexican War Letters of Adolph Engelmann, 1846-1847," *Journal of the Illinois State Historical Society*, XXVI, 443.

[22] Justin H. Smith, *op. cit.*, I, 394; Carleton, *op. cit.*, 107-111.

[23] Carleton, *op. cit.*, 111; Wallace, *op. cit.*, 174-175.

[24] Henry, *op. cit.*, 315; Carleton, *op. cit.*, 116.

[25] Fletcher H. Archer to Mrs. Prudence Archer, May 30, 1847, Petersburg, Virginia, newspaper clipping in possession of Severn L. Nottingham of Orange, Virginia; Carleton, *op. cit.*, 116; Perry, *op. cit.*, 191; Charles W. Upham, *Eulogy on the Life and Character of Zachary Taylor* (1850), 29-30.

[26] Carleton, *op. cit.*, 114-115.

[27] Ramsey, *op. cit.*, 127-128; Carleton, *op. cit.*, 116-119; French, *op cit.*, 83; Perry, *op. cit.*, 190.

[28] Edgar Erskine Hume, *Colonel Theodore O'Hara, Author of the Bivouac of the Dead* (1936), 20-21.

[29] Justin H. Smith, *op. cit.*, I, 396-397; Carleton, *op. cit.*, 127; Pace, "The Diary and Letters of William P. Rogers, 1846-1862," *loc. cit.*, 277n-278n.

[30] Ramsey, *op. cit.*, 132.

[31] Carleton, *op. cit.*, 130-131; Pace, "The Diary and Letters of William P. Rogers, 1846-1862," *loc. cit.*, 278n.

## CHAPTER XVIII

[1] Wilfrid Hardy Callcott, *Santa Anna, the Story of an Enigma Who Once Was Mexico* (1936), 252-253.

[2] Taylor to Joseph P. Taylor, March 27, 1847, Zachary Taylor Papers, Manuscript Division, Library of Congress, Washington.

[3] Taylor to Dr. Robert C. Wood, March 20, 1847, William H. Samson (editor), *Letters of Zachary Taylor from the Battle-fields of the Mexican War* (1908), 91.

[4] Taylor to Wood, April 4, 1847, *ibid.*, 95.

[5] Taylor to Wood, March 20, 1847, *ibid.*, 90.

[6] Taylor to Jones, March 6, 1847, *Senate Executive Document 1, Thirtieth Congress, First Session*, 134, 138-139.

[7] Albert J. Beveridge, *Abraham Lincoln*, 1809-1858 (1928), I, 461.

[8] Taylor to Henry Clay, senior, March 1, 1847, Oliver Otis Howard, *General Taylor* (1892), 283.

[9] Taylor to Wood, April 4, 1847, Samson, *op. cit.*, 96.

[10] Taylor to Wood, July 13, 1847, *ibid.*, 113; Taylor to Mary Elizabeth Taylor, June 23, 1847, *The Autograph*, I, 198.

[11] [Thomas B. Thorpe], *Taylor Anecdote Book* (1848), 114.

[12] Fletcher H. Archer to Mrs. Prudence Archer, May 30, 1847, Petersburg, Virginia, newspaper clipping in possession of Severn L. Nottingham, Orange, Virginia.

[13] George Lockhart Rives, *The United States and Mexico, 1821-1848* (1913), II, *passim*; Justin H. Smith, *The War with Mexico* (1919), II, *passim*.

[14] Taylor to Wood, October 27, 1847, Samson, *op. cit.*, 145.

[15] New Orleans *Picayune*, November 30, 1847; Taylor to Wood, November 17, 1847, Samson, *op. cit.*, 151.

[16] New Orleans *Picayune*, December 1, 1847. At Brazos Island, Taylor wrote a number of political and semi-political letters. In one, typical of all, he stated: "I have no wish or intention of changing the position in which I stand toward the people of the country in relation to the Presidency" (Taylor to Andrew Stewart, November 25, 1847, Zachary Taylor Papers, Hamilton Collection, Fort Wayne, Indiana).

[17] J. Reese Fry and Robert T. Conrad, *A Life of Gen. Zachary Taylor* (1848), 331.

[18] New Orleans *Picayune*, December 1, 1847.

[19] *Ibid.*, December 2, 1847.

[20] *Ibid.*, December 4, 1847.

[21] [J. Reese Fry], *Our Battles in Mexico* (1850), 327.

[22] Bliss Perry, *Walt Whitman, His Life and Work* (1906), 42.

[23] Fry, *op. cit.*, 327.

[24] New Orleans *Picayune*, December 4, 1847.

[25] Fry, *op. cit.*, 327-328.

[26] *Ibid.*, 328.

[27] *Ibid.*, 328-329

[28] *Ibid.*, 330.

[29] *Idem;* New Orleans *Picayune*, December 3, 1847.

[30] New Orleans *Picayune*, December 4, 1847.

[31] New Orleans *Commercial Times*, December 6, 1847; New Orleans *Picayune*, December 4, 1847.

[32] Eleanor Custis Lewis Scrapbook, Taylor Family Papers, Trist Wood Collection, New Orleans.

[33] *Semi-Weekly Natchez Courier*, December 14, 1847.

BIBLIOGRAPHY

# BIBLIOGRAPHY

[In compiling this bibliography, no attempt has been made to include scores of campaign "lives" and other unreliable works, utterly worthless from the standpoint of accurate and impartial history. Only those original manuscript sources, articles, brochures and books on which the author could depend in whole or in part—or which he found worthy of citation—are included here. Contributions made by individuals and institutions are set forth in the remarks headed "Personal Acknowledgments."]

## MANUSCRIPT SOURCES

### PUBLIC COLLECTIONS

Adjutant General's Office, War Department, Washington, Officers' Division, official records.

Adjutant General's Office, War Department, Washington, Old Files Section, Executive Division, official correspondence.

Adjutant General's Office, War Department, Washington, Organization Records Section, Old Records Division, official correspondence.

Burton Historical Collection, Detroit Public Library, Detroit, Electus Backus Papers.

Feliciana (now West Feliciana) Parish, Saint Francisville, Louisiana, land records.

Filson Club Archives, Louisville, Madison Mills Diary, typewritten copy.

Historical Society of Pennsylvania, Philadelphia, Presidential Papers.

Jefferson County, Fayette, Mississippi, land records.

Jefferson County, Louisville, Kentucky, marriage and land records.

Kentucky State Historical Society, Frankfort, Jefferson County (Kentucky) tax records.

Kentucky State Historical Society, Frankfort, Philip Fall Taylor Collection.

Kentucky State Historical Society, Frankfort, Zachary Taylor Papers.

Library of Congress, Washington, James Henry Hammond Papers.

Library of Congress, Washington, Ethan Allen Hitchcock Papers.

Library of Congress, Washington, James Madison Papers.

Library of Congress, Washington, Zachary Taylor Papers.

Missouri Historical Society, Saint Louis, Manuscript Journal of the Missouri Legislative Committee on the Florida Campaign.

Missouri Historical Society, Saint Louis, Presidential Papers.

Newberry Library, Chicago, Edward E. Ayer Collection.

Office of Indian Affairs, Department of the Interior, Washington, Cherokee Agency Papers, Western Superintendency File, official correspondence.

305

Office of Indian Affairs, Department of the Interior, Washington, Choctaw Agency Papers, Western Superintendency File, official correspondence.

William Henry Smith Memorial Library, Indiana Historical Society, Indianapolis, Zachary Taylor Papers.

Texas State Capitol, Austin, Governors' Letters.

West Feliciana Parish, Saint Francisville, Louisiana, land records.

Wilkinson County, Woodville, Mississippi, land records.

Wisconsin State Historical Society, Madison, Kentucky Papers, Draper Collection.

## PRIVATE COLLECTIONS

R. Alexander Bate, Louisville.

James F. Drake, New York City.

Holman Hamilton, Fort Wayne, Indiana.

Miss Irene Hawes, Yellow Springs, Ohio.

Mrs. Roy V. Ott, Ocala, Florida.

The late Mrs. Walter R. Stauffer, New Orleans.

Jaquelin P. Taylor, Orange and Richmond, Virginia.

Reuben Thornton Taylor, Bagdad, Kentucky.

Miss Alice E. Trabue, Louisville.

Miss Lola M. Wood, Maddox, Saint Mary's County, Maryland.

Trist Wood, New Orleans.

## PRINTED SOURCES

Henry Adams, *History of the United States of America* ... (1889-1891).

Fred W. Allsopp, *Folklore of Romantic Arkansas* (1931).

*American State Papers, Military Affairs.*

Kitty Anderson, "Soldiers Retreat; A Historic House and Its Famous People," *Register of the Kentucky State Historical Society*, XVII, Number 51.

*Arkansas Intelligencer* (Van Buren), May 27, 1842.

*Army and Navy Chronicle.*

*Army and Navy Chronicle, and Scientific Repository.*

Caleb Atwater, *Remarks Made on a Tour to Prairie du Chien; Thence to Washington City, in 1829* (1831).

*The Autograph.*

Elkanah Babcock and S. T. Fiske, junior, *A War History of the Sixth U. S. Infantry ... from 1798 to 1903* (1903).

Manuel Balbontin, *La Invasión Americana* (1883).

R. Alexander Bate, *Commodore Richard Taylor, A Colonial Sketch* (1924).

Henry Putney Beers, *The Western Military Frontier, 1815-1846* (1935).

Albert J. Beveridge, *Abraham Lincoln, 1809-1858* (1928).

*Biographical Encyclopaedia of Kentucky* (1878).

Farnham Bishop, *Our First War in Mexico* (1916).

Emma J. Blackwood (editor), *To Mexico with Scott, Letters of Captain E. Kirby Smith to His Wife* (1917).

John H. Bliss, "Reminiscences of Fort Snelling," *Minnesota Historical Society Collections,* VI.

*Boston Public Library Monthly Bulletin.*

Wilhelmus Bogart Bryan, *A History of the National Capital* (1916).

*Calendar of Virginia State Papers.*

Wilfrid Hardy Callcott, *Santa Anna, the Story of an Enigma Who Once Was Mexico* (1936).

James Henry Carleton, *The Battle of Buena Vista* · (1848).

Frances Manwaring Caulkins, *History of Norwich, Connecticut* (1866).

Harry E. Chambers, *Mississippi Valley Beginnings* (1922).

John E. Chapin, "Sketch of Cutting Marsh," *Wisconsin State Historical Society Collections,* XV.

W. H. Chatfield, *The Twin Cities of the Border* (1893).

Hiram Martin Chittenden, *The Fur American Trade of the Far West* (1902).

J. F. H. Claiborne, *Life and Correspondence of John A. Quitman* (1860).

*The Collector.*

Lewis Collins and Richard H. Collins, *History of Kentucky* (1874).

[George S. Cottman (editor)], "Some Letters of John Gibson," *Indiana Magazine of History,* I.

W. A. Croffut (editor), *Fifty Years in Camp and Field, the Diary of Major General Ethan Allen Hitchcock, U. S. A.* (1909), published by G. P. Putnam's Sons.

George W. Cullum, *Biographical Register of the Officers and Graduates . . . of West Point* (1879).

Varina Jefferson Davis, *Jefferson Davis, a Memoir* (1890).

Rhoda van Bibber Tanner Doubleday (editor), *Journals of the Late Brevet Major Philip Norbourne Barbour . . . and His Wife . . .* (1936).

Louis C. Duncan, "A Medical History of General Zachary Taylor's Army of Occupation in Texas and Mexico, 1845-1847," *The Military Surgeon,* XLVIII.

Reuben T. Durrett, *The Centenary of Louisville* (1893).

John M. Ellicott, *Life of John Ancrum Winslow* (1902).

Charles Winslow Elliott, *Winfield Scott, the Soldier and the Man* (1937).

Otto B. Engelmann (editor), "The Second Illinois in the Mexican War, Mexican War Letters of Adolph Engelmann, 1846-1847," *Journal of the Illinois State Historical Society,* XXVI.

Logan Esarey, *History of Indiana* (1918).

Logan Esarey (editor), *Messages and Letters of William Henry Harrison* (1922).

William L. Evans, "The Military History of Green Bay," *Proceedings of the State Historical Society of Wisconsin, 1899* (1900).

Walter L. Fleming, "The Early Life of Jefferson Davis," *Mississippi Valley Historical Review,* IX.

Walter L. Fleming, "Jefferson Davis' First Marriage," *Mississippi Historical Society Publications,* XII.

John H. Fonda, "Early Reminiscences of Wisconsin," *Wisconsin State Historical Society Collections*, V.

Carolyn Thomas Foreman (editor), "Journal of a Tour in the Indian Territory," *Chronicles of Oklahoma*, X.

Grant Foreman, *Advancing the Frontier, 1830-1860* (1933).

Grant Foreman, *Indian Removal* (1932).

Samuel G. French, *Two Wars: An Autobiography* (1901).

[J. Reese Fry], *Our Battles in Mexico* (1850).

J. Reese Fry and Robert T. Conrad, *A Life of Gen. Zachary Taylor* (1848).

George C. Furber, *The Twelve Months Volunteer; or, Journal of a Private . . . in Mexico* (1857).

Thomas Benton Gentry, *Souvenir of General Richard Gentry: A Missouri Pioneer and Soldier* (1899).

William Richard Gentry, junior, *"Full Justice": The Story of Richard Gentry and His Missouri Volunteers in the Seminole War* (1937).

[Luther Giddings], *Sketches of the Campaign in Northern Mexico* (1853).

Parke Godwin (editor), *Prose Writings of William Cullen Bryant* (1884).

Armistead C. Gordon, *Jefferson Davis* (1918).

[Ulysses S. Grant], *Personal Memoirs of U. S. Grant* (1885).

Frank C. Hanighen, *Santa Anna, the Napoleon of the West* (1934).

Alfred Jackson Hanna, *Fort Maitland, Its Origin and History* (1936).

Marcus L. Hansen, *Old Fort Snelling, 1819-1858* (1918).

J. Fair Hardin, "Four Forgotten Frontier Posts of Western Louisiana," *Louisiana Historical Quarterly*, XVI, XVII.

*John Heise Autograph Catalogue*, Number 2468.

F. B. Heitman, *Historical Register of Officers of the Continental Army During the War of the Revolution* (1893).

F. B. Heitman, *Historical Register of the United States Army from . . . September 29, 1789, to September 29, 1889* (1890).

W. S. Henry, *Campaign Sketches of the War with Mexico* (1847).

Frederick W. Hodge (editor), *Handbook of American Indians* (1912).

Charles Fenno Hoffman, *A Winter in the West* (1882).

James K. Holland, "Diary of a Texas Volunteer in the Mexican War," *Southwestern Historical Quarterly*, XXX.

*House of Representatives Executive Documents.*

Oliver Otis Howard, *General Taylor* (1892).

M. A. DeWolfe Howe, *Life and Letters of George Bancroft* (1908).

Edgar Erskine Hume, *Colonel Theodore O'Hara, Author of The Bivouac of the Dead* (1936).

Edward P. Humphrey and Thomas H. Cleland, *Memoirs of the Rev. Thomas Cleland . . .* (1859).

Elijah Iles, *Sketches of Early Life and Times in Kentucky, Missouri and Illinois* (1883).

J. B. S. Jacobs, senior, "List of Inhabitants at Green Bay, September 14, 1818," *Wisconsin State Historical Society Collections*, X.

Marquis James, *Andrew Jackson, the Border Captain* (1933).

Joseph Jefferson, *Autobiography of Joseph Jefferson* (1897).

Allen Johnson and Dumas Malone (editors), *Dictionary of American Biography* (1928-1936).

J. Stoddard Johnston, "Sketch of Theodore O'Hara," *Register of the Kentucky State Historical Society*, XI, Number 33.

William Preston Johnston, *The Life of Albert Sidney Johnston* (1879).

Louise Phelps Kellogg (editor), *Frontier Advance on the Upper Ohio, 1778-1779* (1916).

Louise Phelps Kellogg, "Old Fort Howard," *Wisconsin Magazine of History*, XVIII.

John R. Kenly, *Memoirs of a Maryland Volunteer* (1873).

*Kentucky Gazette* (Lexington), November 7, 1814.

John T. Kingston, "Early Western Days," *Wisconsin State Historical Society Collections*, VII.

Ludie J. Kinkead (editor), "Minute Book No. 1, Jefferson County, Kentucky, April 6, 1784-December 7, 1785," *Filson Club History Quarterly*, VI.

"Lawe and Grignon Papers, 1794-1821," *Wisconsin State Historical Society Collections*, X.

Sarah Jane Line, "The Indians on the Mississinewa," *Indiana Magazine of History*, IX.

James H. Lockwood, "Early Times and Events in Wisconsin," *Wisconsin State Historical Society Collections*, II.

Benson J. Lossing, *The Pictorial Field-Book of the War of 1812* (1869).

Louisville *Courier-Journal*, December 13, 1873; July 16, 1893; July 9, 1934.

Louisville *Herald*, July 4, 1909.

Louisville *Weekly Courier*, July 1, 1848; November 11, 1848.

George A. McCall, *Letters from the Frontier* (1868).

William A. McClintock, "Journal of a Trip through Texas and Northern Mexico in 1846-1847," *Southwestern Historical Quarterly*, XXXIV.

Eugene I. McCormac, *James K. Polk, a Political Biography* (1922).

Robert McElroy, *Jefferson Davis, the Unreal and the Real* (1937).

Bruce E. Mahan, *Old Fort Crawford and the Frontier* (1926).

Deborah B. Martin, *History of Brown County, Wisconsin, Past and Present* (1913).

Nehemiah Matson, *Memories of Shaubena* (1878).

George Meade, *The Life and Letters of George Gordon Meade* (1913).

William E. Meese, "Credit Island, 1814-1914," *Journal of the Illinois State Historical Society*, VII.

Henry Merrell, "Pioneer Life in Wisconsin," *Wisconsin State Historical Society Collections*, VII.

*Missouri Argus* (Saint Louis), April 3, 1838.

*Missouri Gazette* (Saint Louis), September 3, 1814.

Charles W. Moore, "Was Gen. Taylor a Mason?", *Freemasons' Monthly Magazine* (Boston), IX.

Rob. Morris, *History of Freemasonry in Kentucky* (1859).

Rob. Morris, "Masonic Recollections," *Masonic Review* (Cincinnati), LVII.

Charles Augustus Murray, *Travels in North America During the Years 1834, 1835, and 1836* (1839).

F. D. Neill, "Occurrences in and around Fort Snelling, from 1819 to 1840," *Minnesota Historical Society Collections*, II.

Ella Hoes Neville *et al.*, *Historic Green Bay, 1634-1840* (1893).

Allan Nevins (editor), *The Diary of Philip Hone, 1828-1851* (1927).

Allan Nevins (editor), *Polk, the Diary of a President* (1929).

*New England Genealogical Register.*

New Orleans *Commercial Times*, December 6, 1847.

New Orleans *Picayune*, 1846, 1847, various dates.

New York Southern Society, *President Zachary Taylor Sesqui-centennial Celebration* (1934).

New York *Times*, October 20, 1906.

John G. Nicolay and John Hay (editors), *Complete Works of Abraham Lincoln* (1894).

*Niles' National Register.*

Norwich (Connecticut) *Chronicle*, December 22, 1858.

Eleanor Damon Pace (editor), "The Diary and Letters of William P. Rogers, 1846-1862," *Southwestern Historical Quarterly*, XXXII.

George Pence, "General Joseph Bartholomew," *Indiana Magazine of History*, XIV.

George Pence, "Indian History of Bartholomew County," *Indiana Magazine of History*, XXIII.

Bliss Perry, *Walt Whitman, His Life and His Work* (1906).

Oran Perry (editor), *Indiana in the Mexican War* (1908).

Milo M. Quaife (editor), *The Diary of James K. Polk* (1910).

Milo M. Quaife, "A Forgotten Hero of Rock Island," *Journal of the Illinois State Historical Society*, XXIII.

Milo M. Quaife, "The Northwestern Career of Jefferson Davis," *Journal of the Illinois State Historical Society*, XVI.

A. C. Quisenberry, "Colonel George Croghan, the Hero of Fort Stephenson," *Register of the Kentucky State Historical Society*, X, Number 29.

A. C. Quisenberry, "The Battle of New Orleans," *Register of the Kentucky State Historical Society*, XIII, Number 37.

William E. Railey, "Woodford County, Kentucky," *Register of the Kentucky State Historical Society*, XIX.

Albert C. Ramsey (editor), *The Other Side: or Notes for the History of the War between Mexico and the United States* (1850).

Thomas P. Reep, *Lincoln at New Salem* (1927).

Samuel C. Reid, junior, *The Scouting Expeditions of McCulloch's Texas Rangers* (1848).

James D. Richardson (editor), *Messages and Papers of the Presidents* (1897).

George Lockhart Rives, *The United States and Mexico, 1821-1848* (1913).

*The Rough and Ready* (Louisville), October 9, 1847.

William H. Samson (editor), *Letters of Zachary Taylor from the Battle-fields of the Mexican War* (1908).

Joseph Schafer, *A History of the Pacific Northwest* (1905).

Florence Johnson Scott, *Old Rough and Ready on the Rio Grande* (1935).

William Wallace Scott, *History of Orange County, Virginia* . . . (1907).

[Winfield Scott], *Memoirs of Lieut.-General Scott, LL.D., Written by Himself* (1864).

J. T. Scovell *et al.* (editors), *Fort Harrison on the Banks of the Wabash, 1812-1912* (1912).

Don C. Seitz, *The James Gordon Bennetts, Father and Son* (1928).

*Semi-Weekly Natchez Courier*, December 14, 1847.

*Senate Executive Documents.*

John Shaw, "Shaw's Narrative," *Wisconsin State Historical Society Collections*, II.

Isaac Smith, *Reminiscences of a Campaign in Mexico* (1848).

Justin H. Smith, *The War with Mexico* (1919).

John T. Sprague, *Origin, Progress and Conclusion of the Florida War* (1848).

Frank E. Stevens, *The Black Hawk War* (1903).

Frank E. Stevens, "Illinois in the War of 1812-1814," *Transactions of the Illinois State Historical Society*, VI.

Samuel A. Storrow, "The Northwest in 1817, a Contemporary Letter," *Wisconsin State Historical Society Collections*, VI.

John Chaplin Strother *et al.*, "The Strother Family," *Register of the Kentucky State Historical Society*, XXV.

Lawrence Taliaferro, "Autobiography of Maj. Lawrence Taliaferro," *Minnesota Historical Collections*, VI.

Tallahassee *Floridian*, August 25, 1838.

Fred G. Taylor *et al.*, *James Taylor, Emigrant* (1933).

Thomas B. Thorpe, *Our Army at Monterey* (1848).

[Thomas B. Thorpe], *Taylor Anecdote Book* (1848).

Reuben Gold Thwaites (editor), *Early Western Travels, 1748-1846* (1904).

Reuben Gold Thwaites, "The Story of the Black Hawk War," *Wisconsin State Historical Society Collections*, XII.

Alice E. Trabue, *A Corner in Celebrities* (1922).

Alice E. Trabue, " 'Spring Hill,' Oldham County, Kentucky," *Register of the Kentucky State Historical Society*, XVIII.

Charles W. Upham, *Eulogy on the Life and Character of Zachary Taylor* (1850).

Emory Upton, *The Military Policy of the United States* (1912).

Virginia Historical Register, IV.
[Lew Wallace], *Lew Wallace, an Autobiography* (1906).
*The War* (New York), October 10, 1812.
Washington *National Intelligencer*, 1812, 1826, various dates.
Walter Prescott Webb, *The Texas Rangers* (1935).
Harriet A. Weed (editor), *Autobiography of Thurlow Weed* (1883).
Edgar Bruce Wesley, "James Callaway in the War of 1812," *Missouri Historical Society Collections*, V.
*William and Mary College Quarterly*, First Series, XVIII.
Nathaniel Parker Willis, *American Scenery* (1840).
*Wisconsin State Historical Society Collections*, IX.

PERSONAL ACKNOWLEDGMENTS

# PERSONAL ACKNOWLEDGMENTS

*Zachary Taylor: Soldier of the Republic* is the product not of one mind, but of many. Good companions, met along the avenues and bypaths of research, have made this book possible. Some were friends and enemies of the doughty old General; these praised or blamed him on the printed page of half-forgotten tomes now gathering dust on the shelves of the Library of Congress. Others were born generations after Zachary Taylor died, and, whether by inheritance or by native curiosity, came into possession of vital documents without which the story might never have been told. Descendants of Old Rough and Ready, direct and collateral, gave freely of their time and energy to provide material of lasting worth. Librarians, teachers, journalists, historians professional and amateur made contributions. To this loyal band of selfless men and women, the author is profoundly grateful. It is with a sense of abiding pleasure that he presents the roster of his comrades met and cherished throughout the great adventure in quest of truth.

The Taylor family tree has many branches. One man knows every twig. No attempt to untangle the involved kinships of the Taylor clan, however well intentioned, could be successful without the guidance of Trist Wood of New Orleans. Mr. Wood, great-grandson of Zachary Taylor, has made a lifelong study of Taylor parents and grandparents, the sisters and the cousins and the aunts. I found him an ideal ally in the work of genealogy, accurate almost to a fault, expert in his knowledge of the New Orleans of Taylor's time, and with many a rare anecdote handed down from his own father who as a boy knew the General and lived under his roof. Trist Wood has in his possession under lock and key an invaluable cache of Tayloriana: Zachary Taylor's own family register, in which he personally recorded the dates of his children's births and deaths; letters of Sarah Knox Taylor to her father and to her husband, Jefferson Davis; data concerning Taylor's birthplace, boyhood, marriage, and youth. Whatever sound scholarship may be found in my Taylor family material is due, in great measure, to Trist Wood's unfailing counsel and support.

In Kentucky, where Zachary Taylor spent nearly half of his years, Otto A. Rothert was my guide, philosopher and friend. A master of Kentuckiana, Mr. Rothert is Secretary of the Filson Club in Louisville. He placed the club's archives at my disposal, and with apparent eagerness devoted time and talent to the Kentucky period in Taylor's life. Not only did he contribute freely of his own resources, reading and criticizing the first eight chapters of the book in manuscript; he also prevailed upon history-minded friends to illuminate the dark alleys which previous biographers failed to enter. Through him I met Mrs. Jouett Taylor Cannon, Secretary of the Kentucky State Historical Society, Frankfort; J. Winston Coleman and Charles R. Staples of Lexington, Kentucky; the Reverend Lucien V. Rule of Goshen,

Kentucky; Reuben Thornton Taylor of Bagdad, Kentucky; Miss Mabel C. Weaks of New York City; W. C. Barrickman of Austin, Texas; and Dr. R. Alexander Bate, Colonel Lucien Beckner, Miss Evelyn R. Dale, Miss Ludie J. Kinkead, Hambleton Tapp, and R. C. Ballard Thruston of Louisville. I am indebted to Otto Rothert and to his fellow Filsonians. The name of Louisville will always conjure up fond recollections of spring and autumn days well spent in the spacious brick building on Breckinridge Street.

In Indiana, where Taylor's first laurels were won, several prominent scholars have been my benefactors. Louis A. Warren, Director of the Lincoln National Life Foundation in Fort Wayne, encouraged my earliest efforts and placed at my disposal obscure printed sources which caused the signposts of research to point in the right direction. In times of intellectual stress I have felt free to turn to Doctor Warren and to his former assistant, R. Gerald McMurtry, now a member of the faculty of Lincoln Memorial University, Harrogate, Tennessee. These gentlemen have been especially helpful on problems rising out of the Black Hawk War. Together with Dr. Christopher B. Coleman, Secretary of the Indiana Historical Society, and the latter's associates Miss Esther U. McNitt, Miss Caroline Dunn, Richard C. Smith, and the late Miss Florence Venn of Indianapolis, they have lightened the burden of the Indiana research.

In Virginia, where Taylor was born, I had the exciting experience of shaking a hand that shook the hand of Taylor. It was in Winchester in 1935, through the kindness of Mr. and Mrs. Melvin Green, that I made the acquaintance of Mrs. Arabella Taylor Clarke, then ninety-seven years of age and since deceased. Mrs. Clarke was Zachary Taylor's own niece, the daughter of his brother Joseph. As a little girl she had played in the White House during her uncle's administration. She remembered him vividly, verified certain Taylor traditions, denied others, and supplied details which could have been secured from no less unusual source. The author is in debt to Mr. and Mrs. Green for leading him to the bedside of this gracious southern gentlewoman. Other Virginians who have been generous in extending aid are: Dr. H. J. Eckenrode, Director of the Virginia Division of History and Archaeology, Richmond; Dr. Earl G. Swem of the College of William and Mary, Williamsburg; Wilmer L. Hall, Virginia State Librarian, Richmond; Mrs. Winifred Brent Russell of Gordonsville; Jaquelin P. Taylor of Orange and Richmond; and S. C. Trimmer, Severn L. Nottingham, and J. W. Browning of Orange. To this company I add the name of the Honorable R. Walton Moore, Counselor of the United States Department of State, whom I had the pleasure of meeting in the national capital. Mr. Moore, a native of Virginia, was for a number of years one of the Old Dominion's representatives in Congress. Deeply interested in Virginia history, he has made a special study of Zachary Taylor and has delivered several addresses on the high spots of Taylor's life. To him credit is due for arousing in the minds of fellow Virginians a new appreciation of Taylor's worth.

Masses of Taylor letters are now available in the National Archives, Washington. My own acquaintance with War Department manuscripts began prior to their removal from the State, War and Navy Building on Pennsylvania Avenue. I am grateful to the memory of the late Secretary of War, the Honorable George Henry Dern, to successive Adjutants General of the United States Army and to their subordinates for patience and for trust. Both in the Officers' Division and in the Executive Division of the Adjutant General's Office, and also in the Old Records Division then located in the Munitions Building, I spent long hours familiarizing myself with Tayloriana. Many copies were typed, many photostats taken. More than half of my information on General Taylor's forty years of Army service was derived directly from War Department correspondence.

In the Library of Congress, on Capitol Hill, the researcher finds printed and manuscript material which cannot be unearthed elsewhere. He meets a corps of seasoned advisers, who stand ready to give him the benefit of experience and taste. I express my appreciation to Dr. Herbert Putnam, Librarian of Congress during the years when I paid frequent visits; to Dr. Thomas P. Martin, then acting chief of the Division of Manuscripts; and to Martin A. Roberts and his colleagues of the Circulating Division. Among many Washington friends who helped produce this biography, Miss Omo E. Greener merits particular mention. Miss Greener traced down odds and ends when I was unable to visit Washington; I am grateful for her resourceful aid.

Dr. Milo Milton Quaife, Secretary of the Burton Historical Collection, Detroit Public Library, Detroit, is an acknowledged authority on the Old Northwest. To him I have turned for clarification of questions connected with Taylor's residence on the banks of the Upper Mississippi. I have profited by the assistance of Dr. Paul M. Angle, Secretary of the Illinois State Historical Society, Springfield; John H. Hauberg of Rock Island, Illinois, who has made an extensive study of the Battle of Credit Island; Dr. Louise Phelps Kellogg and Miss Annie A. Nunns of the Wisconsin State Historical Society, Madison; and Professor Edgar Bruce Wesley of the University of Minnesota, Minneapolis, one of whose historical hobbies has been Zachary Taylor's Credit Island campaign of 1814. Excluded from the preceding bibliography are two titles which came to the present author's attention only after he completed his own chapters on Taylor's north-western years. Cyrenus Cole's *I Am a Man: The Indian Black Hawk* and Peter Lawrence Scanlan's *Prairie du Chien: French, British, American* are products of sound scholarship in fields too infrequently explored. The fact that many of the conclusions reached by Doctor Scanlan and Mr. Cole parallel the author's independent conclusions is, not unnaturally, a source of valued encouragement. I gladly recommend the two works to persons interested in probing phases of Wisconsin, Iowa, and Illinois history barely touched between the covers of this book.

With regard to Taylor's Florida years, the author delights in thanking Professor Alfred Jackson Hanna of Rollins College, Winter Park, Florida; Watt Marchman, of the same institution; and Florida State Librarian W. T. Cash of Tallahassee for the assistance they have generously given. William I. Fee of Fort Pierce, Florida, and William Richard Gentry, junior, of Saint

Louis, Missouri, have made rather careful studies of the Battle of Okeechobee. I hold with most of Mr. Fee's conclusions, and with some of Mr. Gentry's. I express my gratitude to these gentlemen, and to the Florida Society of the Daughters of the American Revolution, for erecting a suitable marker on that neglected battlefield which witnessed the turning point of organized Indian resistance in the Second Seminole War.

Every student of Oklahoma history is familiar with Grant Foreman's definitive works on the civilized tribes of southern Indians: Cherokee, Chickasaw, Choctaw, Seminole and Creek. I read Doctor Foreman's books as they were published, found them mines of precious information, and have frequently called on their author to analyze discrepancies in my own research. I thank him, and I thank Harbert Davenport and Joseph K. Wells of Brownsville, Texas, who performed a like function in connection with the Mexican War. With Mr. Davenport I examined the battlegrounds of Palo Alto and Resaca de la Palma, visited the sites where Taylor's troops encamped, and studied the "dry weather" and "wet weather" roads between Point Isabel and old Fort Brown. With Mr. Wells I roamed the streets of Matamoros, across the Rio Grande in Mexico. I am grateful to Mrs. Davenport, herself an authority on the fort of Taylor's time; to Captain Andrew Anderson, Miss Marie V. Blucher and Mrs. Howell Ward of Corpus Christi, Texas; and to Umberto García of Brownsville, each of whom made a contribution to this book.

*Zachary Taylor: Soldier of the Republic* is by no means a "family biography" in the sense that descendants of the General told the author what to write, or how to write it. However, it is a "family biography" to the extent that Taylors and Taylor kinsmen generously made available their manuscripts and memories. One who lent both mind and spirit to the undertaking was the late Mrs. Betty Taylor Stauffer of New Orleans. Mrs. Stauffer was Zachary Taylor's granddaughter, the child of his only son. She produced original letters, documents, newspaper clippings, portraits of intrinsic value, and provided the author with many a pleasing picture of General Richard Taylor and his contemporaries. It is a source of regret that this biography was not completed during her lifetime. To her daughters, Mrs. Lewis Hardie of New Orleans and Mrs. John McIlhenny of Charlottesville, Virginia; to her son, Walter Stauffer of New Orleans; to Zachary Taylor's great-granddaughters, Mrs. William Edwin Brickell of New Orleans and Miss Lola Mackubin Wood of Maddox, Saint Mary's County, Maryland; to Miss Alice Elizabeth Trabue of Louisville; to Mrs. Roy V. Ott of Ocala, Florida; to Miss Corinne Robinson of Orlando, Florida; to Miss Irene Hawes of Yellow Springs, Ohio; to Mrs. William Manly Cartmell of Montclair, New Jersey; and to Major Stuart Zachary Taylor Wood, a great-great-grandson of the General and himself head of the Royal Canadian Mounted Police in Regina, Saskatchewan, Canada, the author expresses his indebtedness.

Other friends have aided, and I thank: Matthew Page Andrews of Baltimore; Frank R. Ayer of Norwich, Connecticut; Mrs. Gerald W. Bennett of Colorado Springs, Colorado; H. M. Bixby of Shanghai, China; the

Honorable Claude G. Bowers of Santiago, Chile; Mrs. Pierce Butler, Custodian of the Edward E. Ayer Collection, Newberry Library, Chicago; Maurice A. Cook of Fort Wayne, Indiana; Brigadier General Blas Corral of Mexico City; John H. Cowles of Washington; Colonel M. L. Crimmins of Fort Sam Houston, Texas; Karl W. Detzer of Leland, Michigan; H. W. Dorsey of the Smithsonian Institution, Washington; Miss Stella M. Drumm, Librarian of the Missouri Historical Society, Saint Louis; Arturo L. Gonzalez of Monterrey, Mexico; Dr. Philip M. Hamer, of the National Archives, Washington; Thomas Robson Hay of Sands Point, Long Island, New York; Dr. Reginald B. Henry of Annapolis, Maryland; Andrew B. Learned of Natchez, Mississippi; Mrs. James J. McLoughlin and Miss Terése Zimmerman of New Orleans; George Fort Milton of Chattanooga, Tennessee; Rex M. Potterf and his associates of the Fort Wayne, Indiana, Public Library; Alexander Burton Randall of Cleveland; Dr. Peter Lawrence Scanlan of Prairie du Chien, Wisconsin; Frank E. Stevens of Springfield, Illinois; Jefferson Davis Stirling of St. Francisville, Louisiana; Mayor W. J. Stockett of Woodville, Mississippi; William M. Sweeny of Astoria, Long Island, New York; Judge Jeff Truly of Fayette, Mississippi; Mrs. Harry Temple Watts of Vincennes, Indiana; Professor Walter Prescott Webb of the University of Texas, Austin; Dr. Julian P. Boyd, William R. G. Hamilton and Dr. Roy Francis Nichols of Philadelphia; and James F. Drake, Henry Needham Flynt, Anson G. Haskell and Arthur Swann of New York City. The late Thomas F. Madigan of New York City, the late Dr. Dunbar Rowland of Jackson, Mississippi, and the late Andrew M. Sea, junior, of Louisville are among those to whose memories I am deeply grateful.

Finally, I wish to thank my father and mother, Dr. and Mrs. Allen Hamilton, to whom this book is affectionately dedicated; my friend of longest standing, Miss Ann Studer; my staunch friends William Albert Kunkel, junior, and Frank Roberts, who from time to time have permitted me to write editorials far from the offices of the Fort Wayne *Journal-Gazette* in order that historical field work might be done. I acknowledge my indebtedness to David Laurance Chambers, president of the publishing house whose imprint this volume bears; to Professor William Orlando Lynch of Indiana University, Bloomington, and especially to Marquis James of Pleasantville, New York, each of whom read the entire manuscript and offered wholesome criticism. To Ambassador Bowers I stand eternally indebted, not alone for contributing the Introduction to this book, but more importantly for inspiring and encouraging its author since the latter's boyhood. Through the years Mr. Bowers has been a devoted friend; were further proof of friendship needed, I should hail the Introduction as that proof. Most important of all, I take this inadequate medium to express heartfelt gratitude to my wife, Suzanne Bowerfind Hamilton. The sacrifices that were hers, the courage and the inspiration, can never be translated into things of ink and paper.

H. H.

Fort Wayne, Indiana,
November 30, 1940.

# ADDITIONAL ACKNOWLEDGMENTS

Grateful acknowledgment is made to the following publishers and individuals for permission to reprint material which is in copyright or of which they are the authorized publishers, as follows:

To D. Appleton-Century Company: for direct quotations from *General Taylor* by O. O. Howard (1892); and from *Prose Writings of William Cullen Bryant*, edited by Parke Godwin (1884).

To Dodd, Mead & Company: for direct quotations from *The Diary of Philip Hone, 1828-1851*, edited by Allan Nevins (1927).

To Rhoda van Bibber Tanner Doubleday: for direct quotations from *Journals of the Late Brevet Major Philip Norbourne Barbour . . . and His Wife*, published by G. P. Putnam's Sons (1936).

To Houghton Mifflin Company: for direct quotations from *Abraham Lincoln, 1809-1858*, by Albert J. Beveridge (1928); *Walt Whitman, His Life and Work*, by Bliss Perry (1906); *The Texas Rangers*, by Walter Prescott Webb (1935).

To The Macmillan Company: for direct quotations from *The War with Mexico*, by Justin H. Smith (1919); *Winfield Scott, The Soldier and the Man*, by Charles W. Elliott (1937).

To A. C. McClurg & Company: for direct quotations from *The Diary of James K. Polk*, edited by Milo M. Quaife (1910).

To The Old Salem Lincoln League: for direct quotation from *Lincoln at New Salem*, by Thomas P. Reep (1927).

To Charles Scribner's Sons: for direct quotations from *The Life and Letters of George Gordon Meade*, by George Meade (1913); *Our First War in Mexico*, by Farnham Bishop (1916); *Life and Letters of George Bancroft*, by M. A. DeWolfe Howe (1908).

To The State Historical Society of Iowa: for direct quotations from *Old Fort Crawford and the Frontier*, by Bruce E. Mahan (1926); *Old Fort Snelling, 1819-1858*, by Marcus L. Hansen (1918); for permission to reproduce the map of the Black Hawk War by Shirley Ann Briggs which appeared in *I Am a Man*, by Cyrenus Cole (1938).

To Alice E. Trabue: for direct quotations from *A Corner in Celebrities* (1922).

# INDEX

# INDEX

Abercrombie, John J., 115.

Adair, John, bested by Indians, 31.

Adams, John Quincy, and the Monroe Doctrine, 73; absent from Washington, 75.

*Alabama,* takes Taylor and men to Corpus Christi, 162.

Albright, Jacob W., at Fort Knox, 38.

Alexander, Milton K., in Black Hawk War, 94-96.

Allen, George W., in Second Seminole War, 131, 133.

Alligator, Indian chief, 125 *et seq.*

Allison, John Stadler, 74.

Allison, Mrs. John Stadler, 29, 59, 74.

*America,* in Taylor's procession, 250.

American Fur Company, characteristics of, 115-116; Taylor's opinion of, 116.

Ampudia, Pedro de, threatens Taylor, 175; succeeded by Arista, 176, 180; at Palo Alto, 182; at Monterey, 207 *et seq.;* 227, 243; at Buena Vista, 233, 237.

Anderson, Richard Clough, 27.

Anderson, Robert, in Black Hawk War, 83, 91, 98.

Anderson, William P., hatred for Taylor, 54-56.

Apalache Indians, 122.

Arbuckle, Matthew, at Fort Smith, 70; succeeded by Taylor at Fort Gibson, 146.

Arista, Mariano, succeeds Ampudia, 176; traits of, 179-180; at Palo Alto, 177, 181-185; at Resaca de la Palma, 187-190, 243; armistice refused, 192-193; flees, 195.

*Arkansas Intelligencer,* 150.

Armistead, Walker K., succeeds Taylor in Florida, 141.

Armstrong, William, Indian agent, 150.

"Army of the South," 135.

Ashe, Christopher, marries Sarah Knox Taylor and Jefferson Davis, 107.

Astor, John Jacob, president of American Fur Company, 115.

Atkinson, Henry, Indians quelled by, in 1827, 78; characteristics of, 85; management of Black Hawk War, 84-99.

Atwater, Caleb, Indian commissioner, at Fort Crawford, 110.

Atwood, Jesse, paints Taylor, 246.

Ayer, Elisha, teacher of Zachary Taylor, 28-29, 261.

Backus, Electus, 209.

Bad Axe, Battle of, 96-97.

Bancroft, George, Secretary of the Navy, 159, 160, 218.

Barbour, James, Secretary of War, 76.

Barbour, Philip N., in advance to Rio Grande, 174; at Palo Alto, 184; at Resaca de la Palma, 189-190; on Rio Grande, 199, 201; killed at Monterey, 209.

Bartholomew, Joseph, leads expedition into Illinois, 47.

Baton Rouge, 67, 72, 73, 77, 106, 142, 143, 146, 254.

Bay Saint Louis, Mississippi, 66, 68, 70.

Bayou Sara, Louisiana, 65, 68.

Beall, Lloyd J., 157.

Beaumont, William, post surgeon, 81.

Beechland, home of John Gibson Taylor, 74; Sarah Knox Taylor married in, 106.

Belknap, William G., at Palo Alto, 181, 183; at Resaca de la Palma, 188.

Benton, Thomas H., Taylor denounced by, 145; and Mexican War, 221.

Birch, George, superintends log work at Shields's Spring, 71.

Bissell, Daniel, orders works at Baton Rouge, 67; Taylor's opinion of, 68.

Bissell, W. H., at Buena Vista, 236-237.

Black Hawk, denies legality of land cession, 83; recrosses to eastern shore of Mississippi, 84, 87; characteristics of, 85-87; defeated at Battle of Wisconsin Heights, 96; and at Battle of Bad Axe, 97; captured by Sioux, 97; taken down Mississippi, 98.